BARRON'S
ESL PROFICIENCY SERIES

PREPOSITIONS

THIRD EDITION

Jean Yates, Ph.D.

Acknowledgments

The author would like to thank Debbie Edson at Barron's for the opportunity to create this third edition and for her guidance in the process; professor Marichu Bucelli for her examples of preposition usage in Spanish and Italian, and linguist and professor Bill Zolar for his examples of preposition usage in German, Italian, and Spanish.

Thanks also to the rest of the team at Barron's: Kathryn Malm Bourgoine, Megan Buckman, Joanna Graham, Lauren Manoy, and Angela Tartaro for their insightful suggestions and hard work, especially under difficult conditions during the pandemic.

Published by Kaplan, Inc., d/b/a Barron's Educational Series
750 Third Avenue
New York, NY 10017
www.barronseduc.com

ISBN: 978-1-5062-6757-9

10 9 8 7 6 5 4 3 2 1

Kaplan, Inc., d/b/a Barron's Educational Series, Inc. print books are available at special quantity discounts to use for sales promotions, employee premiums, or educational purposes. For more information or to purchase books, please call the Simon & Schuster special sales department at 866-506-1949.

Table of Contents

Introduction..1

Part One: The Prepositions

How to Use Part One 8

Unit 1: About.................................. 11

Unit 2: Above 16

Unit 3: Across 18

Unit 4: After...................................20

Unit 5: Against 23

Unit 6: Ahead Of*.........................26

Unit 7: Along 27

Unit 8: Among 29

Unit 9: Around 30

Unit 10: As 34

Unit 11: At 35

Unit 12: Back To*/Back From* 42

Unit 13: Before 44

Unit 14: Behind.............................45

Unit 15: Below...............................47

Unit 16: Beneath.......................... 48

Unit 17: Beside..............................49

Unit 18: Besides............................50

Unit 19: Between 51

Unit 20: Beyond 53

Unit 21: But 55

Unit 22: By.....................................56

Unit 23: Close To*.........................61

Unit 24: Despite/In Spite Of*......62

Unit 25: Down................................63

Unit 26: During............................. 66

Unit 27: Except 67

Unit 28: Far From* 68

Unit 29: For 69

Unit 30: From 79

Unit 31: In 84

Unit 32: In Back Of* 100

Unit 33: In Front Of* 101

Unit 34: Inside 102

Unit 35: Instead Of* 103

Unit 36: Into 104

Unit 37: Like 107

Unit 38: Near 109

Unit 39: Next To* 110

Unit 40: Of 111

Unit 41: Off 120

Unit 42: On 126

Unit 43: Onto 140

Unit 44: On Top Of* 141

Unit 45: Opposite 142

Unit 46: Out 143

Unit 47: Outside 150

Unit 48: Over 151

Unit 49: Past 157

Unit 50: Through 158

Unit 51: Throughout 163

Unit 52: To 164

Unit 53: Toward 174

Unit 54: Towards 176

Unit 55: Under 177

Unit 56: Underneath 180

Unit 57: Until 181

Unit 58: Up 182

*Two- or three-word combinations that function as prepositions.

Unit 59: With 190

Unit 60: Within 199

Unit 61: Without 201

Part Two: Prepositions by Function

How to Use Part Two 204

Unit 1: Time 205

Unit 2: Location... 208

Unit 3: Direction 213

Unit 4: Number.. 215

Unit 5: Weather 217

Unit 6: Source of Information 218

Unit 7: Affiliation 219

Unit 8: Description... 220

Unit 9: Wearing 221

Unit 10: Topic 222

Unit 11: Recipient 224

Unit 12: State... 226

Unit 13: Separation 228

Unit 14: Attitude 229

Unit 15: Behavior 231

Part Three: Using Prepositions

How to Use Part Three 236

Unit 1: Prepositional Phrases 237

Unit 2: Prepositions in Questions 243

Unit 3: Prepositions in Noun Clauses 247

Unit 4: Prepositions in Adjective Clauses 249

Part Four: Phrasal Verbs

How to Use Part Four 252

Unit 1: Nonseparable Combinations 253

Unit 2: Must-Be-Separated Combinations........ 260

Unit 3: Separable Combinations 262

Unit 4: Nonseparable Combinations with an
Additional Preposition 271

Unit 5: Separable Combinations with an Additional
Preposition.. 272

Unit 6: Intransitive Combinations 275

Unit 7: Intransitive Verb-Adverb Combinations
Followed by a Preposition 281

Unit 8: Phrasal Verbs Used as Nouns 285

Unit 9: Phrasal Verbs Used as Adjectives 288

Part Five: Prepositions as Nouns, Adjectives, and Verbs

Unit 1: Nouns 290

Unit 2: Adjectives 292

Unit 3: Verbs.. 294

Appendices

Appendix 1: Answer Key..................................... 299

Appendix 2: Index of Phrases............................312

Introduction

Prepositions pose more problems for the non-native speaker or learner of English than any other part of speech. Why? Prepositions are just little words that never change in form; they are pronounced softly, in unstressed syllables; they aren't even given capital letters in book titles; native speakers choose the correct ones without thinking. How can they be confusing?

The word *preposition* has a straightforward definition: a word placed before a noun or pronoun to define its relationship with another word in the sentence. For the learner of English, however, prepositions are anything but straightforward.

- Prepositions are difficult, if not impossible, to define without using other prepositions.
  Example:
  In the sentence, "The book is on the table," what does <u>on</u> mean?
  <u>On</u> means "*above* and supported *by*."

- In no other language are the prepositions (if they exist at all) the exact equivalents of English prepositions.
  Examples:

Spanish	*English*
Tíralo <u>a</u> la basura.	Throw it <u>in</u> the trash.
Vamos <u>a</u> la casa de tu hermano.	Let's go <u>to</u> your brother's house.
Está <u>a</u> la izquierda.	It's <u>on</u> the left.
La celebración empieza <u>a</u> medianoche.	The celebration starts <u>at</u> midnight.

Italian	*English*
Abita <u>a</u> Washington.	He lives <u>in</u> Washington.
Penso <u>a</u> te.	I'm thinking <u>about/of</u> you.
Lui e <u>all'</u>aeroporto.	He's <u>at</u> the airport.

German	*English*
Er wohnt <u>auf</u> der New Jersey Avenue.	He lives <u>on</u> New Jersey Avenue.
Er ist <u>auf</u> dem Flughafen.	He is <u>at</u> the airport.
Ich denke <u>an</u> dich.	I'm thinking <u>about/of</u> you.
Werfen Sie es <u>an</u> den Abfall.	Throw it <u>in</u> the trash.

- Many preposition words can also be adverbs or conjunctions.
  Examples:

the preposition <u>down</u>	She walked <u>down</u> the hill.
the adverb <u>down</u>	He put the book <u>down</u>.
the preposition <u>after</u>	She took a nap <u>after</u> lunch.
the conjunction <u>after</u>	She went outside <u>after</u> she put the book down.

- Many prepositions can indicate more than one meaning or relationship.

  Examples with <u>after</u>:

later than	We rested after lunch.
in pursuit of	The cat is after the mouse.
because of	He was angry after the way she acted.
in the style of	This is a painting after Picasso.
continuously	She worked night after night.

- Two or more prepositions can have the same meaning. Sometimes these prepositions are interchangeable.

  Examples:

  She is disappointed <u>in</u> her new job.
  She is disappointed <u>with</u> her new job.

  Sometimes they are not interchangeable.

  Examples:

  He is fascinated <u>with</u> his new job. (but not *in*)
  He is interested <u>in</u> his new job. (but not *with*)
  He is bored <u>by</u> his new job. (*by* or *with*, but not *in*)

- Many prepositions are also used in expressions where their meaning is entirely different from any of their predictable meanings. Expressions like this do not follow any pattern or logic, and do not allow for substitutions. They must be learned as vocabulary units.

  Examples:

  It's <u>about time</u>.
  They are never <u>on time</u>.
  She got here <u>in time</u> to see the whole show.

- A preposition in combination with another word may have multiple meanings.

  Example:

<u>make up</u> your bed	-arrange
<u>make up</u> your face	-paint
<u>make up</u> your mind	-decide
<u>make up</u> a story	-invent
<u>make up</u> a list	-write down
<u>make up</u> the difference	-equalize
<u>make up</u> last week's homework	-do overdue work
<u>make up</u> for lost time	-compensate
<u>make up</u> with your girlfriend	-reestablish a relationship

- Different prepositions can follow the same verb to change its meaning completely.

  Example:

break <u>down</u>	-collapse
break <u>in</u>	-enter by force
break <u>off</u>	-remove
break <u>out</u>	-erupt
break <u>out of</u>	-leave by force
break <u>through</u>	-establish a successful idea
break <u>up</u>	-end a relationship

- New preposition combinations continue to become part of the language.

  The following examples are relatively new:

<u>boot up</u>	-restart a computer
<u>key in</u>	-type text on the computer
<u>log on</u>	-connect to the Internet
<u>act out</u>	-misbehave (traditionally *act up*)
<u>change out</u>	-replace with
<u>swap out</u>	-replace with
<u>scope out</u>	-make a survey of
<u>listen up</u>	-pay attention

- Preposition words are sometimes "made into" other parts of speech.

  Examples:

prepositions as nouns	I want to learn the <u>ins</u> and <u>outs</u> of prepositions.
prepositions as adjectives	The hospital has only a few <u>in</u> patients. There is a <u>down</u> side to his idea.
prepositions as verbs	I heard they were <u>upping</u> the price.

- There are some regional differences in preposition usage among native speakers.

  Examples:

Most of the United States: *stand <u>in</u> line*	New York City: stand <u>on</u> line
Most of the United States: *graduate <u>from</u> high school/ college/etc.*	Northeastern United States: *graduate high school/college/etc.*

As if all this weren't enough, English sentence patterns can also be troublesome, especially when prepositions are involved. The use of articles and pronouns and the formation of questions, adjective clauses, and noun clauses can be tricky.

Prepositions is designed to take the mystery out of prepositions for those whose first language is not English. It is a comprehensive handbook and guide that explains in detail the sixty-one commonly used English prepositions and their usage. It is easy to read and understand, and easy to use for quick reference or for more serious study.

Part One consists of a unit for each of the prepositions. Each unit includes all of the predictable definitions of the preposition, with typical grammar patterns, example sentences, and lists of the verbs and nouns that are most often used for each meaning. Idiomatic expressions and phrasal verbs are also defined and illustrated with examples. There are exercises at the end of each unit, and comprehensive exercises available online at online.barronsbooks.com.

Part Two provides charts and diagrams that illustrate and compare the functional usage of different prepositions. Each unit includes exercises and answers that will help the reader remember the guidelines.

Part Three gives formulas and examples that describe the use of prepositions before pronouns and verbs, in adjective and noun clauses, and in questions. Exercises at the end of each unit provide practice with these patterns.

Part Four is an exploration of phrasal verbs—idiomatic combinations that consist of a verb + a preposition—and of all the different ways these combinations can be used. Exercises follow each unit.

Part Five details cases where prepositions have merged with—and become prefixes to—certain nouns, adjectives, and verbs, giving them more specific meanings. In the appendices you will find answers to the exercises as well as a glossary for reference. This glossary is an alphabetical list of over 3,800 common adjectives, nouns, and verbs with the prepositions that normally precede and/or follow them, with the preposition name and section number of the text where the expression can be found, for further explanation of its meaning and use in a sentence.

To the Teacher

This book is designed to be used as a reference, rather than a textbook to be followed unit by unit. It is adaptable for use with students of every level of proficiency—from beginners to those who are quite advanced and are seeking perfection. You are encouraged to pick and choose the units that best fit your particular classes—and order them in a way that works with your own approach and teaching plan. Exercises are included in every part of the book, but you may wish to devise your own instead, or supplement these with types that you know work for your students. Emphasize to your students that proficiency is best achieved through practice of correct usage, both oral and written, and that repeating the exercises can help them internalize preposition usage so that they will feel confident in speaking and writing.

There are explicit instructions throughout that are meant to help students improve proficiency in using prepositions and to get over occasional plateaus, where they feel they are not progressing. When they begin to see the patterns—and follow those patterns—soon they will be using prepositions naturally and will confidently move on to greater proficiency.

To the Student

No matter what your level of English is, use this book to become more familiar with the patterns of English sentences. Train your ear to hear prepositions in conversations, and your eye to see them when you read. Ask yourself if you know the underlying meaning of each one. By all means, add new words you hear to the lists in the sections where they belong, and write down new expressions and phrasal verbs as you come across them. Mastering English prepositions is a challenge, but a valuable skill that will enhance your understanding and help you express yourself with confidence.

Following are some specific suggestions:

1. Read the introduction at the beginning of the book.
2. If you are a beginning student of English, begin with Part Two.
3. If you are more advanced, begin with Part One, Part Two, Part Three, or Part Four. You decide.
4. Do the exercises that follow each unit.
5. Write your answers on a separate sheet of paper, not in the book.
6. Check your answers with the Answer Key on p. 299.
7. If you have mistakes, write the correct answers down, and make sure you understand them. Repeat the exercises until you have no mistakes.
8. Repeat the exercises at different times in the future. This will help you memorize hundreds of expressions, correct usage, and perfect word order.

Barron's ESL Proficiency Series: Prepositions provides comprehensive exercises online for an optimal learning experience. Visit the Barron's Online Learning Hub:

online.barronsbooks.com

Register now and begin your language-learning journey with Barron's!

PART ONE

The Prepositions

How to Use Part One

1. Each preposition is described the following ways:
   - by its basic meaning

      This is usually a meaning that can be demonstrated and contrasted with the meanings of other prepositions.
   - by its inclusion in common expressions

      Many expressions include prepositions that do not carry their basic meaning. The preposition is invariable—it cannot be replaced with a different one. Each expression should be learned as a single unit.
   - by its use as a phrasal verb

      A phrasal verb is a combination of a verb and a preposition that changes the meaning of the verb. The preposition does not carry its basic meaning. This combination should be considered as a single verb unit that has a unique definition.

2. Each definition of a preposition is followed by one or more *patterns*, which indicate the word order appropriate for the definition.

   The verbs in each pattern can be changed to other tenses.

   Example:

Pattern	verb + *toward* + noun

   > *The money **goes** toward helping the family.*

   This could also be:

   > *The money **went** toward helping the family.*
   > *The money **will go** toward helping the family.*
   > *The money **is going to go** toward helping the family.*

   When a word cannot be substituted, that word is included in the pattern.

   Example:

Pattern	*be* + *after* + noun

   > *The reception **is** after the wedding.*
   > *be* is the only possible verb for this pattern.

   When a word is optional, it is in parentheses.

   Example:

Pattern	*be* + *outside (of)* + noun

   > *The dog is outside the house.*
   > *The dog is outside **of** the house.*

When the word *noun* is in the pattern, use the normal patterns for noun usage, as outlined in Part Three.

Example:

> **Pattern** verb + *against* + noun

> *Dr. Jones is against **the** idea.*

This could also be:

> *Dr. Jones is against **my** idea.*
> *Dr. Jones is against **this** idea.*
> *Dr. Jones is against **our** ideas.*
> *Dr. Jones is against **some of their** ideas.*

When the noun determiner cannot be substituted, it is included in the pattern.

Example:

> **Pattern** verb + *against* + *the* + noun

> *We sailed against **the** wind for an hour.*
> (*the* cannot be replaced by *a, this, my,* or any other word)

When the word *one's* is in the pattern, it can be replaced by any possessive adjective (*my, your, his, her, its, our, their*)

Example:

> **Pattern** *to* + *one's* + noun

> *Someone will come to **your** aid.*
> *Someone will come to **his** aid.*
> *Someone will come to **our** aid.*

When no noun determiner is used, the symbol ø is in the pattern. The symbol ø means no normally acceptable or grammatically necessary word, such as *the*, is used in the expression, as in *to school* or *at home* or *in class*.

Example:

> **Pattern** verb + *against* + ø + noun

> *I drive against traffic every morning.*

The typical verbs, nouns, and adjectives listed with each pattern are the most common words that are used with the preposition. It is a good idea to think of the combinations as units. As an exercise, you may wish to write sentences with the suggested words, following the pattern and keeping the meaning of the combination in mind.

About

Basic Meaning

1. About identifies a topic.

Pattern 1 noun + *be* + *about* + noun

> *This book is **about** prepositions.*

Nouns commonly used before *about*:

argument, article, book, conversation, disagreement, discussion, joke, lecture, movie, news, play, program, report, speech, story

Pattern 2 noun + *about* + noun

> *She gave me advice **about** my loan.*

Nouns commonly used before *about*:

assurance, comment, complaint, gossip, lie, question, statement, truth

Pattern 3 verb + *about* + noun

> *He often talks **about** his job.*

Verbs commonly used before *about*:

agree, argue, brag, care, complain, cry, do, dream, forget, groan, hear, joke, know, laugh, lie, moan, pray, read, say, scream, sing, talk, think, wonder, worry, yell

Related Expressions

to see about

- to delay a decision until more information is known

> *We want to buy a house, but we will **see about** that later.*

- to get information about

> *I called that office **to see about** getting a job there.*

to find out about to get information about

> *She called the school **to find out about** her daughter's behavior.*

Pattern 4 verb + noun + *about*

> *She knows something **about** airplanes.*

Typical verbs used with this pattern:

ask, find out, know, learn, say

Typical nouns used before *about*:

a little, a lot, nothing, quite a bit, something, very little

Pattern 5 verb + indirect object + *about* + noun

*They asked me **about** my trip.*

Verbs commonly used with this pattern:

advise, ask, bother, contact, harass, inform, question, remind, teach, tell, write, warn

Pattern 6 adjective + *about* + noun

*They were very kind **about** our late arrival.*

Adjectives commonly used before *about*:

charming, kind, nasty, nice, mean, rude, sweet, understanding, unkind

2. **About** can identify the **cause of an emotion or condition.**

Pattern adjective + *about* + noun

*We are excited **about** our vacation.*

Adjectives commonly used before *about*:

angry, anxious, bashful, concerned, confused, crazy, excited, glad, happy, mad, nervous, objective, optimistic, pessimistic, right, sick, silly, unhappy, upset, worried

3. **About** can mean **approximately.**

Pattern *about* + number

*It is **about** nine o'clock.*
*We have **about** ten dollars each.*

4. **About** can mean **in all parts of.**

Pattern 1 *be* + noun + *about* + noun

*There is a lot of excitement **about** town.*

Pattern 2 past participle of verb + *about* + noun

*Papers were scattered **about** the house.*

Typical past participles used before *about*:

scattered, sprinkled, strewn, thrown

5. **About** can **describe a noun.**

> **Pattern** *something/nothing* + **(adjective)** + *about* + **noun**

> > *There is something **about** her that I like.*
> > *There is something adorable **about** her.*
> > *There is nothing nice **about** that.*

Adjectives commonly used before *about*:

adorable, attractive, bad, cute, exotic, fascinating, familiar, fishy, funny, good, interesting, nice, peculiar, special, strange, unusual, weird, wonderful

6. **About** can mean **in all directions.**

> **Pattern 1** **motion verb** + *about* + **noun**

> > *We wandered **about** town for a few hours.*

> **Pattern 2** **motion verb** + *about* **(adverb)**

> > *The baby crawls **about** the house.*

Verbs commonly used with these patterns:

crawl, go, jump, look, move, poke, run, walk, wander

7. **About** (adverb) can mean **almost.**

> **Pattern** *be* + *about* + **adjective**

> > *She is **about** ready.*

Adjectives commonly used after *about*:

complete, done, finished, perfect, ready, right, through

Expressions

about + **infinitive**   ready to

> *The show is **about to begin**.*

to be about time   an expression of annoyance that a person or thing has arrived late.

> *"It's **about time** you got here," said the mother when her daughter came home late.*

to have an air about one   to seem uncaring or unfriendly

> *That new guy **has an air about him**.*

not about (adverb) + **infinitive**   not willing to

> *I'm **not about to sign** that agreement.*
> *They're **not about to go** home early.*

about face

1. (verb) a military command to turn halfway around, and face the opposite direction

    *The sergeant ordered, "**About face!**"*

    *He told his men **to about face**.*

2. (noun) a complete change of opinion

    *He did **an about face** when he learned the facts.*

Phrasal Verbs

bring about (separable)   cause

    *The storm **brought about** problems.*

    *The storm **brought** them **about**.*

come about (intransitive)   happen

    *How did that situation **come about**?*

to get about (intransitive)   to be able to walk

    *He is ninety years old, and he **gets about** very well.*

to find out about (nonseparable)   to get information or news about something

    *When did **you find out about** the accident?*

PRACTICE

1-1. Choose the best word or words for each blank.

1. This _____ is about dogs.

    airplane   house   story   car

2. There was a _____ about my report.

    complaint   traffic accident   secretary   police officer

3. He always _____ about his problems.

    drives   runs   jokes   studies

4. We need to _____ about the law.

    try   learn   work   study

5. They _____ us about the accident.

    learned   finished   told   arrested

6. Her sister was _____ about my mistake.

    crazy   unkind   silly   ridiculous

7. The students are _____ about the field trip.

    good   bad   silly   excited

8. I have about _____ in my pocket.

| my lesson | my keys | twenty dollars | nothing |

9. We are about _____.

| learning | the trip | finished | read |

10. Her clothes were _____ about the bedroom.

| ironed | scattered | washed | bought |

1-2. Use an expression with *about* to express the following:

1. We are not willing to go there.

2. She changed her mind completely.

1-3. Use *about* in a phrasal verb to express the following:

1. The president's announcement <u>caused</u> riots in the street.

2. Is your great-grandmother able to <u>walk</u> by herself?

Above

Basic Meanings

1. **Above** can mean **in or at a higher place.**

> **Pattern 1** *be* + *above* + noun
>
> > *A dark cloud **was above** the house.*

> **Pattern 2** verb + noun + *above* + noun
>
> > *Let's hang the picture **above** the sofa.*

Verbs commonly used before *above*:

arrange, carry, hang, hold, keep, place, put, set

2. **Above** can mean **at a higher level, value, or rank.**

> *Her blood pressure is **above** normal.*
> *The children in her class are all **above** average.*
> *In the navy, a captain is **above** a commander.*

3. **Above** indicates that a person is **too good** to commit the stated negative action.

> **Pattern 1** *be* + *above* + noun
>
> > *The policeman is **above** cruelty.*

Nouns often used after *above*:

cruelty, dishonesty, meanness, murder, perjury, theft, treason

> **Pattern 2** *be* + *above* + verb in gerund form
>
> > *He may be poor, but he is **above** stealing.*

Gerunds often used with this meaning:

breaking the law, cheating, gossiping, lying, robbing, snooping, stealing

As other parts of speech:

Above used as an adverb can indicate something **written earlier** in a book, article, or other document.

> *Please see the instructions **above**.*

Above used as an adjective describes something written earlier.

> *Please follow the **above** instructions.*

Expressions

up above (adverb) in heaven

> *Our dear grandmother is now in peace **up above**.*

above and beyond the call of duty action that is more or greater than what is expected of a person

> *My teacher's help after school was **above and beyond the call of duty**.*

aboveboard completely honest and open; legal

> *Our negotiations with the company were **aboveboard**.*

above the law exempt from restrictions of the law

> *People in power sometimes believe they are **above the law**.*

PRACTICE

2-1. Choose the best word or words for each blank.

1. A beautiful painting was above the _____.

   house   car   tree   sofa

2. He wants to _____ the TV above the fireplace.

   throw   hang   carry   drop

3. The _____ at our school is above the teacher.

   principal   assistant teacher   student   bus driver

4. Our teacher is strict, but she is above _____.

   winning   cruelty   having a party   honesty

5. You need to read the above _____.

   book   newspaper   magazine   article

2-2. Use an expression with *above* to express the following:

1. The policeman's help was extra special.

2. Even the president has to obey the law.

Across

Basic Meanings

1. **Across** indicates the direction of **movement from one side of an area to the other.**

   > **Pattern** motion verb + *across* + noun

   > *The girl ran **across** the yard.*

   Verbs often used before *across*:

   crawl, drive, go, limp, move, ride, run, swim, walk

2. **Across** can mean **on the other side of** a place.

   > **Pattern** verb + *across* + noun

   > *My friend lives **across** the street.*

3. **Across from** means **opposite or facing.**

   > **Pattern 1** verb + *across from* + noun

   > *My assistant's office is **across from** mine.*
   > *My secretary sits **across from** me.*

   > **Pattern 2** verb + *across* + noun + *from* + noun

   > *My assistant's office is **across** the hall from mine.*

4. **Across** and **all across** mean **in every area of.**

   > *People **across** the world are using the Internet.*
   > *There is a heat wave **all across** the country.*

Related Expression

across the board   including everyone or everything

> *Everyone got a raise in salary: there was a wage increase of 3 percent **across the board**.*

Phrasal Verbs

come across (nonseparable)   find something unexpectedly

*I **came across** this old picture of you when I was looking for some documents.*

come across (intransitive)   be received by an audience

*The banquet speaker was not sure how well he **came across**.*

run across (nonseparable)   to find something unexpectedly

*I **ran across** a letter you wrote to me when we were children.*

get (something) **across to**   (separable) make something understood

*The young girl tried **to get** it **across** to her boyfriend that she was not ready to get married.*

PRACTICE

3-1. Choose the best word or words for each blank.

1. Let's _____ across the lake.

   walk   ride   run   swim

2. I can walk to the bank; it's just across the _____ from my house.

   town   street   country   state

3. In our school building, the gym is across from the _____.

   library   street   bank   bedroom

4. Wildfires are burning all across the _____.

   bank   library   state   gym

3-2. Use an expression with *across* to express the following:

1. I found this recipe in my mother's cookbook.

2. Her brother tried to make her understand that she should be quiet.

3. I hope my message is clear to the audience.

UNIT 4:
After

Basic Meanings

1. **After** means **later than** or **following.**

> **Pattern 1**   *be + after + noun*
>
> *The reception is **after** the wedding ceremony.*

> **Pattern 2**   *after + gerund form of verb + noun*
>
> ***After** finishing your homework, you can watch television.*

Used as a conjunction with related meaning:

> **Pattern 1**   *after + subject noun + verb*
>
> ***After** you finish your homework, you can watch television.*

> **Pattern 2**   subject + verb + *after* + subject + verb
>
> *The boss left **after** I came in.*

2. **After** can mean **lower in value or rank.**

> *That school's athletes placed **after** ours in the playoffs.*

3. **After** can mean **in pursuit of.**

> **Pattern**   verb + *after* + noun
>
> *The cat ran **after** the mouse.*

Verbs often used before *after*:

be, come, go, run

4. **After** can mean **because of.**

> **Pattern**   adjective . . . + *after* + noun
>
> *He was mad at her **after** her behavior at the party.*

Typical nouns used after *after*:

attitude, behavior, failure, kindness, manners, outburst, reaction, success

5. After can mean **in spite of.**

> Pattern *after* + verb in gerund form

>> *They never got married, **after** dating for years.*
>> ***After** reading this article three times, I still don't understand it.*

6. After can mean **in the style of.**

> Pattern noun + *after* + noun

>> *The school play was a drama **after** Shakespeare.*

7. After can indicate **continuously.**

> Pattern time period + *after* + same time period

>> *The man waited night **after** night for his telephone to ring.*
>> *Life got harder year **after** year.*
>> *His mother told him time **after** time to clean up his room.*

Nouns often used with this meaning:

day, hour, month, night, time, week, year

Expressions

after all

1. in spite of what happened; nevertheless

> *Our best player got hurt in the first quarter, but we played hard and won the game **after all**.*

2. as a justification

> *Of course I am tired; **after all**, I have been working for twelve hours.*

after all is said and done; eventually

> *I know you feel bad now, but you will be glad about this **after all is said and done**.*

after one's own heart   especially appreciated

> *Her mother always serves us chocolate cake; she is a woman **after my own heart**.*

Phrasal Verbs

come after (nonseparable)   pursue

> *When I saw him, I ran; but he **came after** me.*

look after (nonseparable)   take care of something or somebody

> *She **looks after** our baby on weekends.*

name after (separable)   give a baby the name of someone special

> *They **named** the baby **after** his grandfather.*

take after (nonseparable)   be similar to an older relative

> *The baby **takes after** his father.*

PRACTICE

4-1. Choose the best word for each blank.

1. I did my homework after I _____.
    read the instructions   went to sleep   graduated   finished college

2. My name is last on the list. My name is after _____.
    my teacher   your name   your sister   Mary

3. That dog always runs after ____.
    the school   the school bus   morning   meetings

4. After _____ Spanish in Mexico for six weeks, she still doesn't speak it.
    studies   studied   studying   was studying

5. She works day after _____ in order to pay her bills.
    year   month   hour   day

4-2. Use an expression with *after* to express the following:

1. This course is very difficult, but when we are finished, we will be happy.

2. Even though David didn't study for the test, he got a good grade.

4-3. Use *after* in a phrasal verb to express the following:

1. She looks a lot like her dad.

2. The baby's name is Susan. Her grandmother's name is Susan.

3. The babysitter takes care of the children on Thursday afternoons.

Against

Basic Meanings

1. **Against** means **touching** something or somebody for support.

> **Pattern 1** verb + *against* + noun
>
> > *The man was leaning **against** his car.*
>
> Typical verbs used before *against*:
> **hang, lean, lie, rest, sleep**

> **Pattern 2** verb + noun + *against* + noun
>
> > *They held the mirror **against** the wall.*
>
> Typical verbs used before *against*:
> **butt, hold, keep, lay, lean, place, pull, put, rest, set**

2. **Against** means **touching forcibly.**

> **Pattern** noun + verb + *against* + noun
>
> > *The rain beat **against** the window.*
>
> Verbs often used before *against*:
> **bang, beat, crash, crush, heave, hit, knock, push, splash, throw, thrust**

3. **Against** means **in opposition to.**

> **Pattern** noun + verb + *against* + noun
>
> > *The mayor was **against** the idea of a new day-care center.*
> > *Stealing is **against** the law.*
> > *Our senator voted **against** that bill.*
>
> Typical verbs used before *against*:
> **act, argue, campaign, debate, fight, go, move, play, vote, work**
>
> Nouns often used after *against*:
> **action, bill, concept, enemy, force, idea, law, nomination, orders, plan, precepts, principles, proposal, regulations, religion, rules, suggestion, teachings, team, wishes**

4. **Against** can mean **toward a force in the opposite direction.**

   > **Pattern**   verb + *against* + *the* + noun

   > *Sailing was rough yesterday; we sailed **against** the wind all day.*

   Typical verbs used before *against*:

   drive, fight, go, move, run, sail, struggle, swim, walk

   Nouns often used after *against*:

   current, flow, force, tide, wind

5. **Against** can mean **to the disadvantage of.**

   > **Pattern**   noun + *be* + *against* + noun

   > *You may not get that job because your age **is against** you.*

   Typical nouns before *be against*:

   age, background, height, inexperience, nationality, youth

6. **Against** can mean **in contrast to.**

   > *It is hard to see your black necklace **against** that dark dress.*

7. **Against** can mean **in defense of.**

   > **Pattern**   verb + noun + *against* + noun

   > *They vaccinated the children **against** whooping cough.*
   > *Their heavy coats protect them **against** the cold.*

   Typical verbs before *against*:

   guard, lock up, protect, seal, vaccinate

8. **Against** can mean **in partial payment of.**

   > **Pattern**   noun + *against* + noun

   > *Enclosed is a check for one hundred dollars **against** my bill.*

   Typical nouns after *against*:

   balance, bill, charges, debt, loan

Expressions

against all odds/with all odds against one   having very little chance of success

> *Team A was less experienced than Team B, but they won the game **against all odds**.*
> *Many people come to this country and become successful with **all odds against them**.*

against traffic   in the opposite direction of

*I drive **against traffic** because I live in the city and I work in the suburbs.*

go against the grain   seem very wrong

*Cheating on your test really goes **against the grain**.*

have two strikes against one   be at a strong disadvantage (In baseball, a player is eliminated after three strikes.)

*When you are poor and sick, **you have two strikes against you**.*

Phrasal Verbs

be up against (nonseparable)   be faced with opposition, trouble, or hard work

*My friend **is up against** a lot of problems.*

*When he started his own business, he had no idea what he **was up against**.*

PRACTICE

5-1. Choose the best word or words for each blank.

1. The tired traveler was resting against his _____.
   wallet   suitcase   handkerchief   money

2. It was hard, because we had to swim against the _____.
   current   beach   pool   fish

3. She wasn't accepted on the team because she was too young; her _____ was against her.
   sister   parents   age   teacher

4. The wind crashed against our _____.
   teacher   feet   basement   windows

5. That dark bow doesn't show up against your _____.
   dark hair   light hair   red lipstick   eyeshadow

6. We finally paid off $500 against our _____.
   checks   loan   bank   lawyer

7. The children were vaccinated against _____.
   smoking   drug abuse   the flu   homework

8. My representative in Congress voted against _____.
   gun control   global warming   disease   weather

5-2. Use an expression with *against* to express the following:

1. It seems wrong that teacher salaries are so low.

2. They became prosperous, even though they began with nothing.

3. We are playing the state champions tomorrow night.

UNIT 6:
Ahead Of

Basic Meanings

1. Ahead of means **closer to a destination than** or **in front of.**

> *My friend arrived first, and was **ahead of** me in line.*

2. Ahead of means **before.**

> *You are in a hurry; please go **ahead of** me.*

3. Ahead of can mean **more advanced than.**

> *Because he was absent for two weeks, the other students in his class are **ahead of** him.*

Phrasal Verbs

get ahead (intransitive)   succeed

> *She has struggled all her life to **get ahead**.*

get ahead of (nonseparable)   advance faster or further than someone else

> *They are rivals, always competing to **get ahead of** each other.*

go ahead (intransitive)   do it; begin now

> *I asked for permission, and they told me to **go ahead**.*

PRACTICE

6-1. Choose the best word or words for each blank.

1. He is ahead of me because I got here _____.
    first   before   late   early

2. The other students are ahead of me because I missed _____.
    my mother   five classes   five problems   the baseball game

6-2. Use an expression with *ahead* to express the following:

1. We asked if we could look around, and they said yes.

2. They were just trying to earn a little more money.

3. His brother is trying to be better than he is at tennis.

UNIT 7:
Along

Basic Meanings

1. Along means **following the boundary** of something.

> **Pattern**   verb + *along* + noun

> *We walked **along** the water's edge at the beach last night.*

Typical verbs before *along*:

jog, run, stroll, walk

2. Along with means **together.**

> **Pattern**   verb + *along with* + noun

> *He used to sing **along with** me.*

Typical verbs used before *along with*:

hum, play, run, sing, walk, work

Expression

Used as an adverb:

all along   the whole past time

> *They have been enemies **all along**.*

Phrasal Verbs

get along (intransitive)   live together in harmony

> *She and her old roommate didn't **get along**.*

get along with (nonseparable)   to live in harmony with someone

> *I hope she **gets along with** her new roommate.*

PRACTICE

7-1. Choose the best word or words for each blank.

1. She walked along the _____ to be sure she didn't get lost.

   parking lot   shopping center   path   ocean

2. When you _____ along with me, it's easier.

   complain   work   worry   ask questions

7-2. Use an expression with *along* to express the following:

1. You thought we were angry, but we were just pretending the whole time.

7-3. Use a phrasal verb with *along* to express the following:

1. It's important to have a good relationship with your classmates.

UNIT 8:
Among

Basic Meanings

1. Among can mean **surrounded by.**

> **Pattern**   verb + *among* + plural (three or more) noun
>
> *They camped in the woods **among** the trees.*

2. Among can mean **with each other.**

> **Pattern**   verb + *among* + plural (three or more) noun
>
> *The children quarreled **among** themselves.*

Typical verbs before *among*:

argue, celebrate, debate, discuss something, fight, play, share something, talk

3. Among can mean **to the individuals in a group.**

> **Pattern**   verb + *among* + plural (three or more) noun
>
> *They distributed the flyers **among** the students.*

Typical verbs before *among*:

distribute, hand out, pass out

4. Among can mean **included in a group.**

> *Your friends are **among** the survivors.*

5. Among can indicate **many of a group.**

> *Latin dancing is popular **among** the college students.*

PRACTICE

8-1. Choose the best word or words for each blank.

1. We need to discuss this among _____.

   them   themselves   ourselves   yourself

2. Her son is among the _____.

   school   captain   loser   winners

3. It's pleasant to be in the meadow among the _____.

   mud   rain   flowers   spring

Basic Meanings

1. **Around** means **following a boundary, in a circular direction.**

   | Pattern | motion verb + *around* + noun |

   We walked around the block.

   Verbs commonly used before *around*:

   drive, fly, race, ride, run, skip, travel, walk

   Nouns commonly used after *around*:

   block, building, house, room, track, world

2. **Around** indicates **movement in a circular direction in place.**

   | Pattern | verb + *around (on)* |

   *The earth spins **around on** its axis as it travels around the sun.*

   Typical verbs used before *around*:

   spin, turn, whirl

3. **Around** means **enclosing.**

   | Pattern | verb + noun + *around* + noun |

   *The teacher drew a circle **around** each mistake.*
   *The rancher put a rope **around** the cow's neck.*

   Verbs commonly used with this pattern:

   draw, fasten, put, tie, wrap

4. **(All) around** means **in all areas of.**

   *There is crime **all around** this city.*

5. **(All) around** can mean **on all sides of.**

   *People were screaming **all around** me.*

6. **Around** means **on another side of.**

   *The bank is **around** the corner. Their farm is just **around** the bend.*

7. Around (adverb) means **approximately.**

Pattern   *around* + number

> We have **around** twenty dollars in our pockets.
> I'll see you at **around** three o'clock.

8. (All) around can mean **in many directions, randomly**

Pattern   motion verb + *around* + noun

> The new teacher looked **around** the room.

Verbs often used before *around*:

drive, flit, go, jump, look, march, move, play, run, search, shop, snoop, walk, wander

9. Around can mean **do nothing.**

Pattern   verb + *around* + place

> Those teenagers just hang **around** the mall with nothing to do.

Verbs used before *around*:

drag, fool, goof, hang, lie, lurk, mope, sit

Expressions

turn around (adverb)   face the opposite direction
> You are going east; to go west, you have to **turn around**.

turn something around   (adverb) reverse the position of something
> **Turn your chair around** and talk to me.

around back   at the back of a building
> Go **around back** to pick up your merchandise.

go around the bend   be crazy
> I am so busy, I think I am **going around the bend**.

give someone the runaround   avoid taking action by giving long explanations
> When I tried to return my broken air conditioner, the store manager **gave me the runaround**.

Phrasal Verbs

get around (intransitive)   often visit a lot of places and meet a lot of people
> He seems to know everybody; he really **gets around**.

get around to (nonseparable)   finally make the effort to do something
> One day I will **get around to** cleaning out my files.

31

kick somebody **around** (separable)   mistreat someone by controlling him or her

> *He left that job because the boss always **kicked him around**.*

kick something **around** (separable)   consider the pros and cons of an idea

> *We are **kicking around** the idea of moving to Florida.*

kid around (intransitive)   have fun

> *Our babysitter is great because she likes to **kid around** with us.*

show someone **around** (separable)   take someone on a tour of a place

> *He **showed me around** the campus when I first arrived.*

hang around with someone (nonseparable)   often be with someone

> *She **hangs around with** a boy who lives up the street.*

run around with someone (nonseparable)   often go out with someone

> *She is **running around with** a new group of friends.*

PRACTICE

9-1. Choose the best word or words for each blank.

1. After dinner, the children like to go outside and run around the _____.

    mountain   road   horse   house

2. There is global warming all around the _____.

    world   mountain   street   river

3. You can't see the school, but it is just around the _____.

    road   corner   world   country

4. She wrapped a _____ around her neck.

    scarf   hat   cushion   sweater

5. She has been _____ around the house all day.

    laughing   pushing   moping   standing

6. The detective came in and _____ around the bedroom.

    talked   sat   snooped   stopped

7. I have around _____ in my pocket.

    twenty-five dollars   notes   wallet   maps

8. I'll meet you at around _____.

    the corner   my ankle   the house   five o'clock

9-2. Use an expression with *around* to express the following:

1. Drive to the back of the building.

2. You are going in the wrong direction.

3. He keeps asking her out, and she keeps saying she is too busy.

9-3. Use a phrasal verb with *around* to express the following:

1. She seems to know everybody.

2. Can you give me a tour of the campus?

3. We are just staying home and doing nothing.

4. His older brother bullies him.

UNIT 10:
As

Basic Meaning

1. As means in the role of.

Pattern 1 verb + *as* + noun

*She is a trained teacher, but she works **as** a secretary in our office.*

Typical verbs used before *as*:

act, serve, substitute, volunteer, work

Pattern 2 verb + noun + *as* + noun

*We have selected you **as** the captain of the team.*

Typical verbs:

choose, elect, nominate, pick, select, use

Expression

As for me regarding me

*They all went to the movies; **as for me**, I stayed home.*

PRACTICE

10-1. Choose the best word or words for each blank.

1. He is a student, but he _____ as a volunteer on weekends.
   studies   works   sleeps   goes to the movies

2. They chose me to serve as the _____ of the team.
   brother   action   leader   last

UNIT 11:
At

Basic Meanings

1. At can indicate **location**

Pattern 1   *at + the +* place within a city or town

> *The women are **at the** supermarket.*

Nouns commonly used with this pattern:

apartment, bus stop, factory, hospital, hotel, house, mall, office, park, parking lot, restaurant, station, store, theater, university

Pattern 2   *at +* an address

> *She lives **at** 3757 North 52nd Street, apartment 10.*
> *You can contact him by e-mail @ xyz.com.*
> (The symbol @ is pronounced "*at*.")

Pattern 3   *at + the +* place within another place

> *He was waiting in the room **at the** door.*
>
> *He likes to sit in her apartment **at the** window facing the park.*

Nouns commonly used with this pattern:

counter, desk, table, window

2. At indicates a **place of attendance.**

Pattern 1   *be + at +* ø place or meal of regular attendance

> *The children **are at** school.*
>
> *We aren't allowed to watch television when we **are at** dinner.*

Nouns used with this pattern:

church, class, home, practice, school, work
breakfast, lunch, dinner

Pattern 2   *be + at +* noun of event

> *They **are at** the movies.*
>
> *She **is at** a meeting.*

Nouns commonly used with this pattern:

breakfast, brunch, celebration, concert, conference, dance, debate, dinner, forum, function, funeral, game, lecture, luncheon, meeting, movies, parade, party, play, program, reading, reunion, show, wedding

3. **At** can indicate **in the direction of; toward.**

    Pattern 1   **verb** + *at* + **noun**

    > *The teacher smiled **at** the new girl.*

    Verbs commonly used with this pattern:

    aim, frown, glare, grab, grin, growl, hit, howl, laugh, leer, look, rush, shoot, shout, slap, smile, snatch, stare, swear, swing, wink, yell

    Pattern 2   **verb** + **noun** + *at* + **noun**

    > *The small boy threw a rock **at** the window.*

    Typical verbs:

    swing, throw, toss

4. **At** is used to express **time.**

    Pattern   *at* + **specific time**

    > *We are leaving **at** four thirty.*
    > *They went home **at** midnight.*
    > *We always eat lunch **at** noon.*

Related Expressions

at first   when something started

> ***At first** we thought this hike would be easy.*

at last   finally

> *After that long drive, we are home **at last**.*

at length   for a long time, thoroughly

> *We discussed that topic **at length** at our meeting.*

at night   when it is night

> *I always read or study **at night**.*

at once   immediately (see also *number at a time*, below)

> *We must pack up and leave **at once**.*

at present   now

> ***At present** they are sleeping.*

at the beginning   at first, when something started

> ***At the beginning** we tried to go too fast.*

at the end   when something ended

> ***At the end** of the story, everybody was happy.*

at the moment   at present, now

> *I am very busy **at the moment**.*

(number) at a time   ratio per instance or unit

> *The tall boy liked to go up the steps two or three **at a time**.*

at once   several things together

> *Try to learn one step at a time, rather than three or four **at once**.*

5.   At can mean **busy using** something; **working.**

Pattern 1	*at + the + noun*

> *I have been **at the** computer all day.*

Nouns often used after *at the*:

cash register, computer, fax machine, ironing board, sewing machine, stove, (steering) wheel

Pattern 2	*be + at + work*
	be + at + it

> *You must not bother him; he **is at work**.*
>
> *He **has been at it** for four hours.*

6.   At can indicate a **condition.**

Pattern	*be + at + ø noun*

> *Those two countries **have been at** peace for ten years.*

Nouns used after *at*:

attention, ease, peace, rest, risk, war

7.   At can indicate **reaction.**

Pattern 1	adjective of state + *at* + noun

> *We were shocked **at** the condition of the classrooms.*

Typical adjectives used before *at*:

aghast, amazed, astonished, astounded, indignant, shocked, speechless, surprised, thrilled, upset

Pattern 2	verb + *at* + noun

> *The crowd rejoiced **at** the good news.*

Verbs commonly used before *at*:

cheer, grumble, guess, hint, hoot, laugh, rebel, rejoice, snort, tremble

8. **At** indicates a **degree of skill.**

| **Pattern 1** | **adjective + *at* + noun** |

*Your son is good **at** tennis, but not very good **at** hockey.*

| **Pattern 2** | **adjective + *at* + verb in gerund form** |

*That couple is really great **at dancing** the tango.*

Typical adjectives used before *at*:

bad, excellent, good, great, lousy, skilled, terrible

9. **At** can indicate a **rate** or **level**

| **Pattern 1** | ***at* + noun indicating price** |

*At the market they are selling apples **at** sixty-nine cents a pound.*

*I wish we could buy mangoes **at** that price.*

*Her husband tries to buy everything **at** a discount.*

| **Pattern 2** | **@* + number + *a* + noun indicating a unit of measurement** |

*They are selling apples @ **69¢ a lb**.*

| **Pattern 3** | ***at* + noun indicating level of age or distance** |

*You shouldn't work so hard **at** your age.*

*He was still singing **at** (the age of) eighty.*

*We can't see very well **at** this distance.*

*The plane was flying **at** three thousand feet.*

Related Expressions

at a distance   from far away

*I saw the new baby **at a distance**, and he looked beautiful.*

at arm's length   not close

*I try to stay **at arm's length** from him to avoid an argument.*

---

*@ is pronounced *at*. This meaning and the one for an email address (section 11.1) are the only acceptable uses of this symbol.

> **Pattern 4** *at* + noun indicating level of speed

> *She shouldn't drive **at** that speed.*

> ***At** twenty-five miles an hour on the freeway, she should get a ticket.*

EXCEPTION: **When speed is expressed in numbers after a verb, *at* is omitted.**

> *That driver is going eighty miles an hour.*

> *He drove sixty miles an hour the whole way home.*

10. **At** can indicate the highest possible **degree** in value.

> **Pattern** *at* + superlative adjective used as noun

> ***At** best she is an adequate typist.*

> *She works **at** least nine hours every day.*

> *You should be here by five o'clock **at** the latest.*

Superlatives commonly used with this pattern:

best, least, most, worst
the earliest, the latest

Expressions

at the sound, thought, or prospect of   when one experiences

> *She gets nervous **at the sound of** his voice.*

> *We shudder **at the thought of** moving again.*

> *He is **excited at the prospect of** going to South America.*

make a pass at   indicate romantic interest toward

> *The young man **made a pass at** the beautiful woman he met at the party.*

keep at it   not stop working

> *He wanted to go home, but he **kept at it** until the work was finished.*

be sick at heart   be sad

> *We **were sick at heart** when the dog died.*

be an old hand at   be very experienced with

> *Our professor **is an old hand at** government operations.*

be at an advantage   be in a better-than-average position

> *He **is at an advantage** because his family has influence.*

be at a disadvantage   be in a less-than-average position

> *When you are a newcomer at work, you **are at a disadvantage**.*

down at the heels   shabby

> *His brother looked **down at the heels** when he was without work.*

at one's mercy   in someone else's power

> *I was **at the intruder's mercy** because he had a gun in my back.*

at one's discretion   someone's own decision

> *We can go home when we are ready, **at our own discretion**.*

at that

1.   at that point, not any more or further

> *You did a good job; leave it **at that**.*

2.   illogically

> *We got lost, and in our hometown **at that**!*

be getting at   meaning, but not saying

> *The manager didn't exactly say his employer had been dishonest, but we all knew what he **was getting at**.*

Phrasal Verb

pick at something (nonseparable)   agitate with one's fingernails

> *The child **picked at** the scab on his knee.*

PRACTICE

11-1. Choose the best word or words for each blank.

1.   Stella isn't here now. She's at _____.
     the school   school   store   movies

2.   He lives at _____.
     Oak Street, 123   123 Oak Street   Street Oak, 123   Oak Street, #123

3.   The old man _____ at the nurse.
     smiled   walked   talked   threw

4.   She has been at the _____ all day.
     bed   chair   computer   lamp

5.   The two countries are fighting. They are at _____.
     war   enemies   jungle   battlefield

6.   Don't be late. Be here by six o'clock, at the _____.
     earliest   soonest   latest   tomorrow

7.   Please don't drive at _____.
     speed   75 miles per hour   so fast   highway

8.   They are selling bananas at _____.
     on sale   grocery store   40 cents per pound supermarket

9. The airplane was flying at _____.
    wind   clouds   low   3,000 feet

10. We were upset at _____.
    the news   the newspaper   newspaper   news

11-2. Use an expression with *at* to express the following:

1. They are working now.
2. Don't try to do everything together.
3. We finally arrived.
4. When we first arrived, we were happy.
5. He has a better chance than the others.
6. I stay away from her.
7. He keeps talking, but I don't know what he means.
8. He showed romantic interest in me.

11-3. Use a phrasal verb with *at* to express the following:

1. The child scratched the scab on his knee, trying to take it off.

UNIT 12:
Back To/Back From

Basic Meanings

1. **Back to** indicates **return.**

> **Pattern 1**   verb + *back* to + noun of place or time

> *Please go **back to** the beginning of your story.*
> *The children went **back to** the museum to see the new exhibit.*

Verbs often used before *back to*:

crawl, drive, fly, go, hark, jump, look, move, race, run, think, walk

> **Pattern 2**   verb + noun + *back to* + noun

> *We took the train **back to** the city.*

Typical verbs:

bring, carry, drive, pull, push, take

2. **Back from** indicates **return to a starting place from a different place.**

> **Pattern**   verb + *back from* + noun of place

> *I'll be **back (home) from** the store in about ten minutes.*
> *We can't leave until your mother gets **back from** her trip.*

Typical verbs before *back from*:

be, come, drive, fly, get, move, run, walk

3. **Back** indicates a **return of something.**

> **Pattern 1**   verb + noun + *back* (+ *to* + noun)

> *Please give this plate **back to** your mother.*
> *I took the dress **back to** the store because it didn't fit.*

Typical verbs:

bring, give, pay, send, take

> **Pattern 2**   verb + noun + *back* (+ *from* + noun)

> *Please get my suit **back from** the cleaners.*

Pattern 3	verb + noun + *back* (adverb)

*I called you **back** when I got home.*

Typical verbs:

call, bring, pay, put, take

Phrasal Verbs

get back (intransitive) move out of the way

*We wanted to see the action, but they made us **get back**.*

get back at someone (nonseparable) do harm in return for a wrong

*After he was fired, he tried to **get back at** his boss.*

get back to someone (nonseparable) call someone with new information

*As soon as I know the figures, I will **get back to** you.*

get someone **back** (separable) do harm in return for a wrong

*He hurt my feelings, but I **got** him **back** by hanging up the phone.*

cut back (intransitive) spend less

*With a lower salary he had to **cut back**.*

cut back on (nonseparable) spend less on something

*With a lower salary he had to **cut back on** entertainment.*

PRACTICE

12-1. Choose the best word or words for each blank.

1. We took the coffee maker back to _____ because it didn't work.

   the store   store   shop   shops

2. Our neighbors _____ back from their trip.

   went   came   took   fly

3. I didn't hear the telephone. Please _____ me back.

   throw   hit   speak   call

12-2. Use a phrasal verb with *back* to express the following:

1. She stepped in front of the crowd, but the officer told her to move out of the way.

2. She took my wallet, and I wanted revenge.

3. I will call you when I have the information.

4. We need to spend less money on movies.

UNIT 13:
Before

Basic Meanings

1. **Before** means **earlier than.**

    *We must leave **before** four o'clock.*

2. **Before** can mean **in a more important position than.**

    *She is so ambitious that she puts her job **before** her family.*

3. **Before** can mean **facing.**

    *The handsome singer had many adoring fans **before** him.*

4. **Before** can mean **in the future.**

    *The bride smiled as she thought of the happiness **before** her.*

5. **Before** can mean **in the presence of.**

    *I was told to appear **before** the judge.*

PRACTICE

13-1. Choose the best word or words for each blank.

1. The speaker had _____ before him.

    a lot of people   a lot of money   a lot of time   a lot of cars

2. It takes an hour to get there. We have to arrive at five P.M., so we need to leave here before _____.

    six P.M.   four P.M.   eight P.M.   midnight

3. When you go to traffic court, I hope you don't have to appear before _____.

    the trial   the desk   the classroom   the judge

Behind

Basic Meanings

1. **Behind** means **in the rear of.**

> *The trash can is **behind** the chair.*
> *My friend sits **behind** me in class.*

2. **Behind** can mean **less advanced than.**

> *Miss Thompson's class is studying lesson three; the other classes are studying lesson four. Miss Thompson's class is **behind** the other classes.*

3. **Behind** can mean **left in the past.**

> *He is rich now; all his financial problems are **behind** him.*

4. **Behind** can mean **late.**

behind schedule   later than usual

> *The train is **behind schedule**.*

behind in payments   late in making a regular payment

> *She is always **behind in** her rent payments.*

5. **Behind** can mean **encouraging or supporting.**

> **Pattern**   noun + *behind* + noun

> *The successful man had an ambitious woman **behind** him.*
> *Those candidates have a lot of money **behind** them.*
> *There must be a greedy person **behind** this scheme.*

Typical nouns after *behind*:

a person or people
idea, plan, plot, project, scheme

Expressions

behind the scenes   not seen

*The lawyer knew all the facts about the case; he had a lot of help **behind the scenes**.*

behind the times   old-fashioned/old-school

*Her dad still uses a typewriter; he is really **behind the times**.*

PRACTICE

14-1. Choose the best word or words for each blank.

1. Maria sits in Row 6. Estéban sits in Row 7. I sit in Row 8. Estéban sits behind _____.

    me   Maria   the teacher   him

2. Miss Evans's class is reading chapter eight. Mrs. Martínez's class is reading chapter ten.
    Our class is reading chapter seven. Our class is behind _____.

    Mrs. Martínez's class   the school   Mrs. Martínez's and Miss Evans's classes   Miss Evans's
    class

3. Who is behind this ridiculous _____?

    train   idea   house   car

4. He is happy now. His _____ are behind him.

    problems   cars   plans   ideas

14-2. Use an expression with *behind* to express the following:

1. The bus is later than usual.

2. You are very old-fashioned.

Below

Basic Meanings

1. Below means lower in number or degree than.

> *Your body temperature is 97 degrees Fahrenheit; it is **below** normal, which is 98.6.*

2. Below can mean lower in rank or level than.

> *In our company the supervisors are **below** the directors.*
>
> *Our offices are on the fourth floor; theirs are **below** ours, on the third floor.*

Expression

below the belt   unfairly, not according to the rules

> *He pretended to be her friend, then applied for her job. That was really **below the belt**.*

PRACTICE

15-1. Choose the best word or words for each blank.

1. If your body temperature is 93 degrees Fahrenheit, it is below _____.

   the belt   par   normal   the roof

2. My bedroom is on the third floor. My sister's bedroom is on the second floor. Her bedroom is below _____.

   mine   herself   our parents'   the roof

15-2. Use an expression with *below* to express the following:

1. It was unfair that my friend told my secret to everyone.

UNIT 16:
Beneath

Basic Meanings

1. Beneath means **under and concealed by.**

> *My glasses were **beneath** the newspaper.*
> *The daffodils sprouted **beneath** the snow.*

2. Beneath can mean **less worthy than.**

> *Now that she is rich and famous, she thinks her family is **beneath** her.*

3. Beneath can mean **unlikely, because of goodness or pride.**

Pattern 1   *it + be + beneath + noun of person + infinitive*

> *She was a little wild, but **it was beneath** her to commit a crime.*

Typical verbs after *beneath*:

break the law, commit a crime, commit adultery, commit perjury, gossip, lie, murder, steal

Pattern 2   **noun/gerund form of verb + be + beneath + person**

> *She was a little wild, but committing a crime **was beneath** her.*

Typical nouns before *be beneath*:

adultery, breaking the law, committing a crime, forgery, lying, murder, stealing

---

PRACTICE

16-1. Choose the best word or words for each blank.

1. He is famous, but arrogant; he thinks _____ are beneath him.

   the class   everybody   other people   his brother

2. I finally found my phone. It was beneath my _____.

   pillow   library   classroom   wall

3. I don't like him, but I think _____ is beneath him.

   walking to school   cheating   taking a test   working

Basic Meaning

1. Beside means **next to.**

> **Pattern** verb + *beside* + noun

> *Please come over here and sit **beside** me.*

Verbs commonly used with this pattern:

be, kneel, lie (down), rest, sit (down), sleep, stand, stay, walk, work

Expressions

beside the point irrelevant

> *He always wastes time at our meetings by talking about things that are **beside the point**.*

beside oneself extremely agitated

> *My mother is **beside herself** because she doesn't know where my brother is.*

PRACTICE

17-1. Choose the best word or words for each blank.

1. My best friend likes to _____ beside me at school.

   fight   go to school   talk   sit

2. He is dizzy; please _____ beside him.

   run   sing   walk   work

17-2. Use an expression with "beside" to express the following:

1. Her comment was <u>on a different topic</u>.

2. The teacher is <u>very upset</u>.

UNIT 18:
Besides

Basic Meaning

1.   Besides means **excepting.**

*Everyone **besides** me is at the beach.*

18-1.   Choose the best word or words for each blank.

1.   _____ besides Cecelia are at school.

   The girl   The girls   All the girls   The boy

2.   Besides _____, I invited all my friends to the party.
   my brothers   my games   my toys   my house

Between

Basic Meanings

1. Between indicates **separation of two things.**

> **Pattern** noun + *between* + noun

> *My neighbor and I built a fence **between** our backyards.*

2. Between can show **connection of two places.**

> *Route 395 goes **between** New York and Washington, D.C.*

3. Between can indicate **a choice of.**

> **Pattern** verb + *between* + noun + *and* + noun

> *You can have only one dessert, so please decide **between** cake and ice cream.*

Verbs often used before *between*:

choose, decide, judge, pick, select

4. Between means **not lower or higher in number.**

> *We have saved **between** three and four thousand dollars.*
> *It is hot today. It must be **between** 80 and 85 degrees.*

5. Between means **from a time to another time.**

> *She will be away all weekend, so don't call her **between** Friday night and Monday morning.*

6. Between can mean **shared by.**

> *We are on a diet, so we will have one piece of cake **between** us.*
> *They only had five dollars **between** them.*

7. Between can mean **together.**

> *The newlyweds painted their new house **between** them.*

As an adverb:

In between means **at a middle point**

> *He isn't old or young; he is **in between**.*

Expression

between you and me   confidentially

*I don't like to spread gossip, but **between you and me**, they got married last week.*

PRACTICE

19-1. Choose the best word or words for each blank.

1. Is there is a _____ between your house and theirs?

   car   fence   dog   lamp

2. Ali has three dollars. I have two dollars. We have _____ dollars between us.

   four   six   ten   five

3. She is on vacation this week. She won't be at the office between _____.

   Thursday and Sunday   Tuesday and Saturday   Monday and Friday   Saturday and Sunday

4. It's very cold today. The temperature is between _____ degrees.

   33 and 40   50 and 60   55 and 75   80 and 90

5. That route goes from east to west. It goes between _____.

   New York and Florida   New York and California   Washington and Boston   New York and Boston

6. I like all the desserts. I can't _____ between ice cream and pie.

   save   want   love   decide

19-2. Use an expression with *between* to express the following:

1. This is a secret, but I am not voting for that politician.

Beyond

Basic Meanings

1. Beyond means **on the other side of.**

> Our street is **beyond** the traffic light.
>
> If you are traveling west, New Mexico is **beyond** Texas.

2. Beyond means **past the limits of.**

> **Pattern 1** *be + beyond + noun*
>
> The sick child **was beyond** help.
>
> That situation **is beyond** my understanding.

> **Pattern 2** *be + adjective + beyond + noun*
>
> The palace **was** beautiful **beyond** description.

Nouns commonly used after *beyond*:

belief, comprehension, help, one's wildest dreams, salvation, saving, understanding

3. Beyond can mean **later than.**

> **Pattern** *beyond + noun*
>
> The guests were having so much fun that they stayed well **beyond** midnight.
>
> In this town nothing is open **beyond** ten o'clock.

Expressions

beyond one not understandable by someone

> This puzzle is **beyond me**.
>
> That technical article was **beyond him**.

beyond the pale totally unacceptable

> His rude jokes at that formal reception were **beyond the pale**.

the great beyond (adverb) heaven

> She said there would be perfect peace in **the great beyond**.

PRACTICE

20-1. Choose the best word or words for each blank.

1. If you are traveling east from San Francisco, Philadelphia is beyond _____.
   Chicago   New York   Washington   Miami

2. I don't understand this _____. It is beyond me.
   homework   library   classroom   teacher

20-2. Use an expression with *beyond* to express the following:

1. His behavior was totally unacceptable.

UNIT 21:
But

Basic Meaning

1. **But** means **except.**

   *She works every day **but** Friday.*

21-1. Choose the best word or words for each blank.

1. They work six days a week. They work every day but _____.
   Saturday and Sunday   Monday and Tuesday   Thursday and Saturday   Monday

By

Basic Meanings

1. **By** indicates an **actor, instrument, or cause**

   | Pattern | *be* + past participle + *by* + noun |

   > The work **was** done **by** a carpenter.
   > The mark **was** made **by** a hammer.
   > The damage **was** caused **by** the storm.

2. **By** means **following the boundary of something; along**

   > They walked **by** the side of the road.

3. **By** indicates a **method** or **way.**

   | Pattern | verb + (noun) + *by* + noun |

   > She **made** a little money **by** begging.
   > We **sent** the letter **by** mail.
   > They **went** to the mountains **by** Route 66.

4. **By** can mean **according to** a form, period of time, packaging, weight, number, or amount

   | Pattern | verb + (noun) + *by* + *the* + noun |

   > He makes his decisions **by the** rules.
   > She charges **by the** hour.
   > We buy eggs **by the** dozen.

   Typical nouns after *by the*:

   day, hour, month, week

   job, piece

   bag, barrel, box, bucket, bushel, cup, drop, gallon, ounce, pint, pound, quart, ream, tablespoonful, teaspoonful

5. **By** can mean **not later than.**

   > You must be here **by** 6 A.M. sharp.
   > I'm worried; they should have arrived **by** now.

6. **By** means **near** or **next to.**

> *His desk is **by** mine.*
>
> *I hope you will stay **by** me.*

7. **By** indicates **multiplication, division,** and **square measurement.**

> *We multiplied four **by** three. (4 · 3 = 12)*
>
> *They divided ten **by** two. (10 ÷ 2 = 5)*
>
> *That room measures ten feet **by** twelve feet. It measures 120 square feet.*

8. **By** can mean **a lot of.**

> **Pattern** *by + the +* **noun**

> *He gets letters **by the** hundreds every day.*

Typical nouns used after *by the*:

dozens, hundreds, thousands, truckload

9. **By** can indicate **the extent of a win or a loss.**

> *That horse won **by** a nose.*
>
> *They lost the basketball game **by** three points.*

Expressions

by the time   when

> ***By the time** you get up, I'll be in New York.*

by a mile   by a lot; to a great extent

> *We won the game **by a mile**.*

by far   without question

> *He is **by far** the strongest man here.*

by all means   certainly

> *You should **by all means** visit the art gallery.*

(all) by oneself   alone; without help

> *The children are at home **by themselves**.*
>
> *The girl made the cake **all by herself**.*

by day   during the day; **by night**   during the night

> *Most people work **by day** and sleep **by night**.*

by chance   for no apparent reason

> *I saw my teacher at the mall **by chance**.*

by (any) chance   perhaps

> Do you **by any chance** have change for a dollar?

by the way   incidentally

> **By the way**, my aunt is coming to visit next week. Why don't you come see her?

little by little (adverb)   slowly

> He practiced every day, and **little by little**, began to show improvement.

one by one   one at a time; **two by two**   two at a time

> **One by one**, she picked up the pearls from her broken necklace.
>
> The schoolchildren walked to the museum, **two by two**, holding hands.

by profession   indicates one's job

> He is a teacher **by profession**.

by nature/by disposition   naturally

> She is generous **by nature**.
>
> He is nervous **by disposition**.

by reputation   indicates common belief

> She is a good lawyer **by reputation**.

go by the board   be ignored

> Our suggestions for improving the company **went by the board**.

by and by (adverb)   one day, in the future

> We'll meet again, **by and by**.

by and large (adverb)   almost completely

> The company is doing well, **by and large**.

Phrasal Verbs

do well by (nonseparable)   be responsible for someone's benefit

> She was a good mother; she **did well by** her children.

stand by (intransitive)   wait in hopes of success

> I didn't have a reservation, but I decided **to stand by**, and got on the flight.

stand by (nonseparable)   to support

> She **stood by** me when I was in trouble.

swear by (nonseparable)   have complete faith in the worth of something

> My mother **swears by** that cleaning product.

drop by (intransitive)   visit without notice

> Your friends **dropped by** this afternoon, but you weren't here.

drop by (separable)   to deliver

> A boy **dropped** this package **by** today.

get by (intransitive)   live, but with difficulty

> He's feeble, but he **gets by**.

go by (nonseparable)   pass in front of

> *We **went by** your house last night.*

put by (separable)   store

> *She **put** her dreams **by** for a while.*

run by (separable)   to tell in detail

> *She **ran** her story **by** me several times this afternoon.*

PRACTICE

22-1. Choose the best word or words for each blank.

1. Our new cabinet was built by an expert _____.
   policeman   father   carpenter   tailor

2. The children must be home before dinner. They must be here by _____.
   5 P.M.   noon   midnight   10 P.M.

3. Gasoline for a car is sold by the _____.
   cup   pint   quart   gallon

4. The apartment measures 30 feet by 60 feet. It measures _____ square feet.
   600   1,600   1,800   2,000

5. We earn extra money by _____.
   studying   babysitting   eating   exercising

6. There are a lot of _____ by the side of the creek.
   sand   rocks   mud   water

7. We won the game by _____.
   three miles   a hundred   10 points   close

22-2. Use an expression with *by* to express the following:

1. You should certainly ask for help if you need it.

2. Her nature is to be kind.

3. Incidentally, don't forget the meeting next week.

4. Some people work at night, and sleep in the daytime.

5. Nobody was with her.

6. I found this old photo when I wasn't looking for it.

7. Do you know my father, perhaps?

22-3. Use a phrasal verb with *by* to express the following:

1. He supported me when I needed help.

2. Could you tell me that story again?

3. She lives, with difficulty.

4. Can we visit you this afternoon?

5. I pass your house on my way home from work.

UNIT 23:
Close To

Basic Meanings

1. **Close to** means **near.**

   *Your house is **close to** the metro station.*
   *They are sitting **close to** each other.*

2. **Close to** indicates **a very friendly** or **intimate relationship.**

   *She is very **close to** her older sister.*

3. **Close to** can mean **almost.**

   *I wrote **close to** fifty invitations this morning.*

PRACTICE

23-1. Choose the word or words that best fill each blank.

1. Our teacher lives one block from our school. She lives close to _____.

   the bank   downtown   us   work

2. They are twins. They are very close to _____.

   school   work   each other   him

3. The exam was from 1 P.M. until 3:45 P.M. It lasted close to _____.

   two hours   three hours   an hour   five hours

UNIT 24:
Despite/In Spite Of

Basic Meanings

1. **Despite** indicates **an illogical occurrence.**

   *We had a good time **despite** the bad weather.*

2. **In spite of** has the same meaning and usage as *despite.*

   *We had a good time **in spite of** the bad weather.*

24-1. Choose the best word or words for each blank.

1. He did a good job despite his _____.

   lack of experience   expertise   good education   good manners

2. We arrived on time in spite of the _____.

   street   traffic   parking lot   help

Basic Meanings

1. **Down** indicates **movement from a higher place.**

Pattern   noun + verb + *down* + noun

> *The rocks rolled **down** the mountain.*

Typical verbs used before *down*:

come, fall, go, move, roll, run, slide, walk

2. **Down** means **following the way of; along**

Pattern 1   noun + verb + *down* + noun

> *The old man went **down** the road on foot.*

Typical verbs used before *down*:

come, drive, go, move, run, skate, walk

Pattern 2   noun + verb + noun + *down* + noun

> *The boys rode their bikes **down** the street this morning.*

Typical verbs before *down*:

bring, carry, drive, move, pull, push, ride, take

Typical nouns after *down*:

freeway, highway, path, road, sidewalk, street, turnpike

3. **Down** indicates **destruction.**

Pattern 1   noun + verb + *down* + noun

> *The intruder broke **down** the door.*

Typical verbs used before *down*:

blow, break, bring, burn, cut, strike, take, tear

Pattern 2   verb + noun + *down*

> *The intruder broke the door **down**.*

Expression

upside down   turned so that the bottom is on top

> *The cups go in the dishwasher **upside down**.*

Phrasal Verbs

back down (intransitive)   retreat

> *The dog **backed down** when I called his name.*

calm down (separable)   soothe; tranquilize

> *We had to **calm** the children **down** after the excitement.*

close down (separable)   stop business activity, temporarily or permanently

> *We **close** the shop **down** at four o'clock every day.*
>
> *They plan to **close** that business **down** for good.*

come down with (nonseparable)   become sick

> *She missed the picnic because she **came down with** the flu.*

crack down on (nonseparable)   impose restrictions

> *The police are **cracking down on** street violence.*

let down (separable)   disappoint

> *She **let** me **down** when she didn't help me with my party.*

look down on (nonseparable)   feel superior to

> *The older students tend to **look down on** the younger ones.*

mark down (separable)   lower in price

> *I bought this shirt after they **marked** it **down** to ten dollars.*

put down (separable)   insult

> *She shouldn't go out with him; he **puts** her **down** all the time.*

run down (separable)   criticize negatively

> *She always **runs** her hometown **down**.*

shut down (separable)   turn off a computer; end a business

> *She worked all night and didn't **shut** her computer **down** until morning.*
>
> *They **shut** that shop **down** two years ago.*

turn down (separable)   reject

> *He got a job offer today but he is going to **turn** it **down**.*

write down (separable)   put on paper for future reference

> *She didn't know my phone number, so I **wrote** it **down** for her.*

PRACTICE

25-1. Choose the best word or words for each blank.

1. The children like to _____ down the hill on their sleds.

   run   walk   slide   crawl

2. They cut the _____ down with a saw.

   tree   house   school   grass

3. He took the trash down to the _____ for collection.

   highway   movies   street   party

25-2. Use an expression with *down* to express the following:

1. He hung the picture in the wrong direction.

25-3. Use a phrasal verb with *down* to express the following:

1. The government is imposing restrictions on homelessness.

2. I hope you don't get a cold.

3. Julia's mother will soothe her.

4. Please command your dog to retreat.

5. Please don't disappoint your teacher.

6. Are you going to reject the offer?

7. Let's buy the computer when the price is lower.

8. She feels superior to the newcomers.

9. It's a good idea to make a note of your passwords.

10. Stop criticizing me in front of your friends.

During

Basic Meanings

1. **During** indicates **within a period of time.**

    *We slept **during** the day.*
    *They practiced basketball **during** the summer.*

2. **During** means **at the same time as another event.**

    *I slept **during** the football game.*
    *They lived in the north **during** the war.*

PRACTICE

26-1. Choose the best word or words for each blank.

1. She needs to _____ during the day because she works at night.
    work   sleep   go to parties   smoke

2. What are you going to do during the _____?
    office   field   football game   soccer goal

UNIT 27:
Except

Basic Meaning

1. **Except** means **excluding.**

> *Everyone went to the movies **except** me.*
> *We work every day **except** Sunday.*

27-1. **Choose the best word or words for blank.**

1. My brothers are called Abe, Brian, Carlos, and David. I saw Brian, David, and Carlos last night.
   I saw all of my brothers except _____.

   David   Carlos   Brian   Abe

2. We go to school on weekdays. We go to school every day except _____.

   Saturdays and   Mondays and   Tuesdays and   Tuesdays and
   Sundays   Fridays   Wednesdays   Thursdays

Far From

Basic Meanings

1. **Far (away) from** indicates **a great distance between places or people.**

> *Their office isn't **far (away) from** here.*
> *His sister moved **far from** home a long time ago.*

Before an adjective:

2. **Far from** can mean **not.**

> **Pattern** *far from* + **adjective**

> *His wife is **far from** perfect.*

Adjectives often used with this pattern:
ideal, perfect, wonderful

PRACTICE

28-1. **Choose the best word or words for each blank.**

1. We live two blocks from school. Our school isn't far from _____.

   our friends   our house   our mother   your house

2. He has lied to us many times. He is far from _____.

   handsome   honest   trickery   illegal

For

Basic Meanings

1. For indicates a **recipient** or **beneficiary**.

Pattern 1 noun + *for* + noun

> *I have a present **for** you.*

Nouns often used before *for*:

answer, cure, gift, idea, job, letter, message, plan, present, project, question, secret, suggestion, surprise

Pattern 2 noun + *for* + ø noun

> *We have news **for** you.*

Typical nouns before *for*:

advice, help, information, news, nothing, something

Pattern 3 verb + noun + *for* + noun

> *She sang a song **for** me.*
>
> *He only wants the best **for** you.*

Verbs often used before *for*:

bake, build, buy, care, cook, create, dance, design, do, get, make, perform, play, sing, want, win, work, write

2. For indicates **a special purpose**.

Pattern 1 noun + *for* + noun

> *You need a coat **for** winter.*
>
> *He has a bicycle **for** transportation.*

Pattern 2 noun + *for* + verb in gerund form

> *They have a special place **for** washing cars.*
>
> *The doctor has a machine **for** measuring blood pressure.*

Related Expression

room for/space for   enough space to hold an event or accommodate a number of people or things

> *We need **room for** twenty people for our party.*
>
> *We don't have **room for** a grand piano.*

3. **For** can indicate the **intended result** of an action.

Pattern 1	verb + *for* + noun

> *The boys were screaming **for** help.*
>
> *What are you looking **for**?*

Verbs often used before *for*:

apply, ask, audition, beg, call, campaign, compete, cry, fight, go, go out, hope, long, look, petition, plead, pray, register, run, scream, send, shop, shout, stand in line, strive, study, train, try out, wait, whistle, wish, work, yell

Related Expression

run for office   be a candidate in an election

Pattern 2	verb + someone + *for* + noun

> *We nominated him **for** president of the club.*

Typical verbs:

ask, need, nominate, send, train, want

Pattern 3	noun + *for* + noun

> *I hope they are developing a cure **for** the flu.*
>
> *Do you have a good recipe **for** lemon pie?*

Nouns often used before *for*:

cure, directions, idea, instructions, lesson, need, pattern, plan, program, project, recipe, system

Pattern 4	*be* + adjective of condition + *for* + noun

> *I **am** hungry **for** steak and french fries.*
>
> *They **are** ready **for** the ball game.*

Adjectives often used before *for*:

anxious, eager, greedy, hungry, impatient, prepared, ready, starved, thirsty

4. **For** can explain the **reason** of an action or fact.

Pattern 1	verb + *for* + noun

> *He apologized **for** his absence.*

Pattern 2	verb + *for* + gerund form of verb

> *He apologized **for** arriving late.*

Pattern 3 verb + someone + *for* + noun

> *They rewarded her* **for** *bravery.*
>
> *They congratulated him* **for** *graduating.*

Verbs often used before *for*:

book, chide, cite, compensate, congratulate, criticize, expel, fine, get, honor, pay, praise, punish, reimburse, reprimand, reward, scold, tease

Pattern 4 *be* + adjective + *for* + noun

> *She* **is** *famous* **for** *her great parties.*
>
> *She* **is** *famous* **for** *giving great parties.*

Adjectives often used before *for*:

famous, feared, known, notorious, popular, loved, well known

5. **For** can indicate the **expected benefit** of an action.

Pattern verb + *for* + noun

> *We play soccer* **for** *fun.*

Typical nouns after *for*:

exercise, fun, happiness, kicks, money, peace, pleasure, practice, relaxation, security

6. **For** can indicate the **effect** of an adjective.

Pattern 1 *be* + adjective + *for* + noun

> *Calcium* **is** *good* **for** *your bones and teeth.*

Adjectives often used before *for*:

accessible, available, bad, crucial, good, healthy, helpful, important, necessary, unhealthy, useful

Pattern 2 *It* + *be* + adjective + *for* + object + infinitive

> *It* **was** *hard* **for** *him to make good grades.*

Adjectives often used before *for*:

bad, better, challenging, customary, crucial, good, helpful, important, impossible, necessary, possible, ridiculous, unimportant, unnecessary, unusual, useful, useless, usual, wasteful, worse

Pattern 3 *be* + (not) adjective + *enough* + *for* + noun

> *This apartment* **is** *good* **enough for** *me.*

Pattern 4 *be* + *too* + **adjective** + *for* + **noun**

> *That course **was too** hard **for** him.*
>
> *This apartment **is too** small **for** three people.*

7.   **For** can indicate the **recipient** of someone's feelings.

Pattern *be* + **adjective** + *for* + **noun (person)**

> *We **are** happy **for** her on her wedding day.*
>
> *Why **are** you sorry **for** yourself?*

Typical adjectives before *for*:

delighted, happy, pleased, sorry, thrilled

8.   **For** can indicate activity or preparation on an **occasion.**

Pattern **verb** + **(noun)** + *for* + **noun**

> *What do you want **for** your birthday?*
>
> *What did you have **for** dinner?*

Typical nouns after *for*:

**one's anniversary, birthday, graduation
breakfast, dinner, the holidays, lunch**

9.   **For** indicates **a substitute.**

Pattern 1 **noun** + *for* + **noun**

> *We had to use a newspaper **for** an umbrella.*
>
> *I'm sorry, I mistook you **for** someone else.*

Pattern 2 **verb** + *for* + **noun**

> *He taught the class **for** our teacher, who was sick.*

Verbs often used with this meaning:

**act, conduct, direct, drive, fill in, manage, operate, run, speak, stand in, substitute,
teach, work**

10. **For** can mean **available.**

Pattern **noun** + *for* + **noun**

> *The house is **for** sale.*
>
> *The pianos are **for** use by the students.*

Nouns often used after *for*:

hire, practice, purchase, rent, sale, use

Related Expression

up for grabs   available to many people

>*The chairmanship is **up for grabs**.*

11. **For** can indicate a **destination.**

Pattern   **verb** + *for* + **noun**

>*We are leaving **for** Spain in two weeks.*

Verbs used before *for*:

head, leave, plan, set out, start out, take off

12. **For** can indicate **representation.**

>*Red is **for** stop; yellow is **for** caution; green is **for** go.*
>*M is **for** Mary.*

13. **For** can indicate **equality in an exchange.**

Pattern 1   *be* + **noun** + *for* + **noun**

>*The bananas **are** two pounds **for** a dollar.*

Pattern 2   **verb** + **noun** + *for* + **noun**

>*We bought three books **for** twenty-five dollars.*

Typical verbs:

buy, do, exchange, hand over, make, rent, sell, take, trade, want

Pattern 3   **verb** + *for* + **noun**

>*He works **for** twenty dollars an hour.*

Related Expressions

for free   without charge
for nothing   without charge

14. **For** can indicate **amount.**

Pattern   **noun** + *for* + **noun**

>*The mechanic sent them a bill **for** three hundred dollars.*

Nouns often used before *for*:

bill, check, invoice, receipt, request

15. For can indicate **length of time.**

> *He was here **for** ten years.*

Related Expressions

for good   forever

> *He came to live in this country **for good**.*

for life   until death

> *They sent him to prison **for life**.*

16. For can indicate **need on a future date.**

> *She needs the musicians **for** Thursday afternoon.*

17. For can mean **despite.**

> **Pattern**   *for* + *all* + **possessive pronoun** + **noun**

> **For all** *her experience, she's not a very good secretary.*

Nouns often used with this meaning:

education, experience, expertise, knowledge, popularity, qualifications, training

18. For indicates the **person or people responsible for an action.**

> **Pattern**   *for* + **person** + **infinitive**

> *Your final grade is **for** the teacher to decide.*
>
> *That problem is **for** you to solve.*

19. For can describe a **sense** or **talent.**

> **Pattern**   *have* + **noun** + *for* + **noun**

> *He has an ear **for** music.*
>
> *She has a touch **for** the piano.*

Nouns often used before *for*:

aptitude, ear, eye, knack, rhythm, talent, touch, voice

Related Expressions

have a nose for gossip   often hear and spread news about others

have an eye for the girls   often admire pretty women

20. For can indicate an **unusual fact or exception.**

> **Pattern 1**   adjective + *for* + noun
>
> > *That boy is tall **for** his age.*
> > *It's warm **for** February.*

> **Pattern 2**   adverb + *for* + noun
>
> > *She plays very well **for** a beginner.*

21. For can indicate **purpose** or **outcome**

> **Pattern**   verb + *for* + noun
>
> > *We are **for** higher wages.*
> >
> > *You have to stand up **for** your rights.*

Verbs often used before *for*:

be, push, stand, stand up, fight, strike, work hard

22. For can mean **because of.**

> *We are thankful **for** your help.*
> *She is grateful **for** her family.*

23. For can mean **favor or support.**

> *I'm cheering **for** my school's team.*

Verbs often used before *for*:

be, cheer, show respect

Related Expression

to have a preference for   to prefer

> *She **has a preference for** the other job.*

As a conjunction

For means **because.**

> *She went home early, **for** she was sick.*

Expressions

for once   for the first time, showing exasperation

> *Would you please be at work on time **for once**!*

once and for all   immediately and forever after

> *She decided to stop smoking **once and for all**.*

word for word   reading or talking slowly, one word at a time

> *He read the letter to me **word for word**.*

for the time being   meanwhile; until something happens to change the situation

> *We can't do anything now, so **for the time being** we will act as usual.*

for fear of   in order to avoid

> *He worked and saved **for fear of** being poor again.*

for a change   as usual, sarcastically

> *It's raining **for a change**.*

be for the best   even though the situation is unpleasant, it may be good

> *I was sad when she died, but it **was for the best**, because she was suffering a lot.*

go for a drive/run/swim/walk   spend a short time doing that activity

> *We always **go for a walk** after lunch.*

see for oneself   investigate personally

> *I couldn't believe her, so I decided to **see for myself**.*

for better or for worse   accepting all conditions, regardless of what happens in the future

> *He promised to stay with her forever, **for better or for worse**.*

for naught   with no result

> *Our efforts were all **for naught**; we lost.*

Phrasal Verbs

go (in) for (nonseparable)   like a lot

> *The college girls really **go for** Latin dancing.*

go out for (nonseparable)   perform in hopes of being selected to play on a team

> *She **went out for** the softball team, but didn't make it.*

care for (nonseparable)   love

> *She really **cares for** him.*

care for (nonseparable)   want

> *She doesn't **care for** more ice cream, thank you.*

fall for (nonseparable)   innocently believe or trust

> *He **falls for** all of her tricks.*

not stand for (nonseparable)   not allow

> *The teacher **won't stand for** talking during a test.*

stand for (nonseparable)   tolerate

> *His mother doesn't **stand for** laziness.*

stand up for (nonseparable)   support publicly

> *His best **friend stood up for** him through all his problems.*

take for (separable)   consider as

> *Don't **take him** for a fool; he is really quite smart.*

try out for   audition or perform in hopes of being selected to play a part in a show, band, orchestra, play, or team

> *He's going to **try out for** the school play.*

PRACTICE

29-1. Choose the best word or words for each blank.

1. I know it's your birthday, and I have a _____ for you.
   heartache   surprise   headache   love

2. They practice yoga for _____.
   necessary   painful   relaxation   boring

3. We stood in line two hours for _____.
   fun   tickets   speed   good luck

4. We congratulated him for _____.
   winning   losing   lying   sleeping

5. It's cold there. You will need _____ for winter.
   a bathing suit   a warm coat   shorts   a straw hat

6. She failed the test; it was too _____ for her.
   difficult   simple   easy   slow

7. *A* is for ant. *B* is for bee. *C* is for _____.
   bear   cat   deer   elephant

8. Anybody can be the Treasurer. The office is up for _____.
   sale   rent   grabs   five dollars

9. I'm _____ for Mexico in two weeks.
   staying   flying   driving   leaving

10. She sent me a _____ for $29.
    bill   paper   letter   cash

11. You don't have to pay for these pencils. You can have them for _____.

    ten cents   free   ten dollars   a dime

12. I'm so _____ for you for your promotion.

    jealous   happy   unhappy   sorry

13. He _____ the car for me when I got tired.

    drove   argued   saved   waited

14. We don't plan on going back. We came here for _____.

    class   good   war   problem

15. She's taking piano lessons because she has a good ear for _____.

    art   violin   music   opera

16. She is 86, and still beautiful. She looks _____ for her age.

    wrinkled   tired   short   good

17. For all her experience in the movies, she's not a great _____.

    actress   waitress   teacher   nurse

18. The workers are striking for _____.

    fun   vacation   higher wages   boss

29-2. Use an expression with *for* to express the following:

1. You never help me! Please help me now!

2. We didn't trust the travel guidebook, so we investigated personally.

3. You're on time—as usual (sarcastically).

4. He decided to stop calling her, period.

5. It was very hot, so I decided to swim for ten or fifteen minutes.

6. We cannot change the situation now; we will stay quiet until things change.

29-3. Use a phrasal verb with *for* to express the following:

1. They supported the mayor when he was accused of misconduct.

2. He loves him mom dearly.

3. She is hoping to be in the play, and has an audition next week.

4. The university does not allow cheating.

5. No, thank you. I don't want any dessert.

UNIT 30:
From

Basic Meanings

1. From indicates a source.

Pattern 1 verb + *from* + noun

*Tony is **from** Alabama.*

*I hear **from** him every week.*

Verbs commonly used before *from*:

be, call, come, derive, hear

Pattern 2 verb + noun + *from* + noun

*We get help **from** our neighbors.*

Verbs commonly used with this pattern:

borrow, bring, buy, collect, copy, get, mail, obtain, receive, send

2. From indicates a point of departure.

Pattern verb + *from* + noun (place)

*The ship sailed **from** San Francisco.*

*Please start **from** the beginning.*

Typical verbs:

begin, depart, drive, fly, go, graduate, move, read, sail, start (over), take off

3. From can indicate separation.

Pattern 1 verb + *away* + *from* + noun

*We ran **away from** the building.*

*Keep **away from** the crowd.*

Typical verbs before *away from*:

drive, get, keep, move, run, walk

Pattern 2 verb + noun + *from* + noun

*We collected the papers **from** the students.*

Verbs commonly used with this pattern:

borrow, buy, chase, collect, delete, dissociate, eliminate, erase, expel, hide, keep (away), protect, release, remove, save, scare (away), separate, shield, steal, subtract, take (away)

4. **From** can indicate **difference.**

   | Pattern 1 | number + *from* + number |

   Three from nine equals six.

   | Pattern 2 | number + noun of time or distance + *from* |

   He lives five miles from here.
   They are only twenty minutes (away) from the city.
   I will see you two weeks from today.

Related Expressions

be different from   not be alike
   My sweater is different from yours.

differ from
   My opinion differs from his.

distinguish from   identify in a comparison
   I can't distinguish her from her twin sister.

tell from   identify in a comparison
   I can't tell her from her twin sister.

know from   identify in a comparison
   I don't know her from her twin sister.

not know someone from Adam   never have met someone
   I'm meeting his brother at the airport, but I don't know him from Adam.

5. **From . . . to** can indicate the lowest and highest limits of an estimate; **between.**

   | Pattern | *from* + number + *to* + number |

   You will earn from ten to fifteen dollars an hour.
   We expect from twenty-five to thirty people.

6. **From . . . to** can give the **starting and ending time or place.**

   *We work **from** 9 A.M. **to** 5 P.M.*

Related Expressions

from beginning to end
from front to back
from May to September
from one place to another
from one side to the other
from start to finish
from top to bottom

7. **From** can indicate the **material** something is composed of.

   | Pattern | *be* + past participle of verb + *from* + noun |

   *This suit **was** made **from** three different fabrics.*
   *A new plant **has been** developed **from** those seeds.*

   Past participles commonly used before *from*:
   crafted, created, derived, developed, fashioned, made, put together, sewn

8. **From** can indicate a **position** for viewing or hearing.

   *I can see the bridge **from** my window.*
   *Let's try to see the problem **from** his point of view.*
   *Can you hear the actors **from** the back of the auditorium?*

Related Expressions

from here, there
from his/her/my/our/their/your point of view
from this/that angle, distance, position, vantage point

9. **From** can indicate a **cause.**

   | Pattern 1 | adjective + *from* + gerund form of verb |

   *They are exhausted **from** working so hard.*

   Adjectives often used with this pattern:
   better, bored, drunk, exhausted, fat, healthy, sick, sore, tired, well, worse

<blockquote>
Pattern 2   verb + noun + from + noun
</blockquote>

> *They knew the songs **from** memory.*
>
> *He learned his lesson **from** hard work.*

Typical nouns after *from*:

hard work, listening, memory, studying

Related Expression

to suffer from   to hurt because of

> *She **suffers from** neglect.*

10. **From** can indicate **avoidance.**

<blockquote>
Pattern 1   verb + from + noun
</blockquote>

> *Try to keep **from** shaking.*
>
> *We can't hide **from** them any longer.*

<blockquote>
Pattern 2   verb + direct object + from + verb in gerund form
</blockquote>

> *Try to keep him **from** shaking.*
>
> *They hope to stop her **from** running away.*

Typical verbs:

keep, prevent, stop

11. **From** can mean **because of.**

<blockquote>
Pattern   from + noun
</blockquote>

> ***From** the way he walks, I think his ankle is sprained.*
>
> ***From** his accent, I believe he is from Boston.*

PRACTICE

30-1. Choose the best word or words for each blank.

1. She has a devoted son. She _____ from him every day.

   calls   texts   hears   loves

2. I finally _____ his name from my account.

   stole   subtracted   borrowed   deleted

3. Where did you _____ from?

   study   graduate   go to college   finish

4. The plane _____ from New York.

   landed   sailed   took off   separated

5. We will be working from _____.

   9 A.M. to 5 P.M.   5 A.M. to 4 A.M.   3 A.M. to 2 A.M.   9 P.M. to 8 P.M.

6. She hopes to earn from _____ a year.

   $70,000 to $60,000 $60,000 to $70,000 $100,000 to $30,000 $90,000 to $85,000

7. He refuses to _____ the problem from my point of view.

   see   know   read   talk

8. We are _____ from working so hard.

   sane   tired   happy   unhappy

9. She's so sad. I'm trying to keep her from _____.

   laughing   crying   telling jokes   swimming

10. They are identical twins. I can't _____ one from the other.

    see   talk   say   tell

UNIT 31:
In

Basic Meanings

1. **In** indicates **location inside** or **within** something else.

> **Pattern 1** verb + *in* + noun

> *We live **in** that house.*
>
> *The pencils are **in** the box.*

Nouns commonly used after *in*:

Geographical areas:

city, continent, country, state, town

> *He lives **in** Seattle, Washington, in the United States.*

Comfortable, protected places:

alcove, cocoon, large chair, nest

> *He sat down **in** the chair and read his novel.*

Inside areas:

attic, balcony, basement, building, corner, hall, kitchen, office, room

> *She is **in** her office, **in** that building, **in** room 302, **in** the corner.*

Vehicles where the passengers cannot walk around:

canoe, car, helicopter, small airplane, small boat

> *We went **in** the car, but they went **in** a helicopter.*

Publications and speeches:

article, book, dictionary, encyclopedia, lecture, magazine, newspaper, speech

> *He didn't say that **in** his speech, but I read it **in** the newspaper.*

> **Pattern 2** *be + in + ø* noun

> *He can't come to the phone because he's **in** bed.*

Nouns commonly used after *in:*

bed, church, class, jail, place, school, town

> **Pattern 3** verb + noun + *in* + noun

> *Put the pencils **in** the box.*

Typical verbs:

drop, get, insert, lay, place, push, put

Typical nouns:

bag, box, drawer, file, folder, notebook, sack, suitcase, trunk, wallet

2. **In** indicates **membership** of a group or category.

    | Pattern | *be* + noun + *in* + noun |

    > There **are** seven people **in** our family.
    > Your brother **is** the expert **in** that office.

    Nouns commonly used after *in*:

    association, category, choir, chorus, club, family, fraternity, group, office, society, sorority

3. **In** can indicate a **period of time.**

    | Pattern | *be* + *in* + time period |

    century
    in + the   *She was born **in the** 1800s.*

    decade
    in + the   *He lived **in** Arkansas **in the** 1950s.*
                                          *Life was quieter **in the** fifties.*

    month
    in + ø   *He took his vacation **in** March.*

    period of the day
    in + the   *I work **in the** morning.*
                                          *My boss works **in the** afternoon.*
                                          *We relax **in the** evening.*

    period of time in general
    in + the   *We lived there **in the** past, and we will live here **in the** future.*

    stage of life   **adulthood, childhood, death, health, life, sickness**
    in + ø   ***In** childhood she was always **in** good health.*

    season   **spring, summer, fall, winter**
    in +/- (ø)   *They always go to Europe **in** (the) summer.*

    year
    in + ø   *Their son was born **in** 1994.*

    during general activities   **actions, deeds, dreams, prayers, thoughts**
    in + one's   *She is always **in our** thoughts.*

4.   **In** can mean **after** a period of **time.**

> **Pattern**   *in* + (number) + noun
>
> > *She will be here **in** five minutes.*

Related Expression

in no time   very soon

> *He will be here **in no time**.*

5.   **In** can mean **movement** or **transfer** from one place into another.

> **Pattern 1**   verb + *in(to)* + noun
>
> > *They went **in** the store.*

Verbs often used with this meaning:

burst, butt, come, get, go, jump, move, run, walk

> **Pattern 2**   verb + noun + *in* + noun
>
> > *Please pour the juice **in** the glass.*

Typical verbs:

draw, drop, fly, lay, place, pour, pull, push, put, ram, shove, squeeze, throw

> **Pattern 3**   verb + object + *in*
>
> > *When you finish your test, hand it **in** (to the teacher).*

Typical verbs:

bring, hand, pass, take, turn

6.   **In** indicates the **number of individual parts** of something.

> **Pattern**   number + plural noun + *in* + noun
>
> > *There are seven days **in** a week.*
> > *There are one hundred cents **in** a dollar.*

7.   **In** means during a type of **weather.**

> **Pattern 1**   *in* + *the* + noun
>
> > *They walked all day **in the** rain.*

Nouns used with this pattern:

cold, fog, heat, humidity, rain, snow, storm, sun

> **Pattern 2** *in + ø + noun*
>
> > *In hot weather we stay inside.*

Nouns used with this pattern:

bad weather, cold weather, foggy weather, good weather, hot weather, rainy weather, sunshine

8. In can indicate separated **parts** of something.

> **Pattern** verb + noun + *in(to)* + plural noun
>
> > *She cut the cake in twelve pieces.*

Verbs commonly used with this pattern:

cut, divide, separate, sever, split

Nouns commonly used after *in*:

halves, parts, pieces, portions, sections

Related Expression

in two   in halves

> *We only had one candy bar, so we cut it in two and shared it.*

9. In can indicate **direction.**

> *The girls came in this direction, and the boys went in the opposite direction.*

As an adjective

in-bound   moving toward the city or town

> *There was a lot of in-bound traffic this morning.*

10. In can indicate **ratio.**

> **Pattern** number + *in* + number
>
> > *He is one in a million.*
> >
> > *Four in ten are employed full-time.*

11. **In** indicates the **style** or **composition** of recorded material.

> **Pattern** *in* + noun
>
> *The letter was written **in** ink.*
>
> *They printed the photographs **in** duplicate.*

Nouns commonly used after *in*:

black and white, bold, capital letters, color, duplicate, ink, italics, lower case, oil, pencil, print, water colors

12. **In** indicates the use of a **language** or **style** of expression.

> **Pattern** *in* + ø noun
>
> *The paper was written **in** English.*
>
> *The girls chorus sang **in** harmony.*

Nouns often used after *in*:

a few words, chorus, code, concert, detail, full, harmony, music, poetry, rhythm, sync, tune, verse

13. **In** indicates **current style.**

> **Pattern** *in* + ø noun
>
> *Her clothes are always **in** fashion.*
>
> *She likes to be **in** style.*

Nouns used with this pattern:

fashion, season, style, vogue

Related Expression

to be in   to be in fashion

> *Platform shoes **are in** again this season.*

14. **In** indicates a **condition.**

> **Pattern 1** *be* + *in* + *a* + noun
>
> *She **is** always **in a** good mood.*

Nouns commonly used with this pattern:

good/bad mood, hurry, mess, rage, stew

Pattern 2 verb + *in* + ø noun

> *We are in good health.*
>
> *She ran into the room in tears.*

Nouns often used with this pattern:

anguish, awe, chaos, comfort, condition, confusion, danger, despair, dire straits, disarray, disaster, disgrace, disorder, doubt, dread, fear, good/bad health, love, need, pain, ruins, shape, sickness, tears, trouble

15. In describes a manner of **behavior.**

Pattern 1 verb + *in* + *a* + noun

> *He spoke in a loud voice.*

Nouns often used with this pattern:

manner, voice, way

Pattern 2 verb + noun + *in* + ø noun

> *He told me that story in confidence.*

Nouns often used after *in*:

cold blood, confidence, fairness, friendship, fun, person, silence, someone's absence, someone's presence, trust

Pattern 3 verb + noun + *in* + adjective

> *She is working on her exams in earnest.*

Typical adjectives after *in*:

earnest, private, public

16. In means **wearing.**

Pattern 1 *in* + noun

> *She came in a long dress, and he was in a suit and tie.*

Typical nouns:

bathing suit, coat, dress, hat, skirt, suit, tie, T-shirt

Pattern 2 *in* + ø noun

> *Everybody went to the party in costume.*

Typical nouns:

black (or any color), braces, braids, costume, curls, disguise, drag, high heels, jeans, jewels, make-up, mourning (black), ponytails, (tennis) shoes, shorts, uniform

Related Expression

in the nude   not wearing anything

*He sleeps **in the nude**.*

17. In indicates **involvement in a career or project**.

> **Pattern**   *be/be involved/work + in + ø noun*

*My uncle **is in** business for himself.*

*She **has worked in** insurance for years.*

*They **are involved in** computers.*

Nouns commonly used with this pattern:

accounting, administration, architecture, banking, business, computers, entertainment, government, insurance, journalism, landscaping, law, medicine, politics, publishing, research, stocks and bonds, teaching, training, the air force, the army, the coast guard, the marines, the military, the navy, the reserves

18. In defines an **arrangement**.

> **Pattern 1**   *in + a + singular noun*

*The children all sat **in a** circle.*

Nouns often used with this meaning:

circle, group, line, pile, row, stack

> **Pattern 2**   *in + plural or noncount noun*

*She put the clothes **in** piles on the floor.*

Nouns often used with this meaning:

bunches, bundles, folds, groups, lines, piles, rows, stacks, alignment, order

19. In indicates **composition of money**.

> **Pattern**   *in + noun*

*She always pays **in** cash.*

*I have six dollars **in** change.*

Nouns used with this meaning:

bills, cash, change, checks, coins, dimes, dollars, nickels, pennies, quarters, ones (one-dollar bills), fives, tens, twenties, fifties, hundreds

20. **In** indicates **purpose.**

| Pattern 1 | *in* + ø **noun** + *of* + **noun** |

> *We are here **in** memory **of** our dear brother.*
> *They came **in** search **of** gold.*

Nouns commonly used with this meaning:

aid, appreciation, celebration, commemoration, dedication, honor, lieu, memory, praise, search

| Pattern 2 | *in* + *order* + *to* + **verb** |

> *She came here **in order to** learn English.*
> *They are saving money **in order to** buy a car.*

21. **In** can define a **measurement.**

| Pattern 1 | **number** + **noun** + *in* + **noun** |

> *The box is one foot **in** height, eight inches **in** depth, and eight inches **in** width.*

| Pattern 2 | **verb** + *in* + **noun** |

> *We weigh **in** pounds; I don't know my weight **in** kilos.*

Typical nouns used after *in*:

centimeters, feet, inches, kilos, meters, miles, ounces, pounds, yards

22. **In** can indicate a **special relationship.**

| Pattern 1 | *in* + ø **noun** + *with* + **noun** |

> *All of the parents are working **in** cooperation **with** the teachers.*

Nouns often used with this meaning:

agreement, alignment, cahoots, collaboration, collusion, combination, common, comparison, competition, conflict, conjunction, connection, contact, cooperation, debate, dispute, good, harmony, rhythm, step, sympathy, touch, trouble

| Pattern 2 | *in* + **noun** + *with* + **noun** |

> *She was **in** a fight **with** him yesterday.*

Typical nouns used before *in*:

argument, debate, exchange, fight, session, situation

23. **In** indicates a **location on the body.**

> **Pattern 1** verb + noun + *in* + *the* + body part
>
> *He kicked the attacker **in the** stomach.*
> *She scratched herself **in the** eye.*

Verbs commonly used with this pattern:

hit, hurt, kick, knock, poke, punch, scratch, slap, strike

> **Pattern 2** *have* + noun + *in* + possessive pronoun + noun
>
> *I **have** a pain **in** my chest.*
> *She **has** an ache **in** her left leg.*

Related Expression

to be a pain in the neck to be annoying

> *Her little sister is eight years old, and **she's a pain in the neck**.*

24. **In** can indicate a **current state.**

> **Pattern 1** *be* + *in* + ø noun
>
> *The papers **are in** circulation.*
> *Your book **is in** demand.*
> *The car **is** not **in** gear.*

Nouns commonly used with this pattern:

bankruptcy, captivity, charge, check, circulation, confinement, conflict, control, debt, demand, jail, power, session, trouble, trust

Nouns referring to the transmission of a car or other vehicle:

drive, first, second, third, fourth, fifth, gear, neutral, park, reverse

25. **In** can indicate a **reaction.**

> **Pattern** verb + *in* + ø noun
>
> *Her friend left **in** disgust.*
> *She hung her head **in** disappointment.*

Nouns commonly used after *in*:

apprehension, approbation, approval, assent, compliance, confusion, consent, contempt, defeat, defiance, delight, desolation, disappointment, disdain, disgrace, disgust, dismay, disobedience, dissent, grief, happiness, pain, reaction, relief, sadness, sorrow, the affirmative

Typical verbs used before *in*:

cry, exclaim, go away, leave, react, scream, smile, sneer, squeal, tremble, weep, hang/nod/shake one's head, stick up one's nose

26. **In** can indicate **quantities.**

> **Pattern** *in* + **plural noun**

> *People came **in** thousands to see the shrine.*

Nouns typically used after *in*:

busloads, carloads, groups of ten, hordes, hundreds, small groups, thousands, truckloads

27. **In** can indicate an **example.**

> **Pattern** **noun** + *in* + **noun that names first noun**

> *She has a good friend **in** Mrs. Jones.*
> *They have a wonderful teacher **in** John Smith.*

28. **In** can mean **when.**

> **Pattern** *in* + **verb in gerund form**

> *She is correct **in** saying that he was lazy.*
> ***In** signing your name, you are admitting guilt.*

29. **In** can refer to the **process of a game.**

> **Pattern** *in* + **name of game**

> ***In** baseball, there are nine players on a team.*
> *The boys have been **in** a game of chess all afternoon.*

Names of common games:

badminton, baseball, bridge, canasta, cards, chess, football, golf, hide-and-seek, hockey, Monopoly, polo, racquetball, solitaire, tag, tennis, volleyball

30. In can mean **on the occasion of.**

> **Pattern** *in* + ø noun

> *She smiled **in** acceptance.*
> *He nodded his head **in** agreement.*

Nouns often used with this meaning:

acceptance, action, comparison, conclusion, contrast, conversation, defeat, practice, return, the end

31. In can indicate a **warning** or **prediction** of a reaction.

> **Pattern** *be* + *in* + *for* + *a* + noun

> *He **is in for a** shock when he gets here tomorrow.*

Nouns used with this meaning:

rude awakening, shock, surprise, treat

32. In can define the **emphasis** or **perspective** of a statement.

> **Pattern 1** *in* + ø noun

> ***In** fact, this is a very good report.*
> *The children behave themselves **in** general.*

Nouns commonly used after *in*:

addition, all, all seriousness, analysis, answer, conclusion, fact, general, particular, question, return, reverse, theory, truth

> **Pattern 2** *in* + *one's* + noun

> ***In my** opinion, this is a mistake.*

Typical nouns:

case, heart, opinion, view

> **Pattern 3** *in* + *the* + noun

> ***In the** end, everything was fine.*

Nouns used with this pattern:

end, final analysis

| Pattern 4 | *in* + noun + *of* + noun |

> *She went to the party **in** spite **of** her mother's wishes.*
> ***In** case **of** fire, leave the building.*

Nouns used with this pattern:
case, light, spite, terms, view

33. In can indicate the **quality** of a noun.

| Pattern 1 | *be* + adjective + *in* + noun |

> *They **are** lacking **in** the necessities of a decent life.*
> *Those people may be poor in commodities, but they **are** rich **in** spirit.*
> *Her sister **is** blind **in** one eye.*

| Pattern 2 | *be* + *the* + superlative adjective + noun + *in* + name of category |

> *He **is the** best student **in** the class.*
> *That **is the** longest river **in** the world.*

34. In can indicate a **topic.**

| Pattern 1 | noun + *in* + noun |

> *There was a big improvement **in** her grades this term.*

Typical nouns before *in*:
advance, change, decline, decrease, improvement, increase

| Pattern 2 | verb + *in* + noun |

> *She participated **in** the planning of the conference.*
> *He persists **in** calling me on the telephone.*

Typical verbs:
assist, cooperate, help, invest, participate, persist

| Pattern 3 | adjective + *in* + noun |

> *This land is rich **in** minerals.*
> *She is very interested **in** antique furniture.*

Typical adjectives:
basking, covered, drowning, interested, rich, steeped, submerged

Expressions

in brief   briefly

> *In brief, we are leaving in five minutes.*

in short   briefly

> *In short, everybody is getting a raise in pay.*

in advance   before an event

> *To get tickets to the concert, you have to pay in advance.*

in no time   very soon

> *He will be here in no time.*

in two   in halves

> *We only had one candy bar, so we cut it in two and shared it*

in a corner   trapped

> *With so many bills, and no job, he was really in a corner.*

in the dark   ignorant of the facts

> *My colleagues kept me in the dark about their plans to leave the company.*

in good hands (with)   well-served, safe

> *I know I am in good hands with my lawyer.*

tongue-in-cheek   sarcastically

> *All the nice things he said about her were said tongue-in-cheek.*

to be in hot water   to be in trouble

> *She has been late three times, and now she's really in hot water with the boss.*

to be in the black   to be out of debt

> *We have paid off all our credit cards; we are finally in the black.*

in deference to   with great respect for

> *We are acting in deference to our chairman's wishes.*

hand-in-hand (adverb)   with hands linked

> *Couples love to walk hand-in-hand.*

arm-in-arm (adverb)   with arms linked

> *She always walked arm-in-arm with her mother.*

to be in line   to be waiting in an orderly fashion, one after the other

> *I've been in line for two hours to get tickets.*

in compensation for   to restore balance, pay for

> *She made me a dress in compensation for the favors I did for her.*

in any case   no matter what happens

> *We will have the party in any case.*

in that case   if that happens

> *In that case, everybody will stay at home.*

in addition to   plus

> *In addition to your car payment, you will have to pay for registration and insurance.*

in the air   an indication that something has been discussed

>*A raise in salaries is **in the air**.*

in sight   an indication that something is visible, or will happen soon

>*We are almost there; the bridge is **in sight**.*

>*The work is almost finished; our vacation is **in sight**.*

Phrasal Verbs

break in (intransitive)   enter without permission, removing a barrier

>*Someone **broke in** yesterday and took their bicycles.*

break in (separable)   use something for first time, as a warm-up; to tame

>*The boy got a new bicycle and couldn't wait to **break** it **in**.*

break in on (nonseparable)   enter without permission, surprising those inside

>*We were having a private conversation when he **broke in on** us.*

butt in (intransitive)   interrupt a private conversation

>*Everything was fine until she **butted in**.*

check in (intransitive)   register

>*After they **checked in** at the desk they went to their room.*

check in (separable)   leave something temporarily in a guarded place

>*The bags were heavy, so he **checked** them **in** right away.*

chip in/pitch in (intransitive)   contribute

>*The students all **chipped in** and bought the teacher a present.*

close in (on) (nonseparable)   approach and surround

>*The people were scared as the enemy **closed in on** them.*

count in (separable)   expect someone's participation

>*If you are looking for volunteers, **count** me **in**.*

do in (separable)   tire

>*I exercised at the gym for two hours, and it **did** me **in**.*

drop in (separable)   let something fall into a deep container

>*After you finish the letter, please **drop** it **in** the mailbox.*

drop in (on) (nonseparable)   visit someone without notice

>*We hadn't seen them in years, and they **dropped in on** us yesterday morning.*

fill in (separable)   complete a form

>*Here is the application form; please **fill** it **in**.*

fill in (for) (nonseparable)   substitute

>*Another doctor is **filling in for** her while she's on vacation.*

get in (nonseparable)   enter, perhaps with slight difficulty

>*The door was locked, but we **got in** through the window.*

get in (separable)   place inside, perhaps with slight difficulty

*The mail slot was too small for the package; I couldn't **get** it **in**.*

give in (to) (nonseparable)   surrender

*I hope she never **gives in to** his wishes; he wants to control her.*

keep in (separable)   not allow to go out

*The child was sick and his mother **kept** him **in**.*

key in (separable)   type into the computer

*First you have to **key in** your password.*

kick in (intransitive)   begin to function, as a backup

*When it gets very cold, the electric heater **kicks in**.*

look in (on) (nonseparable)   occasionally check

*Will you **look in on** my mother every afternoon while I'm away?*

squeeze in (separable)   make room or time for somebody

*The doctor was busy, but he managed to **squeeze** me **in**.*

step in (intransitive)   enter

*I knocked on the door and he told me to **step in**.*

take in (separable)   to make smaller

*The skirt was too big, so she **took** it **in** at the waist.*

take in (separable)   to comprehend

*I'm not sure she **took in** everything you were saying.*

turn in (intransitive)   go to bed

*They were really tired, and had to **turn in**.*

PRACTICE

31-1. Choose the best word or words for each blank space.

1. Lisa is in the _____.

   car   bus   train   ship

2. Please write your answers in your _____.

   paper   purse   notebook   calendar

3. Your brother is the best singer in the _____.

   team   committee   chorus   board

4. That song was popular in the _____.

   80s   morning   last year   school

5. It's 3:30. I'll text you at 4 o'clock. I'll text you in _____.

   3 hours   6 years   4 days   30 minutes

6. Please put the _____ in the recycle bin.

    garbage   banana peels   used paper   clean paper

7. We have to _____ in our papers to the teacher.

    tell   give   hand   foot

8. I'm going to cut the cake in 12 _____.

    plates   cups   saucers   portions

9. He was coming toward me. He was coming in _____ direction.

    this   that   the other   a

10. She was all wet. She must have been in _____.

    the sunshine   the rain   the middle   outside

11. Were the photos in color or in _____?

    blue and green   yellow and gray   black and white   gray

12. The children sang the songs in perfect _____.

    colors   words   letters   rhythm

13. Shannon doesn't buy new clothes every year. She isn't always in _____.

    style   sync   school   store

14. Your hostess is a great cook. You are in for a _____.

    disaster   treat   happy hour   long time

15. Her school work is getting better. She shows a big improvement in her _____.

    talents   book   grades   tablet

31-2. Use an expression with *in* to express the following:

1. He will have to pass a driving test plus a written test.

2. They have discussed a ban on smoking on campus.

31-3. Use a phrasal verb with *in* to express the following:

1. There was a robbery at our house last night.

2. We were having a private conversation, and he kept interrupting.

3. You should register at the hotel as soon as you arrive.

4. Before the plane lands, you have to complete this form.

5. I will definitely participate!

UNIT 32:
In Back Of

Basic Meaning

1. In back of means located **behind.**

> **Pattern 1** noun + *in back of* + noun
>
> *There is a beautiful tree **in back of** our house.*

> **Pattern 2** verb + *in back of* + noun
>
> *Your sister sits **in back of** me in class.*

PRACTICE

32-1. Choose the best word or words for each blank space.

1. Charles sits in the third row. I sit in the fourth row. I sit in back of _____.

   him   her   them   you

2. They are so lucky! They have a big _____ in back of their house.

   hole   fish   tennis court   telephone pole

UNIT 33:
In Front Of

Basic Meanings

1. **In front of** means located **before** or **facing** something.

   | Pattern 1 | noun + *in front of* + noun |

   *There is a van **in front of** their house.*

   | Pattern 2 | verb + *in front of* + noun |

   *The teacher usually stands **in front of** the class.*
   *He was **in front of** me in line.*

2. **In front of** can mean **in the future.**

   *She has a lot of problems **in front of** her.*

33-1. Choose the best word or words for each blank space.

1. Your trip to Spain next month sounds fabulous. You have a lot of new _____ in front of you.
   friends   experiences   bullfighters   flamenco dancers

2. The teacher usually stands in front of the _____.
   office   playground   class   clinic

UNIT 34:
Inside

Basic Meaning

1. Inside means **located in the interior part of something; enclosed in.**

> **Pattern** verb + noun + *inside* + noun

> *There are some little toy animals **inside** the box.*
> *She put the money **inside** the envelope.*

As an adverb

Inside means **indoors,** within a building.

> *It started to rain, so we went **inside**.*

PRACTICE

34-1. Choose the best word or words for each blank space.

1. We can't wait to go inside the _____, to see if it will work for our family.

   box   house   station   airport

2. There is a _____ for you inside the envelope.

   party   tickets   invitation   surprise

UNIT 35:
Instead Of

Basic Meaning

1. Instead of means substituting for.

> **Pattern** verb + noun + *instead of* + noun
>
> *They went to Hawaii **instead of** South America.*
> *She cooks a lot of vegetables **instead of** meat.*

PRACTICE

35-1. Choose the best word or words for each blank space.

1. I have changed my mind. I want to go to the movies instead of _____.
    to the mall   seeing a film   to the cinema   watching a movie

2. They changed our flight. We're going to _____ instead of Africa.
    Nigeria   Kenya   Ghana   Australia

UNIT 36:
Into

Basic Meanings

1. **Into** indicates **entrance.**

> **Pattern 1** verb + *into* + noun

> *We went **into** his office.*
>
> *I drive **into** the city every day.*

Typical verbs before *into*:

blow, break, come, drive, fall, fly, gaze, get, go, look, move, walk, run, sail, stare, stomp, storm

> **Pattern 2** verb + noun + *into* + noun

> *She poured the juice **into** the glass.*

Verbs often used with this pattern:

blow, cram, drive, get, move, place, pour, put, set, throw

2. **Into** can indicate **forced contact.**

> **Pattern** verb + *into* + noun

> *That car crashed **into** a tree.*

Verbs often used before *into*:

crash, push, pull, run, smash, tear

Expression

> **to run something into the ground** to talk about something too much
>
> *We are sick of hearing about his job; he really **runs it into the ground**.*

3. **Into** can indicate **division.**

> **Pattern 1** number + *into* + number = number

> *Three **into** twelve equals four.*

> **Pattern 2** verb + noun + *into* + (number) + noun

> *She cut the pie **into** eight wedges.*
>
> *The vase broke **into** a million pieces.*

Typical verbs before *into*:

arrange, break, cut, divide, separate

Typical nouns after *into*:

bits, parts, pieces, slices, wedges

4. **Into** can indicate a **change in condition or form.**

> **Pattern 1**   *go/get* + *into* + ø **noun**
>
> > *They **went into** debt after the accident.*
> > *He always **gets into** trouble at school.*

Nouns often used after *go into*:

action, bankruptcy, debt

Nouns used after *get into*:

danger, condition, shape, trouble

> **Pattern 2**   *go/get* + *into* + **noun**
>
> > *He **went into** a rage.*
> > *They **got into** an argument.*

Typical nouns after *go into*:

a fit, hysterics, a rage, a tantrum

Typical nouns after *get into*:

an argument, a good/bad mood

Related Expressions

to turn into   to change into a different form

> *The water **turned into** ice.*
> *The stranger **turned into** a friend.*

to turn something into   to change the form of something else

> *The witch **turned** the prince **into** a frog.*

to burst into flames   to suddenly be on fire

> *The trash pile **burst into flames**.*

to get into hot water   to get into trouble

> *We **got into hot water** for skipping class.*

5. **Into** can indicate **interest** or **occupation**.

> | Pattern | *be/go + into +* **noun** |
> | --- | --- |
>
> *Her husband **is** really **into** football.*
> *All of her daughters **went into** law.*

Phrasal Verbs

break into (nonseparable)   begin an activity
> *She was so excited that she **broke into** a song.*

check into (nonseparable)   get information, investigate
> *After she called the police, they went to **check into** the situation.*

look into (nonseparable)   get information, investigate
> *The lawyer promised to **look into** our case.*

run into (nonseparable)   to see an acquaintance by chance
> *We **ran into** each other at the mall yesterday.*

talk into (separable)   to convince someone to do something
> *She didn't want to come with us, but I **talked** her **into** it.*

PRACTICE

36-1. Choose the best word or words for each blank space.

1. He _____ into the room and started shouting orders.

threw	gazed	stomped	fell

2. She has to start saving money or she will go into _____.

jail	debt	poverty	trouble

3. They are always getting into _____.

trouble	football	jail	a frog

36-2. Use an expression with *into* to express the following:

1. I don't want the teacher to catch me doing something wrong!

36-3. Use a phrasal verb with *into* to express the following:

1. They convinced me to go with them.

2. I wonder if I'll see anybody I know at the game.

UNIT 37:
Like

Basic Meanings

1. **Like** can mean **similar to.**

> **Pattern** *be, look, seem + like + noun*
>
> > *She **is like** her sister.*
> > *They don't **look like** their mother.*

2. **Like** can indicate **similar behavior.**

> **Pattern** **verb + *like* + noun**
>
> > *He talks **like** his father.*
> > *She swims **like** a duck.*
>
> Common verbs before *like*:
> **act, behave, play, sing, talk, walk**

3. **Like** can describe **excessive behavior.**

> **Pattern** **verb + noun + *like* + abstract noun**
>
> > *She spends money **like** water.*
>
> Nouns commonly used with this meaning:
> **anything, water**

Related Expressions

> **like crazy** a lot, excessively
> **like mad** a lot; excessively
>
> > *He dances **like** crazy.*
> > *She works **like** mad.*

4. **Like** can indicate an **example.**

> **Pattern** **noun + *like* + noun**
>
> > *They grow root vegetables **like** beets, carrots, radishes, and turnips.*

5. **Like** can mean **characteristic of.**

Pattern *be* + *like* + **noun** + *to* + **verb**

*It's not **like** you **to** complain.*

PRACTICE

37-1. Choose the best word or words for each blank space.

1. I like tropical fruit, like _____.

    apples   pears   mangoes   cherries

2. She never stops dancing. She dances like _____.
    crazy   silly   pretty   graceful

3. He is very cooperative.   It's not like him to _____.
    be quiet   be silly   argue   be normal

UNIT 38:
Near

Basic Meanings

1. Near means **close to** in terms of distance.

> *His house is **near** his office.*
> *She lives **near** San Francisco.*

2. Near means **within a short time.**

> *His birthday is **near** Thanksgiving.*

PRACTICE

38-1. Choose the best word or words for each blank space.

1. We both have birthdays in April. Her birthday is _____ mine.

   like   near   far from   next to

2. The librarian's house is two blocks from the library. She lives near _____.

   her job   the school   the drugstore   her gym

UNIT 39:
Next To

Basic Meaning

1.   Next to means **at the side of.**

> *Her best friend sits **next to** her at the table.*
> *I will put my things in the basket **next to** yours.*

PRACTICE

39-1. Choose the best word or words for each blank space.

1. Charlotte is going to sit next to _____ in the cafeteria.
    me and Taylor   Taylor and I   I and Kim   you and he

2. Basketball is my second favorite game, next to baseball. Baseball is my _____.
    best   worst   second favorite   favorite

Basic Meanings

1. **Of** indicates **belonging** or **connection.**

   a. *Of* identifies a thing as a connection or **part of another thing.**

   the pages of the book
   the leaves of the tree

   b. *Of* identifies people, animals, or plants as **part of a larger group.**

Pattern	noun + *of* + *this/that* + noun

   *the women **of that** family*

   *the people **of that** religion*

   Nouns commonly used after *of*:

   city, club, company, country, culture, descent, faith, family, gender, genus, group, ilk, organization, race, religion, society, species

   c. *Of* identifies ideas or **works with their author,** artist, or composer.

Pattern	noun + *of* + noun

   *the works **of** Shakespeare*

   *the methods **of** the teacher*

   Nouns often used before *of*:

   essays, ideas, method, music, novels, opinion, paintings, plays, poems, poetry, songs, work, writing

   d. *Of* identifies an individual or **special member of a group** or institution.

Pattern	noun + *of* + noun

   *the president **of** the class*

   *the coordinators **of** the program*

   Nouns commonly used before *of*:

   captain, citizen, coordinator, dictator, head, hero, heroine, leader, loser, manager, mayor, member, president, secretary, servant, star, student, teacher, treasurer, villain, winner

   e. *Of* identifies a **person's occupation** or area of specialization.

Pattern	noun + *of* + noun

   *a professor **of** mathematics*

   *students **of** cardiology*

   *practitioner **of** medicine*

   f. *Of* indicates a **connection with a place.**

Pattern noun + *of* + noun

> *a native* **of** *Alaska*
> *the birds and animals* **of** *Australia*

Nouns often used before *of*:

animal, bird, citizen, graduate, inhabitant, native, people, resident

g. *Of* indicates a **connection with a period of time.**

> *the music* **of** *the eighties*
> *the dances* **of** *her youth*
> *the fourth* **of** *July*
> *the last day* **of** *the year*
> *April* **of** *last year*

2. **Of** can name another noun.

Pattern *the* + noun + *of* + noun

> *They established* **the** *city* **of** *Los Angeles.*
> *It is near* **the** *Bay* **of** *Bengal.*
> *I don't know* **the** *name* **of** *the school.*

3. **Of** can indicate the **location of a part.**

Pattern preposition + *the* + noun + *of* + noun

> *The passage is in* **the** *middle* **of** *the page.*
> *I have a knot on* **the** *back* **of** *my head.*
> *The numbers are at* **the** *top* **of** *the page.*

4. **Of** indicates a **category of description.**

Pattern noun + *of* + noun

a. Typical nouns used before *of* indicating **category:**

brand, category, class, color, form, kind, make, pattern, shape, size, sort, style, type

> *What kind* **of** *shoes are you looking for?*
> *The color* **of** *your dress is beautiful.*

b. Nouns used before *of* indicating type of **container:**

bag, bowl, box, can, container, load, loaf, package, piece, plate, tube

> *We bought two boxes* **of** *cereal.*

c. Nouns used before *of* indicating **sensation:**

feel, sense, smell, sound, taste, texture

> *I didn't like the smell **of** that meat.*

d. Nouns before *of* indicating **value:**

cost, price, value

> *The price **of** the dress was outrageous.*

e. Nouns before *of* indicating **measurement:**

depth, height, length, measurement, weight, width

> *Do you know the measurement **of** your waist?*

5. Of indicates a **number** or **proportion.**

Pattern 1 **number/adjective + *of* + plural noun**

> *Three **of** the girls are our daughters.*
> *All **of** the women are from New York.*

Adjectives used before *of*:

all numbers
all, another, any, both, each, either, enough, few, many, most, neither, none, plenty, several, some

Pattern 2 **noun + *of* + plural noun**

> *That store has a couple **of** books I want to buy.*
> *A few **of** them are hard to find.*

Nouns used before *of*:

a couple, a few, a lot, lots

Pattern 3 **adjective + *of* + noncount noun**

> *Much **of** the furniture is damaged.*

Adjectives used before *of*:

all, little, much, some

Pattern 4 **noun + *of* + noncount noun**

> *A little **of** the information is correct.*
> *A lot **of** it is incorrect.*

Nouns used before *of*:

a little, a lot, lots

6. **Of** can **identify** abstract nouns by their source.

a. sound

> **Pattern**   *the* + **noun** + *of* + **noun**

>> *I heard **the** cry **of** a baby.*
>> *There was **the** noise **of** a car.*

Nouns of sound commonly used before *of*:

buzz, crash, cry, growl, hiss, howl, hum, hush, laughter, music, noise, silence, sound, whisper

b. force

> **Pattern**   **noun** + *of* + **noun**

>> *A gust **of** wind blew in my face.*
>> *We all need a breath **of** fresh air.*

Nouns of force often used before *of*:

breath, gush, rush, whiff

c. sight

> **Pattern**   **noun** + *of* + **noun**

>> *She had a vision **of** musicians playing violins.*
>> *The blue of her eyes was the color **of** the ocean.*

Nouns of sight often used before *of*:

blue, color, picture, sight, vision

d. sensation

> **Pattern**   *the* + **noun** + *of* + **noun**

>> ***The** touch **of** his hand made me feel safe.*
>> ***The** smell **of** bread baking was wonderful.*

Nouns of feeling often used before *of*:

feel, sense, smell, taste, texture, touch

e. expression

> **Pattern**   **noun** + *of* + **noun**

>> *He shouted words **of** anger.*
>> *She breathed a sigh **of** relief.*

Nouns of expression often used before *of*:

cry, groan, moan, shout, sigh, smile, tears, word

Nouns of feeling often used after *of*:

anger, anguish, delight, elation, excitement, fear, frustration, happiness, joy, relief, sadness, surprise

7. **Of** can indicate **material** or **composition**.

Pattern   **noun + *be* + past participle + *of* + noun**

> *My new bag **is** made **of** leather.*
>
> *Water **is** made up **of** hydrogen and oxygen.*

Past participles used before *of*:

composed, formed, made, made up (used with natural phenomena)

Nouns often used after *of*:

aluminum, brass, cardboard, clay, copper, cotton, crystal, fabric, glass, gold, iron, jute, leather, metal, nylon, paper, plastic, platinum, polyester, rayon, sand, silk, silver, string, tin, water, wire, wood, wool

8. **Of** can identify **contents** or **topic**.

Pattern 1   **noun + *of* + noun**

> *She ate a salad **of** lettuce, tomatoes, and avocados.*
>
> *My uncle wrote a book **of** short stories.*
>
> *The book has pictures **of** flowers.*
>
> *A group **of** students went to the museum.*

Common expressions:

words of love, a sign of weakness, a method of teaching

Pattern 2   **verb + *of* + noun**

> *I dreamed **of** you.*
>
> *They often talked **of** their youth.*

Verbs commonly used before *of*:

complain, dream, hear, learn, sing, speak, talk, think

Pattern 3   **verb + noun + *of* + noun**

> *She informed me **of** my appointment.*

Verbs used with this pattern:

advise, inform, remind, tell

| Pattern 4 | adjective + *of* + noun |

> *She is capable **of** better work.*
>
> *They are independent **of** their parents.*

Adjectives commonly used with this pattern:

capable, ignorant, proud, repentant, sick, tired

Related Expression

be reminiscent of   to remind someone of

> *Your perfume **is reminiscent of** my mother.*

9. **Of** can indicate dedication of time to a **special purpose.**

| Pattern | noun + *of* + noun |

> *That was a day **of** national mourning.*
>
> *We stood for a moment **of** silence.*

Nouns often used before *of*:

day, moment, month, period, season, semester, time, week, year

Nouns often used after *of*:

celebration, exercise, festivity, fun, happiness, meditation, mourning, prayer, quiet, reading, reflection, rest, silence, studying, thanksgiving, work

10. **Of** can indicate **absence.**

| Pattern | noun + *of* + noun |

> *There is a need **of** cooperation.*
>
> *The lack **of** funds is our biggest problem.*

Nouns commonly used before *of*:

absence, dearth, necessity, need, lack, paucity, scarcity

11. **Of** can indicate **separation.**

| Pattern 1 | verb + *of* + noun |

> *He was cured **of** cancer.*
>
> *The dog died **of** old age.*
>
> *She is rid **of** a nuisance.*

| Pattern 2 | verb + noun + *of* + noun |

*They tried to relieve her **of** pain.*

Related Expression

to get rid of   to cause to no longer have

*I **got rid of** my old car.*

12. **Of** can indicate one's **feelings** toward the object.

| Pattern 1 | noun + *of* + noun |

*We appreciate the pleasure **of** your company.*

*He has a love **of** learning.*

Nouns often used before *of*:

anguish, challenge, delight, desire, distrust, enjoyment, excitement, fear, frustration, happiness, hatred, joy, love, need, pleasure, stress

| Pattern 2 | *to the* + noun + *of* + noun |

*We had a big party, **to the** delight **of** the children.*

Nouns often used before *of*:

anguish, annoyance, delight, disgust, enjoyment, excitement, happiness, pleasure

13. **Of** can indicate an **attitude** toward something.

| Pattern | *be* + adjective + *of* + noun |

*They **are** respectful **of** the environment.*

Adjectives commonly used before *of*:

ashamed, aware, certain, conscious, disrespectful, envious, fond, inconsiderate, mindful, proud, repentant, respectful, sure, suspicious, trusting, uncertain, unsure, wary

14. **Of** can indicate a **reason.**

*I came here because **of** you.*

*She lost all her money on account **of** her husband.*

15. **Of** can describe **behavior.**

Pattern	*be* + adjective + *of* + noun

> It **was** very kind **of** Sally to help us.
>
> It **was** cruel **of** him to ignore her.

Adjectives commonly used with this pattern:

bad, careless, conscientious, crazy, crude, cruel, delightful, evil, good, hateful, ignorant, irresponsible, kind, mean, nice, responsible, rude, selfish, sweet, thoughtful, thoughtless, typical, unconscionable

16. **Of** can **describe** a noun by connecting it to a quality.

Pattern	noun + *of* + noun

> She is a woman **of** honor.
>
> They are people **of** integrity.

Nouns of quality often used after *of*:

dignity, faith, few words, good intentions, honor, integrity, high (low) morals, strength, wisdom

Expressions

a change of scenery/pace   a change in place or activity

> We needed **a change of scenery**, so we went to the Caribbean.

right of way   the legal right to proceed before another person

> The accident was the other driver's fault because I had the **right of way**.

PRACTICE

40-1. Choose the best word or words for each blank space.

1. *A*, *B*, and *C* are the first letters of _____.
   my name   your name   Mrs. Jackson   the alphabet

2. The opinions of the English teacher are _____.
   poetry   spelling   private   writing

3. She teaches algebra. She's a professor of _____.
   numbers   girls   students   mathematics

4. Independence Day in the United States is the _____ of July.
   four   fourth   forth   day

5. We bought six _____ of bread to make sandwiches for the party.
   loaves   loaf   halves   box

6. You can hear the _____ of the helicopters inside the house.
   song   music   noise   talking

7. I only want two pieces of fruit. Please give me _____ of bananas.
   a couple   pair   twice   a bunch

8. His blue eyes were the color of _____.
   money   paint   the sky   blood

9. I gave away all of my old sweaters. I got _____ of them.
   new   old   twenty   rid

10. He won the election, to the _____ of his opponents.
    happiness   excitement   disgust   relief

40-2. Use an expression with *of* to express the following:

1. I didn't have the legal right to drive in that lane.

2. We needed to get away, and took a trip to the beach.

UNIT 41:
Off

Basic Meanings

1. Off indicates **movement** from one place to another.

> **Pattern 1**   verb + *off* + noun
>
> > *The car ran **off** the road.*
> >
> > *We got **off** the train in New Orleans.*
>
> Verbs used with this pattern:
>
> **blow, come, dive, drive, fall, get, go, hop, jump, limp, move, roll, run, slide, slip, walk**

Related Expression

to be off (adverb)   to leave

> *It's late, so we must **be off**.*

> **Pattern 2**   verb + noun + *off* + noun
>
> > *They shoveled the snow **off** the driveway.*
>
> Verbs used with this pattern:
>
> **blow, brush, clean, clear, drive, get, move, pull, push, roll, run, scrape, shove, shovel, slide, slip, sweep, take, wash**

2. Off can indicate **separation.**

> **Pattern**   verb + *off* + noun
>
> > *She cut **off** her beautiful long hair.*
>
> Verbs commonly used with this meaning:
>
> **break, chop, cut, pick, pull, saw, send, shave, take, tear, throw**

3. Off means **connected to** or **not far from.**

> **Pattern**   be + *off* + noun
>
> > *Our street **is off** Main Street.*
>
> Typical nouns after *off*:
>
> **beach, coast, highway, island, road, street, turnpike**

4. **Off** can indicate **behavior** that is not as usual or no longer true.

> **Pattern 1** *be/go* + *off* + ø **noun**
>
> > *The children **are off** school today.*
> >
> > *I'm glad your cousin finally **went off** drugs.*
>
> Nouns commonly used with this meaning:
>
> **alcohol, cigarettes, drugs, duty, school, work**
>
> **Pattern 2** *be/go* + *off* + **one's** + **noun**
>
> > *She **went off** her diet again.*
>
> Typical nouns:
>
> **diet, medication, medicine, pills**

Related Expressions

to be off course   to be going (or thinking) in the wrong direction

> *We got lost, and **were off course** for about three hours.*
>
> *They **got off course** while doing the research, and wasted a lot of time.*

to be off one's game   not be playing as well as usual

> *The golf champion **was off his game** yesterday.*

to be off one's rocker   to be crazy

> *She feeds caviar to her cat; I think **she's off her rocker**.*

5. **Off** can indicate **lack of contact.**

> **Pattern 1** **verb** + *off* + **noun**
>
> > *Please keep **off** the grass.*
>
> Verbs used with this pattern:
>
> **get, keep, lay, stay**
>
> **Pattern 2** **verb** + **noun** + *off* + **noun**
>
> > *Please keep the dog **off** the grass.*
>
> Verbs commonly used with this pattern:
>
> **get, keep, move, take**

6. **Off** means **cause to stop functioning.**

> **Pattern**   verb + *off* + noun

> *Please turn **off** the radio.*

Typical verbs with this meaning:

shut, switch, turn

Typical nouns after *off*:

the music, the lights, the machine, the air conditioning, the heat, the motor, the cellphone, the computer

Expressions

off the record   not official or public
> *This is **off the record**, but I heard that our friends got married last week.*

off the charts   too high or successful to measure
> *Our ratings are **off the charts**.*

off the wall   unacceptable
> *I'm sorry, but your ideas are really **off the wall**.*

off chance (noun)   unlikely possibility
> *I stopped by, on the **off chance** that you would be at home.*

off-limits (adverb)   forbidden territory
> *The bars are **off-limits** for teenagers.*

off-color (adjective)   in very bad taste, with a sexual reference
> *I can't believe that she tells so many **off-color** jokes.*

offhand (adjective, adverb)   very casual, casually
> *He made a few **offhand** remarks that I didn't appreciate.*

hit it off   to become friends right away
> *Your sister and my brother really **hit it off** at the party.*

be well off   to have few problems
> *Now that she has retired, she **is** pretty **well off**.*

be better/worse off   to have fewer or more problems
> *She **is** a lot **better off** than she was before.*

Phrasal Verbs

back off (intransitive)   stop trying
> *The man was too aggressive and was told to **back off**.*

beg off (intransitive)   cancel a commitment
> *Our babysitter didn't come; she **begged off** at the last minute.*

break off (separable)   terminate a relationship

> *They couldn't agree on anything, so they **broke off** their engagement.*

call off (separable)   cancel an event

> *We **called** the picnic **off** because of rain.*

check off (separable)   mark on a list

> *She knows I was there; she **checked off** my name.*

drop off (intransitive)   fall asleep

> *She kept **dropping off** during the meeting.*

get off (nonseparable)   leave a vehicle you can walk around on

> *We **got off** the ship in Jamaica.*

get off (separable)   remove, with some difficulty

> *She's trying to **get** the mud **off** her shoes.*

goof off   waste time

> *Stop **goofing off** and get to work!*

kick off (intransitive)   the beginning of an event

> *The conference starts tomorrow; it will probably **kick off** at about ten.*

kill off (separable)   to destroy all members of a species

> *There is a danger that certain birds will be **killed off**.*

knock off (separable)   to stop doing something

> *I'm sick of your teasing. **Knock** it **off**!*

lay off (separable)   fire from a job

> *They didn't need so many workers, so they **laid** him **off**.*

live off (nonseparable)   eat nothing but

> *We have been **living off** fruit and vegetables for weeks.*

mark off (separable)   to designate areas for a game

> *They are **marking** the field **off** for the soccer match.*

nod off   fall asleep

> *He is jet-lagged, and keeps **nodding off** during the day.*

pull off (separable)   manage to achieve success

> *The clients were difficult, but he managed to **pull off** the sale.*

put off (separable)   postpone

> *They **put** the picnic **off** until Tuesday.*

put off (separable)   repel

> *They didn't invite her back; her bad manners really **put** them **off**.*

round off (separable)   use the nearest whole number

> *Don't use all those fractions; **round off** all the numbers.*

sell off (separable)   to sell everything

> *He **sold off** all his property and left town.*

sign off (intransitive) to end a program

*My favorite radio announcer **signs off** at midnight.*

take off (intransitive) leave

*The plane **took off** at four-thirty.*

take off (separable) remove clothing

*The sweater was too warm so he **took** it **off**.*

wear off (separable) to disappear because of wear

*I **wore off** the tread on my tires when I drove to California.*

wipe off (separable) to erase; to destroy completely

*The gunman **wiped** his fingerprints **off** the weapon.*

write off (separable) to no longer consider someone or something to be of value

*He **wrote off** his sister when she got into trouble.*

*He **wrote off** the money she owed him, as he knew she would never pay it back.*

PRACTICE

41-1. Choose the best word or words for each blank space.

1. She _____ off the diving board and made a beautiful dive.

   slipped   jumped   fell   walked

2. Our house is just off the highway. It is _____ the highway.

   close to   far from   on   in

3. The children have a holiday today. They are off _____.

   cruise   birthday party   school   vacation

4. It's way too bright in here. Please turn off the _____.

   air conditioning   lights   music   heater

41-2. Use an expression with *off* to express the following:

1. This is not official, but I heard that the teacher is going to a different school.

2. His behavior is totally unacceptable.

3. The kids are not allowed to go to that bar.

4. My friends really liked my sister.

5. Her situation has improved.

41-3. Use a phrasal verb with *off* to express the following:

1. They cancelled their wedding.

2. I was falling asleep during the meeting.

3. Hey—stop bullying!

4. He was fired from his job because there were too many workers.

5. Nobody liked his bad manners.

6. What time does your plane leave?

UNIT 42:
On

Basic Meanings

1. **On** indicates location **higher than something and touching it; on top of.**

    Pattern *on* + noun

    > *The newspaper is **on** the table.*
    > *Please sign your name **on** the dotted line.*

2. **On** indicates an **outside location.**

    Pattern *on* + *the* + noun

    > *He was standing **on the** corner of First Street and Maple Avenue.*
    > *Let's have a barbecue **on the** balcony.*

    Typical nouns after *on the*:

    balcony, beach, corner, fence, field, ground, hill, horizon, lawn, patio, porch, roof, terrace

3. **On** indicates a **surface location.**

    Pattern 1 *on* + *the* + noun

    > *She rides her bicycle **on the** sidewalk.*

    Typical nouns after *on the*:

    boardwalk, court, (baseball) diamond, field, highway, path, rink, road, rocks, screen, sidewalk, street

    Pattern 2 *on* + ø noun

    > *That is the only place **on** earth where she feels safe.*

    Typical nouns after *on*:

    earth, land, page one (or any other number), solid ground, water

4. **On** indicates certain **inside surface locations.**

    Pattern *on* + *the* + noun

    > *There is a fly **on the** ceiling.*

    Typical nouns after *on the*:

    ceiling, floor, stairs, steps, wall, window
    first/second (or other number) floor

5. **On** indicates surface **contact.**

> **Pattern** verb + noun + *on* + noun
>
> > *The child pasted the picture **on** the page.*

Typical verbs:

glue, hold, paste, stick

6. **On** indicates **location in a part of an area.**

> **Pattern** *be + on + the + noun + of + noun*
>
> > *The porch **is on the** side **of** the house.*

Typical nouns after *on the*:

border, bottom, edge, end, exterior, inside, interior, left, outside, outskirts, first/second (or other number) page, right, side, surface, top

7. **On** means **facing.**

> **Pattern** *be + on + noun*
>
> > *Their house **is on** the beach.*
> >
> > *What street **is** your house **on**?*

Typical nouns:

beach, highway, river, road, street

8. **On** indicates **movement to** something; **onto.**

> **Pattern 1** verb + *on* + noun
>
> > *It rained **on** your bicycle last night.*
> >
> > *She jumped **on** the bed.*

Typical verbs before *on*:

bounce, climb, fall, get, hop, jump, knock, pounce, pound, rain, stamp, step, tread

> **Pattern 2** verb + noun + *on* + noun
>
> > *She poured water **on** the plant.*
> >
> > *He sprinkled salt **on** the meat.*

Typical verbs:

drip, drop, load, pour, put, shower, smear, spill, splash, spray, spread, sprinkle, squirt, throw

9. **On** indicates **travel in vehicles** in which one can walk.

> *She goes to work **on** the bus.*
>
> *They went **on** the train to Philadelphia.*

Typical nouns:

airplane, bus, ship, train

Typical verbs used before *on*:

get, go, ride, sit, travel

10. **On** indicates an **individual method of travel.**

> *He came over **on** his bike.*
>
> *She was sore from riding **on** a horse.*

Typical nouns:

all fours, bicycle, foot, one's hands and knees, motorcycle, roller blades, scooter, skateboard, skates, skis, sled, snowboard, surfboard, tiptoe, tricycle

11. **On** means **wearing.**

Pattern 1	verb + *on* + noun

> *The man has **on** a suit and tie.*
>
> *The lady put **on** her new dress.*

Pattern 2	verb + noun + *on* + noun

> *She put the bracelet **on** her wrist.*
>
> *He had a hat **on** his head.*

Typical verbs:

get, have, keep, put, try, wear

Related Expression

to put on   to get dressed in

> *She **put on** her shoes and went out.*

12. **On** indicates **physical support.**

Pattern 1	verb + *on* + noun

> *The child leaned **on** his father.*
>
> *The children sat **on** small chairs.*

Typical verbs used before *on*:

cling, hang, lean, lie, rest, sit, sleep, stand

Pattern 2   verb + noun + *on* + noun

> *She draped the cloth **on** the table.*
> *He laid the sick child **on** the bed.*

Typical verbs:

drape, hang, lay, place, put

Pattern 3   *be* + *on* + noun

> *The beads **are on** a string.*
> *The popsicle **is on** a stick.*

Related Expression

to be on one's side   to support in spirit

> *They are my friends; I'm sure they **are on my side**.*

13. On can indicate **trust in something or someone.**

Pattern 1   verb + *on* + noun

> *He relies **on** me to pay his rent.*

Typical verbs used before *on*:

bank, bet, count, depend, rely

Pattern 2   *be* + adjective + *on* + noun

> *She **is** dependent **on** her husband.*

Adjectives used before *on*:

based, dependent, predicated

14. On can indicate **frequency.**

Pattern   *on* + ø noun

> *He visits twice a month **on** average.*

Nouns commonly used after *on*:

average, occasion, weekends, Saturdays (or other days)
nice (or other adjective) mornings, afternoons, evenings, nights

15. **On** can indicate a **form of record.**

| Pattern | *on* + ø noun |

> *He wrote it **on** paper.*
>
> *They recorded the song **on** tape.*

Typical nouns:

cassette, compact disc, disk, film, microfilm, paper, record, tape

16. **On** means **by means of.**

| Pattern 1 | verb + *on* + noun |

> *That car runs **on** diesel fuel.*
>
> *They survive **on** very little food.*

Typical verbs used before *on*:

gain/lose weight, keep alive, live, make do, run, scrape by, survive, thrive, train

Typical nouns used after *on*:

calories, electricity, food, fuel, gas, income, salary

| Pattern 2 | verb + noun + *on* + noun |

> *I bought the furniture **on** credit.*
>
> *He wrote his paper **on** the computer.*

17. **On** can mean **using** at the present time.

| Pattern | *be* + *on* + *the* + noun |

> *The manager can't help you now; she **is on the** telephone.*

Nouns commonly used with this pattern:

computer, Internet, machine, telephone

Expression

to log on   to connect to the Internet

> *Don't interrupt him now; he has just **logged on**.*

18. **On** can indicate the **cause of a mishap.**

| Pattern 1 | verb + noun + *on* + noun |

> *I cut my finger **on** a piece of glass.*
>
> *She hurt herself **on** the swing.*

Pattern 2 verb + *on* + noun

*He tripped **on** a fallen branch.*

Verbs commonly used before *on*:

choke, fall, stumble, trip

19. **On** can indicate a **motive for action.**

Pattern 1 verb + *on* + ø noun

*They went to Houston **on** business.*

Nouns used after *on*:

business, command, instinct, reconnaissance, request, sabbatical, spec, vacation

Related Expressions

on purpose   deliberately

*She didn't want to see him; she stayed home **on purpose**.*

on behalf of   in place of, for the sake of

*I went to the meeting **on behalf of** my mother, who was out of town.*

on account of   because of

The picnic was canceled on account of the rain.

Pattern 2 *on* + *the* + noun + *of*

*They went overseas **on the** orders **of** the commander.*

*I bought the car **on the** recommendation **of** my son.*

Typical nouns:

advice, assumption, authority, calculations, charge, orders, premise, recommendation

20. **On** can indicate a **type of trip.**

Pattern verb + *on* + noun

*The class went **on** an excursion around the city.*

Nouns used after *on*:

cruise, excursion, field trip, flight, honeymoon, journey, mission, outing, safari, trip

21. **On** can indicate a **topic.**

> **Pattern 1** noun + *on* + noun

> *We have a good book **on** gardening.*
> *He wrote a long article **on** the economy.*

Typical nouns before *on*:

article, book, debate, discussion, paper, report, research, speech, thesis, thoughts

> **Pattern 2** verb + *on* + noun

> *She spoke **on** the environment.*
> *I wish he would expound **on** his ideas.*

Typical verbs before *on*:

expound, report, speak, write

22. **On** can show an **effect** of something on something else.

> **Pattern** noun + *on* + noun

> *We got a good buy **on** our car.*
> *There is a new tax **on** perfume.*

Typical nouns used before *on*:

ban, discount, embargo, encumbrance, evidence, good buy, restriction, sale, tax, war

23. **On** can indicate **possession** at the time.

> *She had four dollars **on** her.*
> *He didn't have a gun **on** him.*

24. **On** can indicate **membership** in an exclusive group.

> **Pattern** *be* + *on* + *the* + noun

> *She **is on the** basketball team and the honor roll.*

Typical nouns after *on*:

board, committee, council, crew, faculty, honor roll, jury, list, payroll, squad, staff, team

25. **On** can indicate an **occasion.**

> | Pattern 1 | *on* + noun |

> *Congratulations **on** your graduation.*
>
> *They went out to dinner **on** their anniversary.*

Typical nouns:

anniversary, arrival, birth, birthday, death, departure, news, occasion, wedding, weekend

> | Pattern 2 | *on* + ø noun |

> *They are leaving **on** Saturday (or any day).*

> | Pattern 3 | *on* + *the* + noun |

Example:

> *We are leaving **on the** ninth of August (or any date).*
>
> *They are going to New York **on the** weekend.*

26. **On** (adverb) can indicate **continuation.**

> | Pattern | verb + *on* |

> *They told us to move **on**.*
>
> *He was tired, but he drove **on**.*

Typical verbs:

drag, drive, go, keep, live, move, press, read, run, talk, walk, work

Related Expression

keep on + gerund   continue to do something

> *She told us to **keep on** reading.*

27. **On** expresses **offensive action.**

> | Pattern 1 | verb + *on* + noun |

> *The troops marched **on** the city at dawn.*

Typical expressions before *on*:

march, turn
pull a gun, pull a knife

Pattern 2	**noun + *on* + noun**

*They planned a raid **on** the nightclub.*

Typical nouns:

assault, attack, march, raid

28. **On** can indicate a **state** or condition.

Pattern 1	*be + on + ø noun*

*The new windows **are on** order.*

*Our new line of products **is on** display at the showroom.*

Typical nouns:

approval, board, call, course, display, duty, edge, fire, guard, high/low speed, high/low volume, hold, leave, loan, one's best behavior, order, parole, record, sale, schedule, stand-by, strike, tap, target, track, trial, vacation

Related Expressions

on the whole   weighing the good against the bad

>**On the whole** they enjoy their work.

on hand   available

>He is always **on hand** to help us.

online   connected to the Internet

>Every day more and more people are **online**.

on one's own   independent

>He is twenty-one and he lives **on his own**.

Pattern 2	*be + on + a/the + noun*

*She **is on a** diet.*

Typical nouns with *a*:

budget, diet, roll, spree

Related Expressions

on a roll   to be experiencing repeated success

>He has received four job offers; he is **on a roll**.

Typical nouns with *the*:

brink, edge, line, mark, way

on the spot   to be forced to make a difficult decision

*The young man was **on the spot** when his two best friends had an argument.*

on the fence   to be undecided

*The congressman hasn't decided which way to vote: he is **on the fence**.*

on the air   to be broadcasting on the radio or television

*The news is **on the air** at six o'clock.*

on the bench   to be the judge in court

*Do you know who **is on the bench** at her trial?*

on the blink   to be broken

*We can't copy it; the copier is **on the blink**.*

on the road   to be traveling

*Our band is going to be **on the road** for two weeks.*

on the condition that   if

*You can go on the trip **on the condition** that you pay for it.*

29. On can indicate **means of communication.**

*I heard it **on** the radio.*

*There are a lot of movies **on** television.*

*She found it **on** the Internet.*

Related Expression

to go viral on the Internet/a form of social media   to appear digitally rapidly

*Her video went viral **on** the Internet.*

30. On can indicate the **person who pays.**

*The party is **on** me.*

Expression

on the house   paid for by the management of the restaurant

*The drinks are **on the house**.*

31. On can mean **at the same time as.**

Pattern 1	*on* + **verb in gerund form**

*She fainted **on** hearing the news.*

Pattern 2   *on* + ø noun

*She feeds the baby **on** demand.*

*The car is yours **on** receipt of the title.*

Typical nouns after *on*:

approval, demand, receipt, reflection, second thought, sight

32. **On** can indicate **acquisition.**

Pattern 1   verb + *on* + noun

*They took **on** five new technicians at the plant.*

*She wanted to add **on** a family room.*

Typical verbs used before *on*:

add, bring, build, heap, load, pile, put, take

Pattern 2   verb + noun + *on* + noun

*They forced a new assistant **on** us.*

Typical verbs used before *on*:

add, build, force, heap, load, pile, push, put

Related Expression

to put on   to get dressed in

*She **put on** her shoes and went out.*

33. **On** can indicate **attitude toward the object.**

*Please have pity **on** the people who live there.*

*They agree **on** the important issues.*

Related Expression

have a crush on   to have a frivolous romantic interest in

*The young boy **had a crush on** his teacher.*

34. **On** can indicate **behavior concerning the object.**

| **Pattern 1** | *be* + adjective + *on* + noun |

> *The teacher **is** much too easy **on** the boys.*
>
> *I think I **was** too rough **on** her yesterday.*

Typical adjectives before *on*:

easy, hard, rough, soft, strict, tough

| **Pattern 2** | verb + *on* + noun |

> *The old lady doted **on** her only grandchild.*

Typical verbs before *on*:

center, concentrate, dote, dwell, err, harp, pick, prey, put pressure, wait

Related Expression

to lay hands on   to attack

> *If someone **lays hands on** you, call the police.*

35. **On** can indicate a **consequence to another person.**

| **Pattern** | verb + *on* + noun |

> *We were on a family vacation and my brother got sick **on** us.*
>
> *Please don't fall asleep **on** me; I need you to keep me awake.*

Typical verbs:

cheat, die, faint, fall asleep, get sick, go quiet, rat, tattle, tell

Expressions

on time   at the expected time

> *Mary is always **on time** for class.*

on the contrary   the opposite is true

> *We don't have too many books; **on the contrary**, we don't have enough.*

on the other hand   from another viewpoint

> *She is never on time; **on the other hand**, she is a very hard worker.*

on the tip of my tongue   refers to something almost remembered, but not quite

> *I can't remember his name, but it's right **on the tip of my tongue**.*

on your mark   the first command of three at the start of a race

> ***On your mark**, get set, go!*

to depend on   the outcome is decided by a future event

*I want to have the party outside, but it **depends on** the weather.*

Phrasal Verbs

call on (nonseparable)   ask

*If you need help, **call on** me.*

carry on (intransitive)   to behave a little wildly

*She **carries on** every night.*

carry on with (nonseparable)   continue an effort

*Who is going to **carry on with** the program when he leaves?*

catch on (intransitive)   understand

*My sister isn't interested in him; I'm afraid he will never **catch on**.*

get on (nonseparable)   enter a vehicle you can walk around on; mount a horse or bicycle

*We **got on** the bus in New York.*

get on (separable)   dress with slight difficulty

*See if you can **get** these shoes **on**.*

get on (intransitive)   grow old

*She is **getting on**; she is eighty-seven now.*

log on (intransitive)   to connect to the Internet

*She **logged on** to the Internet to communicate with her friend across the country.*

miss out on   lose an opportunity

*He **missed out on** a good party.*

pass on (separable)   tell or give to somebody else

*When you have finished reading this article, please **pass** it **on**.*

pick on (nonseparable)   selectively mistreat

*That teacher likes the boys but **picks on** the girls.*

turn on (separable)   cause to function

*First, you have to **turn** the machine **on**.*

PRACTICE

42-1. **Choose the best word or words for each blank space.**

1. I saw him outside, _____ on the corner.

   holding   pleasing   standing   driving

2. When we're at the beach, we like to walk on the _____.
   corner   water   sidewalk   boardwalk

3. Our garage is on the left side of the _____.

| house | page | inside | paper |

4. Is your house on this _____?

| city | town | street | neighborhood |

5. The baby can't walk yet, but he gets around on his _____.

| motorcycle | bike | hands and knees | skateboard |

6. Please keep your _____ on, so you don't get cold.

| necktie | gloves | bathing suit | necklace |

7. They always go to the movies on _____.

| evenings | mornings | weekends | weekend |

8. The senator spoke on _____.

| health care | roller skates | newspaper | magazine |

9. She's busy after school, because she's on the _____.

| gym | basketball team | driveway | practice |

10. The parts needed to fix my car aren't here, but they are on _____.

| time | line | mechanic | order |

42-2. Use an expression with *on* to express the following:

1. I'm trying to connect to the Internet.
2. My computer isn't working.
3. Elena is never late.
4. She has a silly romantic interest in the camp counselor.
5. 1-2-3-GO!

42-3. Use a phrasal verb with *on* to express the following:

1. We have to board the bus now.
2. It's hard for her to get dressed.
3. It's too bad you couldn't go to the party.
4. Don't let those bullies tease your little sister.
5. You can connect to the Internet here.

Onto

Basic Meanings

1. **Onto** indicates **movement** from one position to another one.

> **Pattern 1** verb + *onto* + noun
>
> > *The child hopped **onto** the bed.*

Typical verbs used before *onto*:

drip, fall, hop, jump, move, run, spill, step

> **Pattern 2** verb + noun + *onto* + noun
>
> > *We moved all the books **onto** the desk.*

Typical verbs used with this pattern:

drip, drop, move, spill, transfer

2. **Onto** indicates **knowledge of misbehavior.**

> **Pattern** *be* + *onto* + noun.
>
> > *The police **are onto** that gang about the missing money.*

PRACTICE

43-1. Choose the best word or words for each blank space.

1. The milk spilled all over the counter, and then onto the _____.

   floor   top   bowl   glass

2. He _____ on the test, but the teacher is onto him.

   failed   wrote   cheated   passed

UNIT 44:
On Top Of

Basic Meaning

1. **On top of** indicates a position **higher than the object, and usually touching it.**

    Pattern   verb + *on top of* + noun

    > They put the blanket **on top of** the sheets, and the bedspread **on top of** the blanket.
    >
    > I'm sure I left my keys **on top of** the desk.

Expression

to be on top of something   to be sure about one's knowledge or control of something

> Her son had a hard time learning math, but he **is on top of** it now.

44-1. Choose the best word or words for each blank space.

1. For a special treat, she put whipped cream on top of her _____, and a cherry on top of that.

    ice cream   soup   sandwich   milk

2. It was so cold that I put an extra blanket on top of my _____.

    hat   bed   coat   floor

UNIT 45:
Opposite

Basic Meaning

1. **Opposite** means **facing; across from.**

> **Pattern** **verb +** *opposite* **+ noun**
>
> *I sat* **opposite** *him at the library last night.*
> *My house is* **opposite** *the drugstore.*

45-1. **Choose the best word or words for each blank space.**

    1. I _____ opposite a well-known author at the dinner party.

        worked   talked   served   sat

UNIT 46:
Out

Basic Meanings

1. **Out** can indicate **removal** and is separable from the verb used.

   Pattern 1   verb + noun + *out*

   > *Please take the trash **out**.*

   Pattern 2   verb + *out* + noun

   > *Please take **out** the trash.*

   Typical verbs used with *out*:

   carry, cross, cut, get, kick, leave, move, take, tear, throw

2. **Out of** indicates **movement from inside.**

   Pattern 1   verb + *out of* + noun

   > *He was freezing when he got **out of** the water.*

   Typical verbs:

   come, crawl, drink, drive, fall, get, go, hop, jump, run, step

   Pattern 2   verb + noun + *out of* + noun

   > *She took the cake **out of** the oven.*

   Typical verbs:

   drive, get, grab, move, pour, pull, push, rip, sip, squeeze, take, tear

3. **Out** can indicate **distribution** and is separable from the verb used.

   Pattern 1   verb + noun + *out*

   > *The teacher told me to hand these papers **out**.*

   Pattern 2   verb + *out* + noun

   > *The teacher told me to hand **out** these papers.*

   Typical verbs used with *out*:

   give, hand, mail, pass, send

4. Out of indicates absence.

> **Pattern**   *be + out of* + noun

> *The boss **is out of** the office.*
> *My neighbors **are out of** the country this month.*

Related Expression

to be out of town   to be absent from one's place of residence

> *The boss **is out of town** this week.*

5. Out of indicates a distance from.

> **Pattern**   verb + *out of* + noun of place

> *The restaurant is about three miles **out of** town.*
> *They live two blocks **out of** the city limits.*

6. Out of can mean no longer in supply.

> **Pattern**   *be/run + out of* + plural or noncount noun

> *I can't make a cake because I **am out of** eggs.*
> *They had to walk to the gas station because they **ran out of** gas.*

Typical noncount nouns used after *out of*:

breath, gas, luck, money, stock, time, work

7. Out of can mean not as usually expected.

> **Pattern**   *be + out of* + noun

> *All her clothes **are out of** style.*
> *Unfortunately, her children **are out of** control.*

Typical nouns used after *out of*:

commission, context, control, date, fashion, focus, place, practice, reach, season, shape, style, sync, the ordinary, the way, tune

8. Out of indicates the basic ingredients or composition of something.

> **Pattern 1**   verb + noun + *out of* + noun

> *She makes the skirts **out of** scarves.*
> *He crafted the tables **out of** twigs.*

| Pattern 2 | past participle of verb + *out of* + noun |

*The statue was carved **out of** stone.*

*That bread is made **out of** whole wheat flour.*

Typical verbs used before *out of*:

build, carve, craft, create, fabricate, fashion, make, sculpt, sew, shape

9. **Out of** can indicate a **fraction.**

| Pattern 1 | number + *out of* + number + noun |

*Nine **out of** ten people on that street have new cars.*

| Pattern 2 | number + noun + *out of* + noun |

*Only three women **out of** the whole group volunteered to help.*

10. **Out of** can indicate **beyond.**

| Pattern | verb + *out of* + noun |

*We waved until he was **out of** sight.*

*He is **out of** touch with reality.*

Typical nouns used after *out of*:

bounds, danger, hearing, line, order, sight, touch

11. **Out of** can indicate a **reason** for action.

| Pattern | verb + *out of* + abstract noun |

*She invited him to the party **out of** kindness.*

*He only went **out of** curiosity.*

Typical nouns used after *out of*:

animosity, anxiety, compassion, cruelty, curiosity, fear, kindness, love, loyalty, malice, meanness, passion, pity, respect, spite, sympathy

Expressions

out of doors   outside

*The children love to play **out of doors**.*

out of it   not conscious of reality

*He hasn't adjusted to his new lifestyle; he is really **out of it** these days.*

out of the past   exactly as in the past

> *The music and dancing were **out of the past**.*

> *She is so old-fashioned: her ideas are **out of the** (nineteen) **sixties**.*

be put out   be resentful

> *She **was** really **put out** that you didn't invite her to your party.*

Phrasal Verbs

ask out (separable)   invite on a date

> *He **asks** her **out** all the time, but she never goes with him.*

blow out (separable)   to extinguish with air

> *She **blew out** all the candles on her birthday cake.*

break out (intransitive)   start suddenly

> *A fire **broke out** in the field yesterday.*

check out (separable)

1. investigate

> *Our air-conditioning isn't working; the repairman is coming to **check** it **out**.*

2. borrow officially

> *He went to the library to **check out** that book.*

check out (of) (intransitive)   pay the bill at a hotel

> *Your friends **checked out** early this morning.*

> *They **checked out of** the hotel at six o'clock.*

chew out (separable)   scold

> *The boss really **chewed** her **out** for being late for the meeting.*

chicken out (on) (nonseparable)   not act because of fear

> *He wanted to call the boss at home, but he **chickened out**.*

> *He promised to do it, but he **chickened out on** me.*

close out of (nonseparable)   sell all of an item, and no longer carry it

> *That store is **closing out of** small appliances, and is having a huge sale.*

come out (nonseparable)   make public that one is LGBTQ

> *She **came out** as lesbian last summer, after her first year at college.*

count out (separable)   not expect someone's participation

> *If you're planning a meeting for Saturday, **count** me **out**.*

creep out (separable)   to cause nervousness or fear

> *That horror movie really **creeped** me **out**.*

drop out (of) (intransitive)   leave a group or society

> *She didn't enjoy the club, and finally **dropped out**.*

> *She **dropped out** of the club.*

eat out (intransitive)   eat at a restaurant, rather than at home

> *That family **eats out** at least once a week.*

figure out (separable)   solve; understand

> *She can't seem to **figure out** her problems.*

fill out (separable)   complete in writing

> *Please **fill out** these forms.*

find out (separable)   learn by investigating

> *Can you help me **find out** where they live?*

freak out (separable)   to cause heightened emotion

> *The young girls **freaked out** when their favorite singer appeared on stage.*

get out of (nonseparable)   find an excuse to break a commitment

> *She said she was sick, and **got out of** washing the dishes.*

go out with (nonseparable)   date someone

> *She **goes out with** my brother every Saturday night.*

hang out (with) (intransitive)   do nothing, with friends

> *Those kids just **hang out** every day after school.*

> *They **hang out with** other students.*

keep out (of) (intransitive)   not enter

> *They told us to **keep out**.*

> *They told us to **keep out of** their yard.*

knock out (separable)   cause to lose consciousness

> *The champion **knocked** the other boxer **out** in the first round.*

look out (for) (intransitive)   be careful

> *We told them to **look out**.*

> *We told them to **look out for** cars when crossing the street.*

luck out (intransitive)   be lucky

> *Tickets were hard to get, but we **lucked out** and got two in the front row.*

make out (intransitive)   be successful

> *We sold all of our stuff at the garage sale and **made out** pretty well.*

pass out (intransitive)   faint

> *She hadn't eaten all day, and she **passed out**.*

pass out (separable)   distribute

> *They asked us to help **pass out** flyers announcing the new restaurant.*

pick out (separable)   select

> *Here are the strawberries; **pick out** the best ones to serve.*

pig out (intransitive)   to eat excessively

> *The party food was so good that a lot of people really **pigged out**.*

point out (separable)   call attention to

> *The agent **pointed out** that the house was in a convenient neighborhood.*

put out (separable)   extinguish; display

> *He **put out** the fire quickly.*

> *She **put out** all her best china.*

stand out (from) (intransitive)   be noticeable

> *The tall girl in the chorus **stands out**.*

> *She **stands out** from all the short girls.*

step out (of) (intransitive)   leave a room or building

> *It was so hot in there that we decided to **step out** for a few minutes.*

stress out (separable)   to cause tension

> *She loves her job, but it **stresses** her **out** sometimes.*

talk out of (separable)   convince someone not to do something

> *He was going to marry that girl, but his mother **talked** him **out of** it.*

try out (separable)   use before buying, to find out if suitable

> *They let you **try** the car **out** before you buy it.*

try out (for) (nonseparable)   audition

> *She is going to **try out for** the musical show at school.*

turn out (intransitive)   indicates a result

> *How did the dress you were making **turn out**?*

wash out (of) (separable)   remove from clothing with soap and water

> *I tried to **wash** that spot **out** of my dress.*

watch out (for) (intransitive)   be careful

> *He told her to **watch out**.*

> *He told her to **watch out for** danger.*

wear out (separable)   use until ruined

> *I **wore** my shoes **out**, and had to throw them away.*

work out (separable)   solve a problem in a relationship

> *That couple had a lot of problems, but they **worked** them **out**.*

work out (intransitive)   do exercise

> *He **works out** every evening.*

PRACTICE

46-1. **Choose the best word or words for each blank space.**

1. My sweater was full of holes, so I _____ it out.
   gave   threw   took   got

2. In addition to the holes in my sweater, it was also out of _____.
   the country   the blue   style   wool

3. When they saw the fire, they _____ out of the house.
   drove   pushed   ran   stood

4. She's on vacation.   She will be out of the _____ for a week.
   office   door   work   beach

5. He's been running, and now he's out of _____
   money   time   the office   breath

6. The female candidate won the election. _____ out of every four people voted for her.
   One   Two   Three   Six

7. He doesn't have much money, but he gives to the homeless out of _____.
   home   kindness   his heart   his mind

46-2. **Use an expression with *out* or *out of* to express the following:**

1. He invited me for a date.

2. They have already left the hotel and paid their bill.

3. He stopped going to school when he was sixteen.

4. She fainted in class yesterday.

5. Please choose four apples that look good.

6. The firemen extinguished the fire.

7. I spilled coffee on the sofa and tried to remove the spot.

8. They exercise together at the gym.

UNIT 47:
Outside

Basic Meaning

1. Outside (of) means not within.

> **Pattern** verb + *outside (of)* + noun
>
> *Don't worry, the dog is **outside (of)** the house.*

PRACTICE

47-1. Choose the best word or words for the blank space.

1. After the accident, the police officer told me to stay outside of the _____.

   car   house   hospital   ambulance

UNIT 48:
Over

Basic Meanings

1. Over means above.

Pattern 1 verb + *over* + noun

> *The plane flew **over** our building.*
>
> *The pictures were hanging **over** the sofa.*

Typical verbs used before *over*:

be, bend, float, fly, hang, hover, lean, look, shine, watch

Pattern 2 verb + noun + *over* + noun

> *She hung the pictures **over** the sofa.*

Typical verbs used with this pattern:

float, fly, hang, hold, install, nail, place, suspend

Expression

to hold something over one's head   to control, threaten, or punish someone because of a known fact or misdeed

> *She knows he was fired from his last job; now she **holds that over his head**.*

2. Over can mean higher than.

Pattern *be + (way) over + noun*

> *The price of that vacation **is (way) over** our budget.*
>
> *The water at this end of the pool **is over** your head.*

3. Over (adverb) can mean more than.

Pattern *over + number + noun*

> *He was driving at **over** eighty miles an hour.*
>
> *I have gained **over** five pounds this month.*

4. **Over** indicates movement **above** something and **to the other side** of it.

> **Pattern 1** **verb** + *over* + **noun**
>
> > *The children jumped **over** the puddles on their way to school.*
> > *We had to climb **over** the mountain to get here.*

Typical verbs used before *over*:

climb, cross, drive, get, go, hop, jump, look, run, skate, skip, step, stumble, trip

> **Pattern 2** **verb** + **noun** + *over* + **noun**
>
> > *The young player batted the ball **over** the fence.*
> > *We had fun throwing rocks **over** the creek.*

Typical verbs:

bat, carry, drive, hit, throw

5. **Over** can mean **covering** something.

> **Pattern** **verb** + **noun** + *over* + **noun**
>
> > *The child wore a warm jacket **over** her dress.*
> > *The lady sewed patches **over** the holes.*

Typical verbs:

drape, hang, have, paint, place, pour, pull, put, sew, spread, tape, wear

6. **Over** indicates **control.**

> **Pattern 1** *rule/preside* + *over* + **noun**
>
> > *She **rules over** her family like a tyrant.*
> > *The chairman asked me to **preside over** the meeting tonight.*

> **Pattern 2** *have control/power* + *over* + **noun**
>
> > *They **have** no **control over** their actions.*
> > *He likes to **have power over** his associates.*

7. **Over** can mean location **on the other side of** something.

> > *That restaurant is **over** the state line.*
> > *They live **over** the river.*

Typical verbs:

be, be located, dwell, lie, live, reside

8. **(All) over** can mean **in many parts of** a place.

Pattern	verb + *all* + *over* + *the* + noun

   *They have traveled **all over the** world.*

   *She looked **all over the** city for her friend.*

   Typical nouns:

   city, country, field, floor, house, place, playground, sidewalk, state, street, table, town, world, yard

   Typical verbs:

   broadcast, crawl, drive, look, roll, run, send, spill, throw, travel, walk

9. **Over** can mean **during.**

Pattern 1	*over* + noun

   *We had an interesting discussion **over** breakfast this morning.*

   Typical nouns after *over*:

   breakfast, coffee, dinner, drinks, lunch, snacks, tea

Pattern 2	*over* + *the* + noun

   *They decided to read the papers **over the** holidays.*

   *She has been sick **over the** last three weeks.*

   Nouns commonly used with this pattern:

   holidays, summer, weekend, winter
   next (number) hours, days, weeks, months, years
   last (number) hours, days, weeks, months, years

10. **Over** can indicate a **topic.**

Pattern	verb + *over* + noun

    *They argued **over** politics all night.*

    *I wish you wouldn't fight **over** money.*

    Typical verbs used before *over*:

    argue, battle, cry, fight, grieve, gush, puzzle, sigh, worry

11. **Over** (adverb) can mean **again.**

> **Pattern**   verb + noun + *over*

> *She didn't like my work; she told me to do it **over**.*

Typical verbs used before *over*:

do, read, start, write

Expressions

be over one's head   more than one can understand

> *I can do simple math, but that problem **is** way **over my head**.*

over the telephone   by means of telephone

> *She gave me that information **over the telephone**.*

head over heels   completely

> *He is **head over heels** in love with her.*

As an adverb

(all) over   finished

> *The party was **all over** at nine o'clock.*

Phrasal Verbs

blow over (intransitive)   be forgotten

> *Don't worry about your argument with him; I'm sure it will **blow over**.*

fall over (intransitive)   collapse

> *She was sitting at her desk when she suddenly **fell over**.*

go over (nonseparable)   review

> *He **went over** my algebra with me.*

hand over (separable)   give reluctantly

> *The children had to **hand over** all the money they found.*

have over (separable)   invite to one's home

> *We want to **have** you **over** soon.*

look over (separable)   review

> *Please **look over** these papers before the meeting tomorrow.*

pass over (separable)   not give an expected promotion

> *She expected to be promoted to director, but she was **passed over** this year.*

pick over (separable)   find and choose the best of a lot

> *Some of these cherries are not ripe; you will have to **pick** them **over** carefully.*

pull over (intransitive)   drive to the side of the road

> *We were driving too fast, and the police officer made us **pull over**.*

pull over (separable)   move to cover something

>   ***Pull*** *the sweater **over** your head.*

run over   crush with vehicle

>   *She **ran over** the package with her car.*

start over   begin again

>   *I made a lot of mistakes, so I **started** my homework **over**.*

take over (intransitive)   become the boss, or act like a boss

>   *The children don't like to play with that boy because he always tries to **take over**.*

take over (separable)   carry something to another place

>   *Please **take** this letter **over** to your neighbor.*

think over (separable)   consider the pros and cons

>   *Your offer interests us; we will **think** it **over**.*

turn over (intransitive)   change position from face down, face up, or vice versa

>   *Most babies **turn over** in the first six months of life.*

turn over (separable)   move something from top to bottom, or vice versa

>   *Some kids **turned** all the trash cans **over** last night.*

PRACTICE

48-1. Choose the best word or words for each blank space.

1. The airplane was flying over our _____.
    clothing   furniture   building   party

2. Don't go in that end of the swimming pool. The water is over your _____.
    weight   age   height   head

3. He hit a home run. The ball went over the _____.
    street   base   fence   home plate

4. She has no control over her _____.
    dogs   roof   garage   door

5. To get there, you have to go over the _____.
    street   state line   house   horse

6. He drives way too fast.   He always goes over _____.
    55 mph   60 mph   the speed limit   the traffic lights

7. We looked all over the _____ for your keys.
    ceiling   clothing   pockets   hotel room

8. They don't get along. They are always fighting over _____.
    traffic   money   the hotel room   the state line

48-2. Use an expression with *over* to express the following:

1. She is really in love with him.

2. That course is too hard for me.

48-3. Use a phrasal verb with *over* to express the following:

1. Nobody was there when he collapsed.

2. The police officer stopped me when I was driving too fast.

3. He didn't get the promotion.

4. We are considering your offer.

5. Could you please read these contracts before the meeting?

UNIT 49:
Past

Basic Meanings

1. Past means beyond.

> **Pattern** *be* + *past* + **noun referring to a place**
>
> > *The gas station **is** on your left, just **past** the shopping center.*

2. Past indicates movement in front of and beyond a place.

> **Pattern** **verb** + *past* + **noun**
>
> > *We drove **past** your house on our way to the party.*
> >
> > *They often walk **past** the park.*

3. Past means older than.

> **Pattern** *be* + *past* + **noun referring to age**
>
> > *His daughter **is past** her teens now.*
> >
> > *I'm sure he **is past** fifty.*

4. Past means no longer able to do something.

> **Pattern** *be* + *past* + **verb in gerund form**
>
> > *She **is** bitter now, and **past** caring.*
> >
> > *The men **were** exhausted and **past** working.*

5. Past (adverb) means later than.

> **Pattern** *be* + *past* + **noun referring to time**
>
> > *It is ten **past** three in the afternoon.*
> >
> > *They left at half **past** seven.*

PRACTICE

49-1. Choose the best word or words for each blank space.

1. I can take you to work. I go past _____ on the way to mine.

   your apartment　　　　your office　　　　your house　　　　your sister

2. He plans to retire when he is past _____.

   sixty-five　　　　the goalpost　　　　the corner　　　　the state line

Through

Basic Meanings

1. **Through** indicates **passage within** something.

Pattern	verb + *through* + noun

    *The children drank their milkshakes **through** straws.*

    *The highway was closed, and we had to come **through** the city.*

    Typical nouns used after *through*:

    funnel, passage, pipe, straw, tunnel
    a place building, city, country, park, state, town

2. **Through** can indicate a **gateway** or **obstacle** between two places.

Pattern 1	verb + *through* + noun

    *We came **through** the front door.*

    *He drove **through** the red light and got a ticket.*

    Typical nouns:

    barricade, barrier, curtains, customs, door, entrance, gate, hole, intersection, light, slot, stop sign, window

Pattern 2	verb + noun + *through* + noun

    *The mail carrier pushed the letters **through** the slot.*

    Typical verbs used before *through*:

    bring, carry, force, pull, push, receive, send, take

3. **Through** can indicate **vision beyond something.**

Pattern	see/show + *through* + noun

    *The window is so dirty that I can't **see through** it.*

    *The tablecloth needs a liner; the table legs **show through** it.*

    Typical nouns used after *through*:

    clouds, fabric, fog, glass, smoke, window

Related Expression

to see through somebody   to detect insincerity

*That woman pretends to be nice, but I can **see through her**.*

4. **Through** can indicate the **parts beginning, between, and including.**

> **Pattern**   *from* + noun + *through* + noun
>
>> *They have to work **from** Monday **through** Friday.*
>> *Please read **from** chapter one **through** chapter four.*

5. **Through** can mean **finish something that requires effort.**

> **Pattern 1**   verb + *through* + noun
>
>> *I have to get **through** school before I can get married.*

Typical verbs used before *through*:

get, go, live, struggle, suffer

Typical nouns after *through*:

school, training, work

> **Pattern 2**   *be* + *through* + *with* + noun
>
>> ***Are** you **through with** your exams yet?*

Typical nouns used with this pattern:

course, exams, red tape, trouble

Related Expression

to go through   to experience something difficult

> *He is **going through** a divorce.*

6. **Through** can indicate **in all parts of a place; throughout**

> **Pattern 1**   verb + *(all) through* + *the* + noun
>
>> *We walked **all through the** garden.*

> **Pattern 2**   verb + noun + *(all) through* + *the* + noun
>
>> *They distributed flyers **all through the** neighborhood.*

Typical nouns used after *through*:

building, city, country, garden, house, neighborhood, state, town

Related Expression

to go/look through   something to look at all the contents of something, hoping to find something

> *I **went through** my files and found these documents.*

> *I **looked through** my papers, but I couldn't find the certificate.*

Typical nouns used after *through*:

boxes, closets, correspondence, drawers, files, letters, notes, papers, records, things

7. **(All) through** (or **throughout**) can mean **during an entire event** or period.

> **Pattern 1** **verb** + *through* + **noun**

> > *Those women talked **through** the whole game.*

> > *The baby finally slept all **through** the night.*

Typical verbs before *through*:

cheat, cry, laugh, play, sit, sleep, stay, talk, wait, watch, worry

> **Pattern 2** **verb** + **noun** + *through* + **noun**

> > *She cared for her father **through** his illness.*

Verbs commonly used with this pattern:

abuse, care for, help, ignore, wait for, wait on

Typical nouns used after *through*:

afternoon, breakfast, day, dinner, game, illness, life, lunch, meal, month, morning, night, ordeal, performance, play, time, war, wedding, week, year

Related Expressions

to see something through   to stay with something until it is finished.

> *Don't worry, we will **see** your project **through**.*

to see somebody through   to stay with somebody until he is out of trouble.

> *I will **see** you **through** this problem; I promise.*

8. **Through** can mean **by means of.**

> | Pattern | verb + noun + *through* + noun |
> | --- | --- |
>
> > *We heard the news **through** friends.*
> >
> > *They bought that apartment **through** an agency.*
>
> Typical nouns after *through*:
>
> **agency, contacts, friends, gossip, newspaper, translator**
> **instruments of vision binoculars, glasses, lenses, microscope, periscope**

Related Expressions

to hear something through the grapevine   to get news unofficially

> *We **heard** about your engagement **through the grapevine**.*

9. **Through** can indicate a **reason.**

> | Pattern | verb + noun + *through* + noun |
> | --- | --- |
>
> > *She achieved success **through** determination and hard work.*
> >
> > ***Through** an error in our accounting, we have overcharged you.*
>
> Typical nouns after *through*:
>
> **carelessness, determination, fault, frustration, generosity, greed, hard work, help,**
> **kindness, luck, misinformation, negligence, selfishness, an error, a mistake**

Expression

to go through with something   to continue doing something; to not give up

> *I can't believe you are still going **to go through with** your plans.*

Phrasal Verbs

carry/follow through (separable)   complete a project

> *He has some good ideas; I hope he can **carry** them **through**.*

carry/follow through with (nonseparable)   complete

> *I hope he can **carry through with** his plans.*

come through (intransitive)   perform as one has promised

> *She promised to help us; I hope she **comes through**.*

fall through (intransitive)   collapse

> *All his plans to move to California **fell through**.*

show through (separable)   to give someone a tour of a building

> *When we went to Washington, D.C., our congressman **showed** us **through** the Capitol.*

PRACTICE

50-1. Choose the best word or words for each blank space.

1. She got a ticket because she went through a _____.

   counter   red light   concert   movie

2. I can't see through the _____, because it's so dirty.

   couch   chair   garage   window

3. Before I can graduate, I have to get through this _____.

   street   course   office   window

4. She took care of him all through his _____.

   illness   work   concert   bed

5. We got the visas through the _____.

   airplane   passports   embassy   stewardess

50-2. Use a phrasal verb with *through* to express the following:

1. Do you think he will do what he promised?

2. Our contract failed.

3. She gave us a tour of the museum.

Throughout

Basic Meanings

1. **Throughout** means **in all parts** of a place.

   *There are spiders **throughout** the building.*

2. **Throughout** means during **an entire period of time.**

   *She stays at the beach **throughout** the summer.*

PRACTICE

51-1. Choose the best word or words for each blank space.

1. I've had that song in my head throughout the _____.

   building   day   years   city

2. When our team won the championship, there were victory celebrations throughout the _____.

   city   bus station   airport   game

UNIT 52:
To

Basic Meanings

1.   To indicates the **destination of a verb.**

> **Pattern 1**   verb + *to* + ø noun
>
> > *I'm going **to** bed.*
> >
> > *They ride **to** school on the bus.*
>
> Nouns commonly used after *to*:
>
> **bed, breakfast, church, dinner, jail, lunch, school, work**

Exception

> **go ø home**
>
> > *It is time to **go home.***
> >
> > *They **went home** on the bus.*
>
> **Pattern 2**   verb + *to* + *the* + noun
>
> > *We go **to the** park every afternoon.*
> >
> > *Call when you get **to the** office.*
>
> Verbs often used with *to*:
>
> **come, drive, extend, fall, fly, get, go, hike, move, return, ride, rise, run, send, ship, sink, walk**

2.   To indicates the **destination of a noun.**

> **Pattern 1**   noun + *to* + noun
>
> > *The train **to** New York leaves at six o'clock.*
> >
> > *We wanted to go on a cruise **to** the Caribbean.*
>
> Typical nouns used before *to*:
>
> **airplane, bridge, bus, climb, cruise, flight, highway, path, race, road, subway, train, trip, way**
>
> **Pattern 2**   noun + *be* + *to* + noun
>
> > *The train **is to** New York.*
> >
> > *His question **is to** me.*
>
> Typical nouns used before *to*:
>
> **answer, card, donation, explanation, gift, letter, memo, offer, petition, present, proposal, question, request, suggestion**

3. **To** indicates a **transfer** from a person or place.

> **Pattern** verb + noun + *to* + noun
>
> > *He delivers the mail **to** the office.*
> > *She mentioned her plans **to** me.*

Typical verbs used before *to*:

bring, carry, deliver, describe, distribute, donate, explain, give, hand, introduce, lend, mention, pass, present, read, recommend, reveal, send, shout, show, sing, speak, submit, suggest, take, tell, write

4. **To** indicates a **beneficiary.**

> **Pattern 1** verb + noun + *to* + noun
>
> > *They made a toast **to** the bride and groom.*

Typical verbs used with this pattern:

award, dedicate, devote, give, make

Typical nouns used before *to*:

award, dedication, gift, memorial, monument, plaque, present, remark, scholarship, statement, toast

Related Expression

as a favor to   for the benefit of

> *We came to help you **as a favor to** your father.*

> **Pattern 2** *to* + *one's* + noun
>
> > *If you shout, someone will come **to** your aid.*
> > *It is **to** your benefit to join the credit union.*
> > *The police came **to** my rescue when my car broke down.*

5. **To** indicates an **effect on the recipient.**

> **Pattern 1** *be* + noun + *to* + noun
>
> > *He **is** a credit **to** his mother and father.*
> > *The airplane noise **is** a disturbance **to** the neighborhood.*

Nouns commonly used before *to*:

annoyance, bother, challenge, credit, detriment, discredit, disturbance, help, nuisance

Pattern 2	*be* + adjective + *to* + noun

*His calls **are** very annoying **to** me.*

Typical adjectives used before *to*:

abhorrent, acceptable, annoying, beneficial, boring, confusing, crucial, detrimental, distasteful, disturbing, fascinating, gratifying, harmful, helpful, hurtful, important, meaningful, obnoxious, pleasing, precious, preferable, repulsive, satisfying, unacceptable, unfavorable, unimportant, vexing, worrisome

Related Expression

to be to one's taste   to be personally pleasing to someone

*The apartment is large and expensive, but **it's** not **to my taste**.*

Pattern 3	*to* + *one's* + noun

***To my** surprise, everybody was at work on Saturday.*

***To their** delight, the campaign was a great success.*

Typical nouns:

astonishment, chagrin, delight, disappointment, discomfort, disgrace, disgust, embarrassment, horror, satisfaction, surprise

6.   **To** can indicate a **reaction**.

Pattern 1	verb + *to* + noun

*She responded **to** my letter right away.*

*I hope you don't object **to** my offer of help.*

Typical verbs used before *to*:

adapt, admit, agree, appeal, consent, listen, object, pay attention, prefer, react, relate, reply, respond, revert, subscribe

Pattern 2	noun + *to* + noun

*She has an allergy **to** that medicine.*

*Do you have an answer **to** that question?*

Typical nouns:

allergy, answer, appeal, aversion, consent, objection, preference, reaction, relation, reply, response

Pattern 3 *be* + **adjective** + *to* + **noun**

> She **is** allergic **to** that medicine.

> We **are** indebted **to** you for helping us.

Typical adjectives:

accustomed, allergic, grateful, indebted, thankful

7. **To** can indicate someone's **behavior toward another person.**

Pattern *be* + **adjective** + *to* + **noun**

> He **was** very cruel **to** me.

> She **has been** hostile **to** her neighbors.

Typical adjectives:

affectionate, appreciative, attentive, available, charming, cold, considerate, cordial, cruel, devoted, dreadful, faithful, friendly, gracious, hospitable, hostile, inconsiderate, kind, loyal, mean, nice, obedient, open, pleasant, polite, respectful, sassy, warm

8. **To** can indicate **attachment.**

Pattern 1 **verb** + **noun** + *to* + **noun**

> We will paste the wallpaper **to** the bedroom walls.

> She pinned the flowers **to** my lapel.

Pattern 2 *be* + **past participle of verb** + *to* + **noun**

> Your paper **is** stapled **to** mine.

> The gum **is** stuck **to** my shoe.

Typical verbs used with these patterns:

add, adhere, affix, apply, attach, glue, hold, nail, paste, pin, press, screw, sew, staple, stick, tape

9. **To** indicates the **end of a period of time; until.**

Pattern *from* + *to* + **noun**

> They work **from** morning **to** night.

> He was here **from** two **to** five.

10. **To** means **before,** in telling time.

> **Pattern**   *It* + *be* + **number of minutes** + *to* + **hour**

> *It is* ten (minutes) *to* three in the afternoon.
> *It was* a quarter (fifteen minutes) *to* four.

11. **To** can indicate **continuous repetition of an action.**

> **Pattern 1**   **verb** + *from* + **noun** + *to* + **same noun**

> We went *from* door *to* door with our information sheets.
> The bus rocked *from* side *to* side.

Common expressions:

door to door, house to house, place to place, side to side

> **Pattern 2**   **noun** + **hyphen** + *to* + **hyphen** + **same noun** + **noun**

> They have door-*to*-door service.

12. **To** can indicate a **comparison of value.**

> **Pattern 1**   *be* + **adjective** + *to* + **noun**

> His work *is* comparable *to* hers.
> Your car *is* similar *to* mine.

Typical adjectives:

comparable, inferior, preferable, similar, superior

> **Pattern 2**   *compare* + **noun** + *to* + **noun**

> Please don't *compare* my work *to* yours.

> **Pattern 3**   *compared* + *to* + **noun**

> She is of medium height, but *compared to* her sister, she is tall.

13. **To** can indicate a **problem** or **solution.**

> **Pattern**   **noun** + *to* + **noun**

> The strike is a threat *to* our survival.
> She knows the secret *to* success.

Typical nouns used before *to*:

Problems: **barrier, obstacle, threat**
Solutions: **answer, antidote, boost, clue, directions, guide, instructions, key, secret, solution**

14. **To** can indicate **ownership, membership,** and **connection.**

| Pattern 1 | *belong/pertain* + *to* + **noun** |

> The book **belongs to** me.
> Her friends **belong to** that club.
> This discussion does not **pertain to** you.

| Pattern 2 | **adjective** + *to* + **noun** |

> Your comments are not pertinent **to** this topic.

Adjectives used with this meaning:

attached, attributable, committed, connected, dedicated, engaged, exclusive, important, married, obligated, pertinent, promised, related, relevant, seconded, tied

15. **To** can indicate an **exclusive relationship.**

| Pattern | *the* + **noun** + *to* + **noun** |

> This is **the** key **to** my front door.
> Have you seen **the** jacket **to** my new suit?
> She is **the** new secretary **to** the chairman.

Typical nouns:

assistant, case, cover, door, jacket, key, knob, lid, part, secretary, strap, ticket, top

16. **To** indicates the **accompaniment of sound.**

| Pattern | **verb** + *to* + **noun** |

> We danced **to** the rhythm of the music.
> I wake up **to** the noise of the city.

Typical nouns:

beat, blare, buzz, honk, hum, music, noise, rhythm, roar, sound, strum, tune

17. **To** means **leading to an extreme condition.**

| Pattern | **verb** + **noun** + *to* + **noun** |

> He tore the paper **to** pieces.
> She drives him **to** distraction.

Related Expressions

beat/grind to a pulp

bore to death

carry to extremes

chill to the bone

cook to perfection

drive to distraction/insanity

grind to dust

move to tears

push/carry/take to the limits

sing/rock to sleep

smash to bits

soak to the skin

starve/freeze to death

tear to pieces/shreds

18. **To** indicates an **upper limitation** of an approximation.

Pattern	number + *to* + number

*It is two **to** two-and-a-half feet long.*

*He is thirty-eight **to** forty years old.*

19. **To** indicates a **relationship** between the subject and the object.

Pattern 1	noun + *be* + adverb + *to* + **noun,** to show location

*The library **is** close **to** the park.*

*The new theater **is** adjacent **to** the mall.*

Typical adverbs:

at an angle, close, next

Pattern 2	noun + *be* + adjective + *to* + noun

*That line **is** parallel **to** this one.*

Typical adjectives:

adjacent, parallel, perpendicular

Pattern 3	noun + *to* + **noun,** to indicate position

*They sat back **to** back.*

*She came face **to** face with danger.*

Pattern 4	**number + *to* + number,** to give the score of a game

*The score was three **to** two.*

Pattern 5	**amount + *to* + amount,** to show equality

*There are four quarts **to** a gallon.*

Pattern 6	**amount + *to* + amount,** to show ratio

*He gets thirty miles **to** a gallon on the highway in his new car.*

20. **To** can indicate **restriction.**

Pattern 1	**verb + noun + *to* + noun**

*We limited him **to** three meals a day, with no sugary snacks.*
*They confined her **to** jail for thirty-six hours.*

Typical verbs:
bind, confine, hold, limit, restrict, sentence, tie

Pattern 2	**past participle of verb (adjective) + *to* + noun**

*He is limited **to** three meals a day.*
*She is confined **to** jail for thirty-six hours.*

Expressions

to rise to the occasion   to force oneself to act correctly

*I was annoyed when he walked in, but I **rose to the occasion** and shook his hand.*

to subscribe to   to pay for and receive a periodical regularly

*How many magazines do you **subscribe to**?*
*She **subscribes to** three daily newspapers.*

from time to time   occasionally

*He calls me **from time to time**.*

to be used to/to be accustomed to + noun   to have adapted

*He is dizzy because he **is not used to** the altitude.*
*She is nervous because **she is not used** to driving in traffic.*

Phrasal Verbs

come to (intransitive)   regain consciousness

> *She fainted a few minutes ago, but fortunately **came to** right away.*

see to (nonseparable)   take responsibility for a future action

> *You don't have to make reservations; we will **see to** that.*

look forward to (nonseparable)   await with pleasure

> *We are **looking forward to** seeing you soon.*

PRACTICE

52-1. Choose the best word or words for each blank space.

1. After school, the kids went _____.
   | to home | to the home | playground | home |

2. How do the children get to _____?
   | home | school | playground | house |

3. The _____ to Los Angeles leaves at 4 P.M.
   | road | highway | flight | bridge |

4. She _____ her homework to the teacher.
   | handed | threw | found | told |

5. The music award went to the _____.
   | best builder | best pilot | best pianist | best brother |

6. Bad drivers are a danger to the _____.
   | sky | neighborhood | driveway | supermarket |

7. Don't worry.   Soon you will _____ to your new environment.
   | adapt | consent | prefer | respond |

8. Do you have an allergy to _____?
   | the weather | dust | homework | rain |

9. The dog was _____ to its owner.
   | happy | hospitable | obedient | sick |

10. It's 10:45.   It's _____ to eleven.
    | 10 minutes | 45 minutes | a quarter | half |

11. My friends and I belong to the _____.
    | bookshelf | book club | readers | hospital |

12. How many miles to a _____ do you get on the highway?
    | city | speedometer | gallon | quart |

52-2. Use an expression with *to* to express the following:

1. He texts me occasionally.

2. Have you adapted to the climate here?

52-3. Use *to* in a phrasal verb to express the following:

1. She regained consciousness a few minutes ago.

2. I am awaiting your visit with pleasure.

Basic Meanings

1. Toward means **in the direction of a place.**

> **Pattern 1**   verb + *toward* + noun

>> *She ran* **toward** *the playground to see her friends.*
>> *Let's head* **toward** *the park.*

Typical verbs:

blow, fly, go, head, hike, look, march, move, point, run, sail, turn, walk

> **Pattern 2**   verb + noun + *toward* + noun

>> *He guided us* **toward** *the cave.*
>> *They directed the girls* **toward** *the path.*

Typical verbs:

direct, guide, lead, pull, push, shove, throw

2. Toward indicates **attitude** about something.

> **Pattern 1**   *be* + adjective + *toward* + noun

>> *She* **is** *very affectionate* **toward** *her parents.*
>> *They* **have been** *cool* **toward** *his proposals.*

Typical adjectives:

affectionate, charitable, considerate, cool, friendly, gracious, hospitable, inhospitable, menacing, spiteful, warm

> **Pattern 2**   noun + *toward* + noun

>> *His feelings* **toward** *her have not changed.*

Typical nouns before *toward*:

attitude, behavior, conduct, demeanor, feelings

3. **Toward** indicates the **direction of action**.

Pattern	verb + *toward* + noun

   > *They are heading **toward** an agreement.*
   > *We worked **toward** a happy conclusion for everyone.*

   Typical nouns after *toward*:
   agreement, argument, conclusion, ending, goal, vote

   Typical verbs:
   head, lean, push, take steps, work

4. **Toward** indicates the object of a **contribution** or **partial payment**.

Pattern	verb + *toward* + noun

   > *The money will go **toward** helping the family.*
   > *She contributes **toward** his monthly expenses.*

   Typical verbs:
   contribute, donate, give, go, help

PRACTICE

53-1. Choose the best word or words for each blank space.

1. We are taking _____ toward achieving our goals.

   pushes   steps   walks   money

2. She _____ toward his monthly expenses.

   contributes   donates   goes   steps

3. He is very _____ toward his guests.

   happy   confusing   feeling   hospitable

4. They _____ us toward the camp.

   followed   found   directed   threw

UNIT 54:
Towards

Basic Meanings

1. Towards means near a period of time.

Pattern 1 *towards* + noun

*I always feel hungry **towards** dinnertime.*

Typical nouns used after *towards*:

dawn, dinnertime, dusk, evening, lunchtime, mid-afternoon, midnight, noon

Pattern 2 *towards + the + end/middle + of + the + noun*

*We start getting ready for school **towards the end of the** summer.*

Typical nouns used with this pattern:

class, concert, course, day, fall, flight, game, month, party, period, season, semester, show, spring, summer, trip, vacation, week, winter, year

---

PRACTICE

54-1. Choose the best word or words for each blank space.

1. Everyone will be leaving towards _____.

   the game   midnight   month   year

2. We'll start practicing for the concert towards the beginning of _____.

   April   the game   midnight   month

UNIT 55:
Under

Basic Meanings

1. **Under** means **in a lower position** than something else.

Pattern 1	verb + *under* + noun

   *We sat **under** the tree and had a picnic.*

Pattern 2	verb + noun + *under* + noun

   *Let's put the desk **under** the window; then we'll have a great view.*

2. **Under** means **covered by something else; underneath.**

Pattern 1	verb + *under* + noun

   *The children hid **under** the table, thinking we couldn't see them.*

   Typical verbs before *under*:

   be, hide, lie, rest, sit, sleep, stand, wait, walk

Pattern 2	verb + noun + *under* + noun

   *She stores all her boxes **under** the bed.*

   Typical verbs:

   bury, find, hide, place, push, put, store, wear

3. **Under** means **less than.**

Pattern	*under* + noun

   *I'm sure she was driving **under** the speed limit.*

   *He has three children **under** age ten.*

   Nouns commonly used after *under*:

   age, any number, average, height, limit, maximum, minimum, norm, weight

Expression

to be under age   to not be old enough to do something

   *She can't vote because she **is under age.***

4. **Under** can indicate **control.**

> **Pattern 1** *under* + noun

> **Under** this boss we have little freedom to express our own ideas.
> You have a lot more benefits **under** the new insurance policy.

Typical nouns used after *under*:

boss, coach, contract, dictator, doctor, general, king, mayor, policy, president, principal, professor, supervisor, teacher

> **Pattern 2** *under* + *the* + noun + *of* + noun

> She is **under the** care **of** a doctor.

Typical nouns after *under the*:

administration, care, control, dictatorship, direction, eye, management, presidency

> **Pattern 3** *under* + ø + noun

> The children are **under** supervision at all times.
> They were arrested **under** orders of the chief.

Typical nouns:

control, orders, supervision, surveillance

5. **Under** can indicate a **current situation or state:**

> **Pattern 1** *be* + *under* + ø noun

> Those two thugs **are under** investigation by the police.
> That problem **is** still **under** discussion by the board.

Typical nouns used after *under*:

consideration, construction, discussion, investigation, suspicion

> **Pattern 2** *be* + *under* + noun

> They are **under** the influence of their new friends.

Typical nouns used after *under*:

circumstances, conditions, impression, influence

6. **Under** can identify the **category of a noun** in written reference material.

> **Pattern** *look up/find* + noun + *under* + name of category

> You can **find** my name **under** "Y" in the directory.
> I **looked up** butterflies **under** "Insects" in my encyclopedia.

PRACTICE

55-1. Choose the best word or words for each blank space.

1. She hides the children's _____ under the bed.

   socks   sweaters   food   gifts

2. They have three young children. They are all under _____.

   seven   twenty   twenty-five   fifteen

3. A lot of _____ were changed under his presidency.

   people   computers   laws   gifts

4. I am under the _____ that you are unhappy.

   impression   influence   condition   investigation

5. To find information about Toronto, look under _____.

   The United States   Mexico   The United Kingdom   Canada

UNIT 56:
Underneath

Basic Meanings

1. Underneath means **in a lower position** than something else.

*The sheets are **underneath** the blankets on the shelf.*

2. Underneath means **covered by.**

*I found my jacket **underneath** the other coats.*

3. Underneath indicates **concealed feelings.**

__Underneath__ her smile there is a lot of heartache.
*He is really very kind **underneath** his stern appearance.*

PRACTICE

56-1. Choose the best word or words for each blank space.

1. The clown has a big smile on his face, but underneath he is _____.
   sad   happy   laughing   silly

2. She wore _____ underneath her clothes because it was so cold.
   a slip   a coat   thermal underwear   a blanket

Until

Basic Meaning

1. **Until** indicates the **time of change** of an activity or situation.

   | Pattern 1 | **verb + *until* + time** |

   *They waited **until** six o'clock.*
   *The boys studied **until** midnight.*

   | Pattern 2 | **verb + *until* + beginning of event** |

   *They lived here **until** their wedding; then they left.*
   *She was busy **until** her graduation.*
   *They didn't watch the game **until** halftime.*

PRACTICE

57-1. Choose the best word or words for each blank space.

1. Please be here by noon. I will wait for you until _____.

   6 P.M.   1 A.M.   12 P.M.   12 A.M.

2. You will have to study this information until you _____ it.

   learn   forget   write   begin

Basic Meanings

1. Up indicates **movement to a higher place.**

> **Pattern 1** verb + *up* + noun

> *The cat climbed **up** the tree.*
> *She always walks **up** the steps to the fifth floor.*

Typical verbs used before *up*:

climb, creep, go, jump, move, pop, race, run, walk

> **Pattern 2** verb + noun + *up* + noun

> *Bring the box **up** the steps.*

Typical verbs used with this pattern:

bring, carry, drag, heave, move, send, take

2. Up (adverb) indicates **location at a high place.**

> **Pattern** be + *up*

> *The balloon **is up**.*

3. Up indicates **location further along** the way.

> **Pattern** verb + *up* + noun

> *Their farm is three miles **up** the road.*
> *She lives two blocks **up** the street.*

4. Up indicates **movement along a way.**

> **Pattern 1** verb + *up* + noun

> *She is going to travel **up** Route 66.*

Nouns commonly used after *up*:

highway, path, road, street, turnpike, way

> **Pattern 2** verb + noun + *up* + noun

> *We will drive four more miles **up** the highway.*

5. **Up** indicates movement **against a current of water.**

> Pattern   verb + *up* + noun
>
> > *They swam **up** the river for exercise.*

Typical verbs used before *up*:

cruise, drive, go, row, sail, swim

6. **Up** indicates a **desired result.**

> Pattern   verb + *up* + noun
>
> > *They are trying to drum **up** support.*

Typical verbs:

drum, round, scrape, work

Related Expression

to get up (enough) energy   to try to force oneself to act

> *She was exhausted, but she **got up enough energy** to cook dinner for her family.*

7. **Up** indicates **creativity.**

> Pattern   verb + *up* + noun
>
> > *We dreamed **up** a wonderful idea.*

Typical verbs used before *up*:

draw, dream, make, think

8. **Up** can indicate **division into pieces.**

> Pattern   verb + *up* + noun
>
> > *She chopped **up** the onions and peppers.*
> > *They divided **up** all the money.*

Typical verbs:

blow, break, chop, cut, divide, tear

Expressions

be up   be awake

> I ***am up*** every day by eight o'clock.

be up to date   have current knowledge or records

> The governor ***is up to date*** on all the important issues.

> It's important to keep the files ***up to date***.

be up to someone   be the responsibility of someone to decide

> I don't care what movie we see; ***it's up to*** you.

be up in arms (about)   protest in anger

> The employees ***are up in arms*** over the decrease in benefits.

be up to one's ears   be extremely busy

> Her brother ***is up to his ears*** in work.

be up a creek   be in a difficult situation

> My partner left with all my money and now ***I'm up a creek***.

count up to   to count as far as a number

> The baby ***can count up to*** ten already.

make up one's mind   decide

> ***Make up your mind*** between the red dress and the black one.

up and down the room   constant movement from one side of the room to the other

> He was so nervous that he walked ***up and down the room*** all night.

Phrasal Verbs

act up (intransitive)   misbehave (**act out** is now commonly used with this meaning)

> The children always ***act up*** just before the school holidays begin.

add up (intransitive)   make sense

> She claims to have lots of friends, yet she is always alone; it doesn't ***add up***.

amp up (separable)   increase in force

> The new government ***amped up*** investigations of private citizens.

back up (intransitive)   reverse

> The hardest part about driving a car is ***backing up***.

blow up (intransitive)   get angry

> The girl's father ***blew up*** when she got home so late.

blow up (separable)   make bigger

> These photographs are too small; we should ***blow*** them ***up***.

bone up on (nonseparable)   do an intensive study or review of

> He wanted to ***bone up on*** European history before he went on the tour.

boot up (separable)   start a computer

> We shut the computer down and then ***booted*** it ***up*** again.

break up (separable)　end

> *The neighbors didn't like our noisy party and told us to **break** it **up**.*

break up (with) (intransitive)　end a relationship

> *It's always sad when a family **breaks up**.*
>
> *The girl cried when she **broke up with** her boyfriend.*

bring up (separable)　raise

> *She **brought** the children **up** by herself.*

bring up (separable)　mention a new topic

> *At the meeting, the lady **brought up** the parking problem in our neighborhood.*

brush up (on) (nonseparable)　practice to relearn old skills

> *He wants to **brush up on** his Spanish before he goes to Mexico.*

burn up (separable)　be destroyed by fire (something small)

> *All of her papers and books **burned up** in the fire.*

burn up (separable)　make angry

> *Those silly gossips really **burn** me **up**.*

call up (separable)　contact someone by telephone

> *He comes home from school and **calls** all his friends **up**.*

catch up on (nonseparable)　get back to a normal situation

> *After staying up late every night, I need to **catch up on** sleep.*

catch up (with) (intransitive)　reach the place or level of another person or people

> *He has been sick and needs some time to **catch up**.*
>
> *It will be hard for him to **catch up with** the other students.*

cheer up (intransitive)　be happier

> *She needs to **cheer up**.*

cheer up (separable)　make someone happier

> *She needs someone to **cheer** her **up**.*

clean up (intransitive)　clean thoroughly

> *They promised to **clean up** after the party.*

clean up (separable)　clean thoroughly

> *They promised to **clean** the house **up** after the party.*

close up (intransitive)　close for business

> *The shops **close up** in the afternoon, and reopen in the evening.*

close up (separable)　stop operating a business

> *They **closed** the shop **up** last year.*

come up to　approach

> *They **came up to** us and asked for help.*

cover up (separable)　hide the facts

> *They committed a crime and then **covered** it **up**.*

dress up   put on more formal clothes than usual

*She always **dresses up** for parties.*

face up to (nonseparable)   confront

*She had to stop dreaming and **face up to** the truth.*

feel up to (nonseparable)   feel good enough for an activity

*He is a lot better, but he still doesn't **feel up to** going to work.*

fill up (separable)   put in all that the container will hold

*If you use my car, please **fill** it **up** with gas.*

get up (intransitive)   rise

*She **gets up** at six o'clock every morning.*

get up (separable)   lift or remove something with some difficulty

*Will you help me **get** these boxes **up** the steps?*

give up (intransitive)   surrender

*We won the game because the other team **gave up** and went home.*

give up (separable)   stop using something

*He tried to stop smoking cigarettes, but found it hard to **give** them **up**.*

give up (on) (intransitive)   stop trying

*She tried to convince her daughter to go back to school, but she finally **gave up**.*

*She finally **gave up on** her daughter.*

grow up (intransitive)   become an adult

*Her son wants to be a doctor when he **grows up**.*

hang up (intransitive)   put the phone down to end a telephone call

*You have called the wrong number; **hang up** and try again.*

hang up (separable)   put clothing on a hook or hanger

*After you wash this dress, you should **hang** it **up**.*

hang up on (nonseparable)   rudely end a telephone call during a conversation

*When she refused his invitation, he got angry and **hung up on** her.*

hold up (intransitive)   continue in good condition

*The bike is in good shape now, but I don't know how long it will **hold up**.*

hold up (separable)   delay

*The traffic on the bridge **held** us **up** for two hours.*

hurry up (intransitive)   go faster

*Please **hurry up**! We're late.*

hype up (separable)   advertise excessively

*They **hyped up** that actress, but she's not really very good.*

keep up (intransitive)   stay at the level of the others

*The other hikers walked faster, and we couldn't **keep up**.*

keep up (separable)   continue

*You are doing a great job. **Keep** it **up**!*

keep up with (nonseparable)   go as fast as

> *Please don't walk so fast; I can't **keep up with** you.*

line up (intransitive)   form a line for service in order

> *We always **line up** to buy tickets.*

line up (separable)   make an arrangement with someone

> *We **lined up** a great band for our dance.*

listen up (intransitive)   pay attention

> *The coach told the boys to **listen up**.*

look up (separable)   search in a guide or directory

> *If you want her phone number, **look** it **up** in the directory.*

look up to (nonseparable)   respect

> *Everybody in the department **looks up to** the director; she is wonderful.*

make up (separable)   do missed work at a later time

> *She missed the test, but the teacher said she could **make** it **up** next week.*

make up to (separable)   do a favor to pay for a damage

> *She hurt his feelings, then **made** it **up to** him by inviting him to her party.*

make up (with) (intransitive)   become friends again after an argument

> *They had a big fight, but they **made up** last night.*

> *They **made up with** each other at the party.*

mark up (separable)   increase the price

> *Those shoes were cheaper last year; they have **marked** them **up**.*

mix up (separable)   confuse

> *The sisters look so much alike; I **mix** them **up** all the time.*

mix up (with) (separable)   put with other things

> *She put the ingredients in a bowl and **mixed** them all **up**.*

> *They **mixed** the eggs **up** with the butter and sugar.*

pass up (separable)   miss an opportunity

> *She had a chance to continue her studies, but she **passed** it **up** to get married.*

pick up (intransitive)   increase in momentum or pace

> *Business is very slow this season; we hope it will **pick up** soon.*

pick up (separable)   lift

> *When I dropped my bracelet on the sidewalk, he **picked** it **up** and handed it to me.*

run up (separable)   increase charges through excessive use

> *He made a lot of long-distance calls and **ran up** my phone bill.*

set up (separable)   arrange

> *We **set** the appointment **up** for November.*

set up (separable)   cause an innocent person to be blamed for something

> *He is not guilty of the theft; the hoodlums **set** him **up**.*

set up (separable)   establish in a career or business

> *His uncle **set** him **up** in the family trade.*

show up (intransitive)   appear

> *We will leave early if everyone **shows up** on time.*

show up (separable)   appear to be better than someone else

> *They practiced the dance steps at home and **showed** everybody else **up** at the party.*

sign up   register

> *We are **signing up** for your course.*

sign up (separable)   arrange an activity for someone

> *They **signed** us **up** to work on Thursday night.*

slip up (intransitive)   make a mistake

> *We intended to send the package last week, but our workers **slipped up**.*

stand up (intransitive)   move to one's feet; be on one's feet

> *When the president entered the room, everyone **stood up**.*

> *When you teach school, you have to **stand up** all day.*

stand up (separable)   miss a commitment without explaining

> *He went to pick her up but she wasn't there; she had **stood** him **up**.*

step up (separable)   increase the speed

> ***Step** it **up** a little; we need to go faster.*

take up (separable)   pursue a new interest

> *She **took up** knitting when she was pregnant.*

take up (separable)   to shorten

> *The pants are too long; we will have to **take** them **up**.*

tear up (separable)   rip into small pieces

> *The letter made her so angry that she **tore** it **up**.*

throw up (intransitive)   vomit

> *The poor child got sick and **threw up**.*

turn up (intransitive)   appear

> *She is very unreliable; we never know if she will **turn up**.*

turn up (separable)   increase in volume or speed

> ***Turn** the radio **up**; this is a great song.*

wake up (intransitive)   open one's eyes after sleeping

> *What time do you usually **wake up**?*

wake up (separable)   cause someone to stop sleeping

> *Please **wake** me **up** in the morning.*

wrap up (separable)   finish a session

> *We've been practicing for three hours; let's **wrap** it **up**.*

write up (separable)   explain in writing

> *His ideas were good, and they asked him to **write** them **up**.*

PRACTICE

58-1. Choose the best word or words for each blank space.

1. The frog _____ up onto the rock.

   ran   walked   hopped   raced

2. Jack and Jill ran up the _____.

   house   well   back yard   hill

3. We aren't there yet. We have to go two more blocks up the _____.

   street   steps   farm   stairs

4. We are trying to _____ up a little money.

   think   hope   scrape   work

5. The children made up a delightful _____.

   fort   playground   swings   game

6. She tore the letter up into little _____.

   pictures   pieces   papers   words

58-2. Use an expression with *up* to express the following:

1. She kept walking from one side of the room to the other.

2. I hope you decide soon.

3. It's your decision.

4. The workers are protesting in anger.

5. I can't go because I have a lot of work to do.

58-3. Use *up* in a phrasal verb to express the following:

1. My mom got really angry when she found out.

2. Please don't talk about that topic at the meeting.

3. He will need to do extra work in order to reach the level of the other students.

4. I hope this news will make you happier.

5. Please move faster!

6. Don't stop doing such a great job!

7. She can't walk as fast as you do.

8. I hope she doesn't refuse this opportunity.

9. She explained her ideas in writing.

UNIT 59:
With

Basic Meanings

1. With means in the company of.

Pattern 1 verb + *with* + noun

> She is **with** her sister.
> I danced **with** him.

Typical verbs used before *with*:

be, chat, converse, dance, drink, eat, go, leave, live, play, stay, study, talk, travel, walk, work

Pattern 2 verb + noun + *with* + noun

> She spent the weekend **with** us.

Typical verbs used with this pattern:

dance, drink, eat, leave, play, spend, study

Related Expressions

to be tied up with   to be occupied with at the moment

> He can't come to the phone; he **is tied up with** a client.

to be in a discussion with   to be talking seriously to

> The boss **is in a discussion with** the manager right now.

2. With means in the same place as.

Pattern 1 *be* + *with* + noun

> My hat **is with** my scarf.

Pattern 2 verb + noun + *with* + noun

> Put your coat **with** mine.
> She left her children **with** the babysitter.

Typical verbs:

keep, leave, put, store

3. **With** can mean **added together.**

> **Pattern** noun + *with* + noun
>
> > *She always drinks her coffee **with** sugar.*
> > *The hotel **with** meals will cost two hundred dollars a day.*

4. **With** can describe something by indicating what it **has.**

> **Pattern 1** noun + *with* + noun
>
> > *Did you see a woman **with** a baby a few minutes ago?*
> > *I have an article **with** pictures for my presentation.*
>
> **Pattern 2** *be* + past participle + *with* + noun
>
> > *You will **be** provided **with** two sets of keys.*

Past participles used with this pattern:

caught, discovered, found, furnished, provided, seen

Related Expression

to be blessed with   to be lucky to have

> *He **is blessed with** good health and good looks.*

5. **With** can describe a **manner of behavior.**

> **Pattern 1** verb + *with* + noun
>
> > *Please handle the piano **with** care.*
> > *They accepted the proposal **with** enthusiasm.*

Typical nouns used after *with*:

anger, care, compassion, courage, delight, discretion, disdain, distress, enthusiasm, fear, feeling, glee, grace, gratitude, happiness, hatred, humility, indifference, joy, kindness, love, optimism, pleasure, pride, regard, sadness, shame, skill, sympathy, tenderness, thanks, understanding

> **Pattern 2** verb + noun + *with* + noun
>
> > *She greeted us **with** a big smile.*
> > *He always starts work **with** a grumble.*

Typical nouns used after *with*:

air, cry, expression, frown, greeting, grumble, grunt, handshake, hug, kiss, look, promise, question, shudder, sigh, smile, smirk, thank you, word

> **Pattern 3** *be* + adjective + *with* + noun (thing)
>
> > *Please **be** careful **with** the piano.*
> > *I hope he **is** successful **with** the mission.*

Typical adjectives:

awkward, careful, clumsy, creative, dexterous, quick, skillful, slow, successful, talented, unsuccessful

> **Pattern 4** *be* + adjective + *with* + noun (person)
>
> > *She **is** very patient **with** me.*
> > *The boss **has been** frank **with** her about her performance.*

Typical adjectives:

awkward, belligerent, curt, flexible, forthcoming, frank, friendly, generous, helpful, honest, impatient, open, patient, stiff, sympathetic, truthful

6. **With** can describe someone's **feelings about something.**

> **Pattern** *be* + adjective + *with* + noun
>
> > *The child **was** bored **with** her toys.*
> > *They **are** very happy **with** their new home.*

Typical adjectives used with this pattern:

bored, comfortable, content, delighted, disappointed, frustrated, happy, impressed, pleased, satisfied, thrilled, uncomfortable, unhappy, upset

Related Expressions

to be in love with   to have a romantic feeling toward

> *He **is** (madly) **in love with** her.*

to be fed up with   to have reached one's limit or patience toward

> *She is leaving her job because she **is fed up with** the restrictions on her creativity.*

7. **With** can indicate **a working relationship.**

> **Pattern 1** *be* + *with* + noun
>
> > *She **is with** a real estate company.*

> **Pattern 2** *be* + past participle + *with* + noun
>
> > *He **is** involved **with** that organization.*
> > *They **are** not concerned **with** our group.*

Pattern 3 *work + with + noun*

> *His mother **works with** us.*

8. **With** can indicate the **instrument or tool used** for an action.

Pattern 1 **verb +** *with* **+ noun**

> *She writes **with** a pen.*

Typical verbs used before *with*:

color, clean, cut, dig, draw, eat, paint, serve, sweep, wash, write

Pattern 2 **verb + noun +** *with* **+ noun**

> *The boy drew a flower **with** his crayons.*
>
> *I swept the garage **with** a big broom.*

Typical verbs:

attach, clean, clear, cut, dig, draw, dry, eat, erase, fasten, hit, move, nail, open, paint, plow, season, serve, sweep, wash, write

9. **With** can indicate a noun that **covers or fills an area.**

Pattern **verb + noun +** *with* **+ noun**

> *She filled the pitcher **with** lemonade.*
>
> *They planted the bed **with** white flowers.*

Typical verbs:

cover, cram, fill, frost, heap, ice, pack, paint, plant, smear, spread, sprinkle, stuff

10. **With** can indicate **struggle**

Pattern 1 **verb +** *with* **+ noun**

> *My colleague disagrees **with** the management.*
>
> *He is always fighting **with** his brother.*

Typical verbs:

argue, clash, compete, conflict, differ, disagree, fight, quarrel, wrestle

Related Expression

to have it out with   to express anger verbally

> *After two years of frustration, he finally **had it out with** his boss.*

> **Pattern 2** *have + a +* noun *+ with*
>
> *She **has an** argument **with** him every morning.*
>
> *They **are having a** quarrel **with** the neighbors right now.*

Typical nouns:

argument, bout, contest, disagreement, fight, match, quarrel

> **Pattern 3** *be + in +* noun *+ with*
>
> *She **is in** competition **with** him for the promotion.*
>
> *It's too bad your ideas **are in** conflict **with** those of the majority.*

11. **With** can indicate **support or cooperation.**

> **Pattern 1** verb *+ with +* noun
>
> *They are cooperating **with** the authorities.*
>
> *You have to comply **with** the rules.*

Typical verbs:

agree, collaborate, comply, concur, cooperate, empathize, harmonize, help, negotiate, sympathize, work

Related Expressions

to get along with   to cooperate with

> *I **get along with** my roommate, even though she is not my best friend.*

to be with   to support

> *Don't be nervous when you are giving your speech; we **are** all **with** you.*

> **Pattern 2** verb *+ a +* noun *+ with +* noun
>
> *She signed **a** contract **with** us.*

Typical nouns:

agreement, business, contract, friendship, partnership, relationship

Expression

to do business with   to have negotiations with

> *We don't **do business with** them anymore.*

Pattern 3   *be* + *in* + noun + *with* + noun

> ***Are*** *you **in** agreement **with** the decisions they made?*

Typical nouns before *with*:

accord, agreement, cahoots, collaboration, compliance, concert, concurrence, cooperation, harmony, partnership, sympathy

12. With means at the same time as.

> *He rises **with** the sun.*
>
> *They opened the show **with** a song.*

Typical verbs:

begin, celebrate, close, dedicate, end, start

13. With means at the same rate as.

> *Wine improves **with** age.*
>
> *Wisdom comes **with** experience.*
>
> ***With** time, you will forget.*

14. With means in the same direction as.

Pattern   verb + *with* + *the* + noun

> *It will take longer because we will be **with the** traffic.*
>
> *They drifted down the river **with the** current.*

Typical verbs used before *with*:

be, cruise, drift, drive, float, go, ride, sail

Typical nouns used after *with the*:

current, flow, tide, traffic, wind

15. With can indicate separation.

Pattern   verb expression + *with* + noun

> *I hate to part **with** my old books.*
>
> *Our company severed relations **with** that client years ago.*
>
> *He is through **with** her; he doesn't want to see her again.*

Typical verb expressions used before *with*:

be finished, be through, break up, cut ties, fall out, part, part company, sever relations, split up

16. **With** is used in a **comparison** or **contrast.**

> **Pattern 1**   noun + verb + *with* + noun
>
> > *Your blouse clashes **with** your skirt.*

Verbs commonly used with this pattern:

clash, compare, contrast, go, look good

> **Pattern 2**   *compare/contrast* + noun + *with* + noun
>
> > *Let's compare this computer **with** that one.*

17. **With** can indicate **equality.**

> **Pattern**   *be* + adjective + *with* + noun
>
> > *This side **is** not even **with** that side.*
> >
> > *Our **team** is tied **with** theirs: the score is two to two.*

Typical adjectives used before *with*:

comparable, even, level, on a par, parallel, tied

18. **With** can indicate the **cause of a condition.**

> **Pattern 1**   adjective + *with* + noun
>
> > *The branches of the trees were heavy **with** snow.*
> >
> > *The girl's face is wet **with** tears.*

> **Pattern 2**   verb in gerund form + *with* + noun
>
> > *The newlyweds were beaming **with** happiness.*

Typical verbs used before *with*:

aching, beaming, crying, dancing, fuming, screaming, shouting, smiling, trembling

Typical nouns used after *with*:

anger, fear, glee, happiness, joy, mirth, rage, shame, zeal

> **Pattern 3**   *with* + *the* + noun
>
> > ***With the** traffic in this city, it takes a long time to get to work.*
> >
> > *Their lifestyle changed completely **with the** birth of their first baby.*

Typical nouns used after *with the*:

arrival, bills, birth, change, crime, death, decrease, departure, guests, increase, move, problems, rain, traffic, trouble, worries

Pattern 4 *with + (all) + possessive noun or pronoun + noun*

> ***With all** his talent, he should be famous.*
>
> *She is quite popular, **with all** her beauty and charm.*

Typical nouns after *with*:

beauty, charm, education, influence, intelligence, money, power, talent

19. With can mean despite.

Pattern *with + (all) + possessive noun or pronoun + noun*

> *I love him **with all** his faults.*
>
> ***With all** her problems, she is quite serene.*

Expressions

to be with someone   to follow or understand

> *Please repeat that; **I'm not with** you.*

to be charged with something   to be formally accused of a crime

> *The boy **was charged with** breaking and entering.*

Down with something   a rallying call to eliminate oppressors

> ***Down with** the tyrants!*

Off with someone   a call for someone to leave

> ***Off with** you, and don't come back!*

Phrasal Verbs

(get) on with (nonseparable)   to start something right away

> *Let's **get on with** this job; I want to go home early.*
>
> ***On with** the show!*

get away with   escape a misdeed without penalty

> *He tore up his parking fine and **got away with** it.*

put up with   tolerate

> *The house is beautiful, but I can't **put up with** the noise of the airplanes.*

PRACTICE

59-1. Choose the best word or words for each blank space.

1. I hope you will _____ with me at the party.
   fight   discuss   dance   look

2. The hotel room is _____ with a double bed.
   built   furnished   seen   discovered

3. The carpenter showed us his work with _____.
   pride   promise   health   saw

4. They need something new to play with. They are bored with their _____.
   days   nights   toys   food

5. Our congressman is not concerned with our _____.
   offers   problems   money   voting

6. She has a new job. She is now with _____.
   a new car   a new husband   a new company   a new hairstyle

7. They get along well. They work in _____ with each other.
   singing   band   chorus   harmony

8. She _____ with him because he was lazy.
   sailed   drove   got tired   broke up

9. He was _____ with anger.
   dancing   beaming   shouting   smiling

10. Does this dress look good with _____?
    these shoes   these bags   these combs   these brushes

59-2. Use an expression with *with* to express the following:

1. They were accused of starting the fire.

2. Remove the dictator!

3. She never argues with her roommate.

59-3. Use *with* in a phrasal verb to express the following:

1. I can't tolerate his attitude.

2. I don't know how he escapes punishment for his crimes.

3. I'm getting impatient. Let's begin!

Within

Basic Meanings

1. **Within** means **not outside a place.**

Pattern	*be + within + noun*

   > *Those schools **are within** the county jurisdiction.*
   > *There is too much commotion **within the** building.*

   Typical nouns used after *within*:

   area, building, city, country, county, jurisdiction, state, territory, walls

2. **Within** means **less than a period of time.**

   > *I will return **within** the hour.*
   > *He will finish **within** five minutes.*

3. **Within** means **less than a distance.**

   > *There is a hospital **within** five miles of the school.*
   > *The storm was **within** ten miles of our town.*

4. **Within** means **possible; not exceeding the limits of something.**

Pattern	*be + within + (one's) noun*

   > *At last, the beach **is within** sight!*
   > *A fortune **is within** our reach if we are lucky.*

   Typical nouns used after *within*:

   bounds, hearing, range, reach, sight, the law, the limit, the rules

Expression

to keep within the family   to not reveal something to anyone who is not a family member

> *That man has a strange history, but they **keep it within the family**.*

PRACTICE

60-1. Choose the best word or words for each blank space.

1. There is some crime within this _____.
    neighborhood   teacher   garage   playground

2. We will be back momentarily. We will be back within _____.
    ten hours   ten years   ten minutes   a year

3. We are almost at the beach. The water is within _____.
    the ocean   the river   noise   sight

Without

Basic Meanings

1. **Without** indicates the **absence of somebody.**

   *I can't live **without** you.*

   *Please don't leave **without** me.*

2. **Without** means **not having.**

Pattern	verb + *without* + *(any)* noun

   *That young mother manages **without any** help.*

   *We are **without** money this month.*

3. **Without** means **not using.**

Pattern	verb + noun + *without* + noun

   *We did the crossword puzzle **without** a dictionary.*

   *She can't read **without** her glasses.*

4. **Without** means **not performing an action.**

Pattern	*without* + verb in gerund form

   *She passed the test **without** studying.*

   *He left **without** saying good-bye.*

Expressions

without a doubt   certainly

   *She is **without a doubt** the best chairperson we have ever had.*

without fail   a demand or promise to do something

   *Be here at six A.M. **without fail**.*

   *I will finish within three days **without fail**.*

without ceremony   immediately and quietly

   *He took charge **without ceremony** and began to work.*

that goes without saying   that is understood to be true

   *You will be paid well for your work; **that goes without saying**.*

PRACTICE

61-1. Choose the best word or words for each blank space.

1. She's freezing. She left school without _____.
   teacher   hat   her coat   homework

2. She can now ride her bicycle without _____.
   handlebars   horn   training wheels   spokes

3. They left the restaurant without _____.
   food   coat   noise   paying

61-2. Use an expression with *without* to express the following:

1. She was certainly my best teacher.

2. We promise to finish the job tomorrow.

3. That is understood to be true.

4. The new boss quietly began to work.

PART TWO

Prepositions by Function

How to Use Part Two

Part Two is the most important section of this book for learning the most basic everyday usage of prepositions. The expressions and formulas described here indicate specific facts and must be used correctly. Incorrect usage could cause great misunderstanding!

1. Begin with Unit 1.

2. Read each example quietly, and make sure you understand its meaning. If you are not sure, ask for help from your teacher, a classmate, or someone who speaks both English and your native language.

3. Read each example aloud. Do this several times, until it sounds and feels natural. If possible, ask a native speaker of English to read each example out loud for you. Then ask that person to listen to your pronunciation and tell you if it is acceptable.

4. Think of a new example sentence for each category, and write it down.

5. When you feel confident that you have memorized each item, do the exercises at the end of the chapter. Write your answers to the exercises in your notebook—not in the book! (This way, you can go back and test yourself often.)

6. Compare your answers with the Answer Key on p. 303. If all of your answers are correct—that is wonderful! If you have any incorrect answers, read the explanation again. Write down the correct answers in complete sentences.

7. When you feel ready, do the entire exercise page again.

8. Continue to do this until you have completed the exercises with no errors.

9. Practice the items you have learned as often as possible.

10. Now begin Unit 2, in the same way as Unit 1. Then continue until you have completed all of Part Two.

11. Test yourself often to make sure you have memorized all the expressions. You will be able to use them in conversation with confidence.

BEFORE

—previous to a time

Ten o'clock is before eleven o'clock.

AFTER

—subsequent to a time

Three o'clock is after two o'clock.

DURING

—for part of a period

He slept during the day. (He slept from 2 P.M. until 4 P.M.)

—at the same time as another event

She slept during the football game.

THROUGH, THROUGHOUT

—for an entire period, and after

He slept through the day. (He slept from 9 A.M. until 9 P.M.)

He slept throughout the day.

AT AROUND, AT ABOUT

—at an approximate time

We will leave at around six.

We will get there at about seven.

BY

—no later than a time

We have to be there by seven-fifteen.

by the time—when

By the time you get here, we will have left.

TO, OF

—minutes before the hour

It's ten to four.

It's ten of four.

TOWARDS

—nearing a period of time

It was towards evening when she called.

BETWEEN

—after a time, and before another time

They will arrive between five and six.

WITHIN

—between now and a length of time

They will be here within ten minutes.

BEYOND, PAST

—after a time

Our guests stayed beyond midnight.

Our guests stayed past midnight.

UNTIL

—up to, but not after a time

The party will last until ten.

FOR

—during a length of time

They have been here for a week.

SINCE

—between a past time and now

They have been here since last Thursday.

IN

in time—not too late for an event

Try to get here in time to help me.

—a century, decade, year, season, month

He lived in the sixteenth century.

That singer was popular in the eighties.

We came here in the fall.

We came here in October.

We came here in 1997.

—after a length of time

She will be here in two weeks.

in the morning, afternoon, evening

They work in the morning.

He comes home in the afternoon.

We are going to go out in the evening.

ON

on time—at the required time

He is punctual; he always arrives on time.

on the dot—at the exact minute

Be here at ten o'clock on the dot.

—a day, days, a date, dates

She is coming on Monday.

She doesn't work on Tuesdays.

I heard that singer on my birthday.

We came here on October sixth.

We came here on October 6, 1997.

AT

at night

He works at night.

—a specific time

He comes home at ten o'clock.

at present—now

We are studying at present.

at the moment—now

I am not working at the moment.

WITH

—at the same time as

She wakes up with the sun.

OUT OF

to be out of time—to have no time left

We didn't finish, and now we are out of time.

to run out of time—use up remaining time.

We didn't eat because we ran out of time.

AHEAD OF

to be ahead of time—to be early

I'm glad you got here ahead of time; you can help me get ready for the party.

UP

time is up—there is no official time remaining for a specific activity.

I sat down when the bell rang because my time was up.

PRACTICE

1-1. Write the correct preposition in each blank:

1. Their daughter was born _____ 1998

   _____ October

   _____ the 18th

   _____ four-thirty

   _____ the afternoon.

2. I haven't seen my friend _____ August.

3. He was here _____ two weeks.

4. The play starts _____ seven o'clock _____ the dot, so be sure to be here _____ six-fifty.

5. Her mother is going to be here _____ the tenth _____ July. She will be here _____ two weeks.

6. Our neighbors always have a party _____ New Year's Eve. It usually starts _____ ten o'clock and lasts _____ the next morning.

7. Some people never go out _____ night because they get up so early _____ the morning.

8. Four o'clock is _____ five o'clock.

9. The baby didn't sleep _____ the night because he was so hungry.

10. I heard a noise _____ the night, but I was too sleepy to get up.

11. _____ the moment we are trying to study.

12. Some of us couldn't finish the test because the time was _____.

Location

IN	ON	AT
—a continent, a country, a state, a city, a town	—a street, a floor	—a building, a house or apartment number
She lives in California.	*She lives on Oak Street.*	*She lives at The Manor.*
She lives in San Francisco.	*She lives on the fourth floor.*	*She lives at 1260 Oak Street.*
		at home—in one's own house
		at work—at one's job
		at school—attending school
		at church—attending church services
—a room, an area of a room	—an outside area	—a work area inside
She is in the kitchen, in the corner.	*He is standing on the corner.*	*She is at the kitchen sink.*
Our theater seats are in the balcony.	*He has an outdoor grill on the balcony.*	
—a comfortable chair	—a straight chair, a sofa, a couch	
He sat in the chair and watched television.	*He sat on the chair and ate his dinner.*	
	We sat on the sofa and watched television.	
in bed—under the covers	**on the bed**—on top of the covers	
—the water, the air, the environment	—facing a coast, a beach	—the coast, the beach
They are swimming in the water.	*The house is on the beach.*	*The whole family is at the beach.*
There is pollution in the air.		
—the center, the middle	—the side, left, right, surface	—the beginning, start, end
Our house is in the center of town.	*Our house is on the left side of the street.*	*Our house is at the end of the street.*

—the north/south/east/west

New England is in the north of the United States.

—a bodily attack

The stone hit me in the face.

—a vehicle one cannot walk around in (car/small boat/small plane/helicopter)

Please ride in the car with us.

—the north side/south side/east side/west side

Our house is on the south side of town.

—the surface of the body

He has a scratch on his arm.

—a vehicle one can walk around on (bus/train/large boat/airplane)

Please ride on the bus with us.

—an individual vehicle (horse, bicycle, motorcycle, skates)

He came over on his bike.

ABOUT, AROUND, THROUGHOUT

—in all areas of a place

The clothes were thrown about the room.

The papers were lying around the house.

There was trash throughout the house.

ACROSS

—in all areas of a flat surface

The toys were scattered across the floor.

WITH

—in the same place as someone or something else

The baby is with the nurse.

I'm going to put my bag with yours on the chair.

OVER, ABOVE

BELOW, BENEATH, UNDER, UNDERNEATH

The white box is **over** the black box.

The white box is **above** the black box.

The black box is **below** the white box.

The black box is **beneath** the white box.

The black box is **under** the white box.

The black box is **underneath** the white box.

AGAINST

BY, BESIDE, NEXT TO

Chair A is **against** Chair B.

Chair B is **by** Chair C.

Chair B is **beside** Chair C.

Chair B is **next to** Chair C.

BETWEEN

AMONG

Chair 2 is **between** Chair 1 and Chair 3.

The black spot is **among** the white spots.

ON, ON TOP OF, UPON

OFF

The white lamp is **on** the table.

The white lamp is **on top of** the table.

The white lamp is **upon** the table.

The black lamp is **off** the table.

IN, INSIDE, WITHIN

OUT OF, OUTSIDE OF

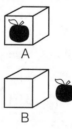

Apple A is **in** the box.

Apple A is **inside** the box.

Apple A is **within** the box.

Apple B is **out of** the box.

Apple B is **outside of** the box.

ACROSS FROM, OPPOSITE	IN FRONT OF, AHEAD OF	IN BACK OF, BEHIND

A   B   C

Chair C is **across from** Chair B.

Chair C is **opposite** Chair B.

Chair B is **in front of** Chair A.

Chair B is **ahead of** Chair A.

Chair A is **in back of** Chair B.

Chair A is **behind** Chair B.

NEAR, CLOSE TO	FAR FROM	BEYOND

A   B   C   D

Chair A is **near** Chair B.

Chair A is **close to** Chair B.

Chair C is **far from** Chair B.

Chair D is **beyond** Chair C.

AT THE TOP OF		AT THE BOTTOM OF

X
Z

The X is **at the top of** the box.

The Z is **at the bottom of** the box.

ON THE TOP OF	ON THE BOTTOM OF	ON THE SIDE OF

6
X Z
2

The number 6 is **on the top of** the box.

The number 2 is **on the bottom of** the box.

The X and the Z are **on the sides of** the box.

PRACTICE

2-1. Write in the correct prepositions:

A. Where is the star?

1. _____ the box

2. _____ the box

3. _____ the box

4. _____ the box

5. _____ the box

6. _____ the box

7. _____ the box

8. _____ the box

9. _____ the box

10. _____ the box

11. _____ the boxes

12. _____ the boxes

B. Her apartment is _____ Florida,

_____ Miami,

_____ The Palms

_____ Ocean Drive

_____ number 407.

She lives _____ the fourth floor

_____ a very nice apartment.

She is often _____ school

or _____ work.

When she is _____ home, she is usually

asleep _____ bed.

However, right now she is

_____ the kitchen,

_____ the stove, cooking.

Soon she will sit down

_____ a dining room chair

_____ the table

_____ the corner, to eat her dinner.

She will probably be out

_____ the balcony after dinner,

sitting _____ a comfortable chair and relaxing.

UNIT 3:
Direction

ACROSS

The line goes **across** the box.

ALONG, BY

The line goes **along** the box.
The line goes **by** the box.

PAST

The line goes **past** the box.

THROUGH

The line goes **through** the box.

AROUND

The line goes **around** the box.

TO, TOWARD

The solid line goes **to** the box.
The dotted line goes **toward** the box.

FROM, AWAY FROM

The line goes **from** the box.
The line goes **away from** the box.

BACK TO

The line goes **back to** the box.

BACK FROM

The dotted line comes **back from** the box.

IN, INTO

The line goes **in** the box.
The line goes **into** the box.

OUT OF

The line goes **out of** the box.

ONTO

The line goes **onto** the table.

OFF

The line goes **off** the table.

OVER

The line goes **over** the hill.

DOWN

The line goes **down** the hill.

UP

The line goes **up** the hill.

WITH

The boat sails **with** the wind.

FOR

Spain

U.S.A.

The plane is leaving **for** Spain.

PRACTICE

3-1. Where is the dotted line going?

1.   _____ the box

2.   _____ the box

3.   _____ the box

4.   _____ the box

5.   _____ the box

6.   _____ the box

7.   _____ the box

8.   _____ the box

9.   _____ the box

10.   _____ the box

11.   _____ the box

12.   _____ the box

13.   _____ the box

14.   _____ the table

15.   _____ the table

Number

About, around, above, over, under, and between are <u>adverbs</u> when used before numbers.

ABOUT, AROUND

—approximately

There were about two hundred people there.

There were around two hundred people there.

ABOVE, OVER

—more than

She has over a hundred books on that subject.

She has above a hundred books on that subject.

UNDER

—less than   **$895**

The car costs under a thousand dollars.

BETWEEN

—higher than one number and lower than another   **$21.50**

The tickets will cost between twenty and twenty-five dollars.

PLUS

—indicates addition $5 + 6 = 11$

Five plus six equals eleven.

FROM

—indicates subtraction $10 - 3 = 7$

Three from ten equals seven.

BY

—indicates multiplication $3 \times 4 = 12$

Three multiplied by four equals twelve.

INTO

—indicates division $3\overline{)12}$ (quotient 4)

Three into twelve equals four.

OF

—indicates a fraction

One-half of twelve is six.	**1/2 x 12 = 6**
One-third of nine is three.	**1/3 x 9 = 3**
Three-quarters of twelve is nine.	**3/4 x 12 = 9**

indicates all, part, or none of a specific plural or noncount noun, following **all, many, much, a lot, lots, plenty, enough, several, some, a few, a little, a bit, none**

All of the books on the table are yours.

Some of the money went to charity.

None of the furniture is valuable.

PRACTICE

4-1. Fill in each blank with the appropriate word:

1. He has (approximately) _____ five hundred dollars in cash.

2. There are (more than) _____ twenty-five people here.

3. I paid (less than) _____ ten dollars for this meal.

4. The number six is _____ one and twelve.

5. $7 + 4 = 11$ Seven _____ four equals eleven.

6. $12 - 2 = 10$ Two _____ twelve equals ten.

7. $2\overline{)12}^{\,6}$ Two _____ twelve equals six.

8. One-tenth _____ one hundred equals ten.

UNIT 5:
Weather

DURING	IN	ON
—weather events (a storm, flood, hurricane, tornado, earthquake)	—types of weather (good, bad, foul, stormy cloudy, humid, wet, dry, hot, cold, sticky)	—types of days, periods of the day (nice days, sunny mornings, humid nights, rainy weekends)
	in the rain **in the snow**	
We stayed at home during the storm.	*They swim in good weather.* *He walked home in the rain.* *The children played in the snow.*	*I sit on the balcony on sunny mornings.* *We play cards on rainy weekends.*

PRACTICE

5-1. Fill in the blanks with the correct prepositions:

1. I don't like to go out _____ bad weather.

2. The children love to play _____ the snow.

3. They have to stay inside _____ the storm.

4. We often go to the beach _____ sunny days.

5. She loves to walk _____ the rain.

6. She gets depressed _____ rainy days.

7. _____ the hurricane we stayed in the basement.

8. _____ cold days you have to wear a warm coat, a hat, and gloves.

9. _____ cold weather it is nice to sit by the fire.

10. What do you do _____ snowy evenings?

UNIT 6:
Source of Information

IN	ON	FROM A PERSON OR PEOPLE
—written material (book, magazine, article, newspaper)	—electronically (the radio, the Internet, the telephone, television social media, _____ (name of social medium or app)	—graphic material (photo, video, picture, movie, film)

I read it in a book.

She found the article in a magazine.

We saw you in a movie.

I heard it on the radio.

They saw him on television.

PRACTICE

6-1. Fill in each blank with the appropriate preposition:

1. I saw your picture _____ the newspaper.

2. He found the information _____ the Internet.

3. She heard the news _____ television last night.

4. The video went viral _____ social media.

5. I read that _____ a book.

6. He got those dates _____ his professor.

7. We watched that show _____ television.

8. The article was _____ a magazine.

9. There was a good program _____ the radio yesterday.

10. Did you talk to her _____ the telephone?

UNIT 7:
Affiliation

IN	OF	ON
—part of a group (association, bureau, category, choir, chorus, clan, club, division, family, fraternity, group, office, organization, society, sorority, union, political party)	—related to origin of place, time, culture, generation, race, religion, sex	—part of an exclusive group (board, committee, jury, panel, team, council, crew, faculty, honor roll, list, payroll, squad, staff)

The children in that family are all good students.

The people of that city are very friendly.

—a special member of a group

She is the president of the college.

The women on that committee are snobs.

PRACTICE

7-1. Fill in the blanks with the appropriate prepositions:

1. She is _____ the female sex.

2. My sister is _____ the jury.

3. She is also _____ the women's chorus.

4. Her son is _____ the softball team.

5. His wife is _____ a different religion.

6. Is your brother _____ a fraternity at college?

7. She was the president _____ the senior class.

8. I think her cousin is _____ the school board.

9. She is _____ the garden club.

10. They are going to put you _____ the payroll next month.

UNIT 8:
Description

ABOUT	ABOVE	LIKE	OF	WITH
—partially describing	—better than	—similar to	—having an unseen characteristic	—having a physical characteristic
There is something cute about him.	*He is above deceit.*	*He is (just) like his father.*	*She is a woman of honor.*	*I'm looking for a woman with red hair.*
I don't see anything funny about that.	*She is above cheating.*	*He looks like his father.*	*They are people of low morals.*	*He is the man with the broken arm.*

8-1. Fill in the blanks with the appropriate prepositions:

1. He is _____ his brother.

2. She may be nasty, but she is _____ cruelty.

3. We don't know anything _____ that.

4. His reputation is spotless; he is a man _____ decency.

5. There is something special _____ him.

6. She's a little crazy, but there is something _____ her that I like.

7. Have you seen a man _____ white hair and glasses? I can't find my father.

8. He is very polite; he is a man _____ good manners.

9. I don't know anybody _____ him.

10. My friend is the girl _____ curly red hair.

UNIT 9:
Wearing

(DRESSED) IN	WITH . . . ON	HAVE . . . ON
He was dressed in black.	*He is the man with the black suit on.*	*The man has a black suit on.*
She came in a red dress.	*She is the lady with the red dress on.*	*The lady has a red dress on.*
They are always in jeans.	*They are the students with jeans on.*	*The students have jeans on.*

PRACTICE

9-1. **Fill in the blanks with the appropriate words:**

1. The lady was dressed _____ red.

2. The lady had a red suit _____.

3. The lady _____ the red suit _____ is my sister.

4. The children who _____ blue jackets _____ are my nephews.

5. The children were _____ blue jackets.

6. The children had blue jackets _____.

7. I saw a man _____ black.

8. I saw a man _____ a black hat _____.

9. I saw a man who had _____ a black hat.

10. The students are always dressed _____ jeans.

UNIT 10:
Topic

Prepositions after Verbs:

ABOUT		AT	IN	OF	ON	OVER
advise	know	aim	assist	advise	agree	argue
agree	laugh	glare	bask	complain	concentrate	battle
argue	lie	grab	cooperate	dream	expound	cry
ask	pray	hit	drown	hear	focus	fight
bother	question	laugh	help	inform	harp	grieve
brag	read	look	interest	know	insist	puzzle
care	remind	rush	invest	learn	report	sigh
complain	say	shoot	participate	remind	speak	worry
contact	sing	snatch	persist	sing	write	
cry	speak	stare	steep	speak		
do	talk	swing	submerge	talk		
dream	teach			tell		
fight	tell			think		
forget	think					
grieve	wonder					
harass	worry					
hear	write					
inform	yell					
joke						

PRACTICE

10-1. Fill in the blanks with the appropriate prepositions:

1. She advised me _____ my schedule.

2. We argued _____ money.

3. They don't know anything _____ cars.

4. He helped us _____ getting a loan.

5. He taught me a lot _____ music.

6. They insisted _____ leaving early.

7. Are you going to invest _____ that business?

8. What are you looking _____?

9. Why did he persist _____ asking that question?

10. The girl is going to report _____ the environment.

11. One shouldn't cry _____ spilled milk.

12. We all tried to participate _____ the discussion.

13. Everybody laughed _____ him when he put on that silly hat.

14. I am dreaming _____ a vacation at the beach.

15. The children are fighting _____ the toys.

16. What subjects are you interested _____?

17. They are aiming _____ very high goals.

18. She reminds me _____ her sister.

19. He is totally focused _____ his job.

20. It's too bad they lied _____ it.

UNIT 11:
Recipient

FOR

—usually indicates benefit to recipient

after verbs:
bake, build, buy, cook, create, dance, design, do, get, make, play, sing, want something, win, work, write

I wrote this poem for you.

after nouns:
advice, answer, cure, gift, help, idea, information, job, letter, present, message, news, nothing, plan, present, project, question, secret, something, surprise

Here is an answer for him.

—indicates effect on recipient

after adjectives:
bad, beneficial, better, crucial, good, harmful, healthy, helpful, important, necessary, unacceptable, unfavorable, unhealthy, unimportant, useful, worse

That environment is unhealthy for you.

ON

Expressions:

have pity/mercy

Please have pity on them.

The boss had mercy on us and let us go home early.

pull a gun/knife on

The thief pulled a gun on the frightened workers.

TO

—usually indicates transfer to recipient

after verbs:
award, bring, carry, dedicate, deliver, describe, devote, distribute, donate, explain, give, hand, introduce, lend, mention, pass, present, read, recommend, reveal, send, shout, show, sing, speak, submit, suggest, take, tell, write

I wrote this letter to you.

after nouns:
answer, award, bill, dedication, gift, letter, memorial, monument, present, plaque, remark, scholarship, statement, toast

They gave the answer to him.

—indicates effect on recipient
beneficial, detrimental, harmful, helpful, useful, unfavorable

His advice was very useful to her.

—indicates recipient's feelings

after adjectives:
abhorrent, acceptable, annoying, boring, confusing, crucial, distasteful, disturbing, fascinating, gratifying, hurtful, important, meaningful, obnoxious, pleasing, precious, preferable, repulsive, satisfying, unacceptable, unimportant, vexing, worrisome

Those comments were hurtful to us.

PRACTICE

11-1. Fill in the blanks with the appropriate prepositions:

1. I hope they give the award _____ him.

2. She cooked a big meal _____ us.

3. The police had mercy _____ the young hooligans and sent them home.

4. The travel agency had a lot of information _____ her.

5. They sent a lot of information _____ her.

6. The information was useful _____ her.

7. This fresh fruit is good _____ you.

8. The news was fascinating _____ him.

9. Is the contract acceptable _____ you?

10. Practicing is very good _____ me.

11. They prepared a wonderful surprise _____ her.

12. Are electronic devices harmful _____ children?

UNIT 12:
State

Nouns after Prepositions

AT	IN		ON	OUT OF	UNDER
attention	a hurry	disarray	a roll	breath	consideration
ease	a mess	disaster	approval	commission	construction
leisure	a mood	disgrace	board	control	discussion
peace	a rage	disorder	call	danger	investigation
play	a stew	doubt	course	focus	suspicion
rest	anguish	dread	display	gear	
risk	awe	fear	duty	luck	
war	bankruptcy	focus	edge	order	
work	captivity	gear	fire	practice	
	chaos	good health	guard		
	charge	hot water	high/low speed		
	check	jail	high/low volume		
	circulation	love	hold		
	comfort	luck	leave		
	commission	need	loan		
	condition	order	one's best behavior		
	confinement	pain	order		
	conflict	power	parole		
	confusion	ruins	record		
	control	session	sale		
	danger	shape	schedule		
	debt	sickness	standby		
	demand	tears	strike		
	despair	trouble	tap		
			target		
			track		
			trial		
			vacation		

PRACTICE

12-1. Fill in the blanks with the appropriate prepositions:

1. The children were _____ breath when they finished the game.

2. The new houses are _____ construction.

3. She is _____ a big hurry.

4. The soldiers stood _____ attention.

5. All of the workers are _____ strike.

6. They sat there _____ comfort all afternoon.

7. I'm afraid she's _____ a lot of trouble.

8. He isn't here; he's _____ vacation.

9. These smart watches are _____ sale this week.

10. The poor man was _____ pain.

11. I hope your parents are _____ good health.

12. We were talking on the phone and he put me _____ hold.

13. That car seems to be _____ control.

14. Our boss is _____ control of the situation.

15. Both boys are _____ investigation.

UNIT 13:
Separation

FROM	OF	OFF	OUT OF	WITH
after verbs: drive, keep, move, run, separate, stay, subtract, walk	**after verbs:** cure, die, relieve, rid	**after verbs:** break, chop, cut, pick, pull, saw, send, shave, take, tear, throw	**after verbs:** come, drive, get, go, grab, move, pour, pull, push, rip, sip, squeeze, take, tear	**after verbs:** be finished, be through, break up, cut ties, fall out, part, part company, sever relations, split up
after adjectives: divorced, separated	**after adjectives:** cured, relieved, rid			

PRACTICE

13-1. Fill in the blanks with the appropriate prepositions:

1. I'm glad you finally got rid _____ that old car.

2. He drove _____ the garage in a big hurry.

3. Are you finished _____ that project yet?

4. She walked _____ school to her apartment every day.

5. They relieved her _____ all her important duties.

6. They are going to send their children _____ to camp for the summer.

7. We can't move into the office until they move _____ it.

8. Before doing the laundry, I want to separate the dark clothes _____ the white ones.

9. Have you seen Sally? She has cut _____ all her hair!

10. It is wonderful; he has been cured _____ cancer.

UNIT 14:
Attitude

Adjectives before Prepositions

ABOUT	AT	BY	FOR	IN	OF	TO	WITH
angry	aghast	amazed	concerned	disappointed	afraid	addicted	annoyed
anxious	amazed	amused	eager	interested	ashamed	committed	bored
bashful	amused	annoyed	grateful*		disrespectful	dedicated	content
concerned	angry	bewildered	prepared		envious	devoted	delighted
confused	annoyed	bored	ready		fond	faithful*	disappointed
crazy	astonished	confused	sorry		in favor	grateful*	disgusted
excited	astounded	disgusted			jealous	opposed	fascinated
faithful*	indignant	embarrassed			mindful		frustrated
glad	shocked	fascinated			proud		happy
happy	speechless	frustrated			repentant		impressed
honest	surprised	irritated			respectful		irritated
mad	thrilled	shocked			scared		pleased
nervous	upset				sure		satisfied
objective					suspicious		thrilled
optimistic					terrified		unhappy
pessimistic					tired		upset
right					trusting		
sad					uncertain		
sick					unsure		
silly					wary		
sorry							
unhappy							
upset							
worried							

*grateful *to* a person/grateful *for* a thing
faithful *to* a person/faithful *about* doing something

PRACTICE

14-1. Fill in the blanks with the correct prepositions:

1. She is ashamed _____ her sloppy work.

2. Are you ready _____ the test?

3. We are grateful _____ you.

4. We are grateful _____ your help.

5. He is very annoyed _____ me.

6. Try to be objective _____ it.

7. They were shocked _____ the child's behavior.

8. I am interested _____ studying there.

9. He seems to be suspicious _____ us.

10. She is a little unsure _____ herself.

11. I am so pleased _____ the new house.

12. Was he embarrassed _____ the gossip?

13. We are optimistic _____ the future.

14. The students were not prepared _____ the exam.

15. She seems to be unhappy _____ something.

Adjectives before Prepositions

OF SOMEONE	ABOUT SOMETHING	WITH SOMETHING OR SOMEONE ELSE	TO SOMEONE ELSE	TOWARD SOMEONE ELSE	ON SOMEONE ELSE
bad	careless	awkward	charming	affectionate	easy
careless	charming	belligerent	considerate	charitable	hard
charming	crazy	careful	courteous	considerate	rough
crazy	cruel	careless	cruel	cool	soft
crude	good	clumsy	faithful	courteous	strict
cruel	honest	curt	friendly	friendly	tough
evil	kind	flexible	good	gracious	
good	mean	forthcoming	gracious	hospitable	
hateful	nasty	frank	hateful	inhospitable	
honest	nice	friendly	helpful	menacing	
ignorant	rude	generous	hospitable	spiteful	
irresponsible	selfish	honest	inhospitable	sympathetic	
kind	sweet	impatient	kind	thoughtful	
mean	thoughtful	open	mean	warm	
nasty	thoughtless	patient	nice		
nice	understanding	stiff	polite		
responsible	unkind	sympathetic	rude		
rude		truthful	sweet		
selfish			sympathetic		
sweet			truthful		
thoughtful			unkind		
thoughtless					
typical					
unconscionable					
understanding					
unkind					

PRACTICE

15-1. Fill in the blanks with the correct prepositions:

1. She was impatient _____ us.

2. He was rude _____ our absence.

3. Try to be courteous _____ everyone.

4. The teacher is too hard _____ him.

5. Thank you for being so hospitable _____ my mother.

6. They have been very sympathetic _____her.

7. The old man was generous _____ his money.

8. Do you think he is being honest _____ us?

9. She is faithful _____ her husband.

10. The landlord was nasty _____ my late payment.

Verbs before Prepositions

AT	ON	TO	TOWARD	WITH
cheer	center	adapt	contribute	agree
grumble	concentrate	admit	donate	collaborate
guess	dote	agree	give	comply
hint	dwell	appeal	go	concur
hoot	err	consent	head	cooperate
laugh	harp	listen	help	empathize
rebel	pick	object	lean	get along
rejoice	prey	pay attention	push	harmonize
snort	put pressure	react	take steps	help
tremble	wait	relate	work	negotiate
	work	reply		sympathize
		respond		work
		revert		
		subscribe		

PRACTICE

15-2. Fill in the blanks with the correct prepositions:

1. He didn't respond _____ my letter.

2. You have to comply _____ the agreement.

3. We are working _____ our goals.

4. Try not to dwell _____ your problems.

5. I don't object _____ their coming.

6. They donated _____ several charities.

7. She is putting a lot of pressure _____ him.

8. I wish you wouldn't laugh _____ my mistakes.

9. They rejoiced _____ the news.

10. The children cried _____ delight.

Prepositions before Nouns

IN	WITH		IN/WITH	
assent	abandon	humility	anger	dread
cold blood	anger	indifference	apprehension	earnest
compliance	care	joy	approbation	fairness
confusion	compassion	kindness	approval	fear
consent	courage	love	compassion	friendship
defeat	delight	malice	confidence	gratitude
desolation	despair	optimism	contempt	grief
disgrace	discretion	pleasure	defiance	happiness
disobedience	disdain	pride	delight	kindness
dissent	distress	regard	despair	pain
fun	enthusiasm	sadness	disappointment	relief
person	fear	shame	disbelief	sadness
private	feeling	skill	disdain	shame
public	glee	sympathy	disgust	sorrow
reaction	grace	tenderness	dismay	sympathy
someone's absence	gratitude	thanks	distress	trust
someone's presence	happiness	understanding		
	hatred			

PRACTICE

15-3. Fill in the blanks with the correct prepositions:

1. He resigned _____ disgrace.

2. She performed her duties _____ grace.

3. She hung her head _____ sorrow.

4. I told you that _____ confidence.

5. You have to deliver it _____ person.

6. The woman was clearly _____ pain.

7. She does her work _____ skill.

8. Please don't talk so loud _____ public.

9. The matter must be treated _____ discretion.

10. She accepted the invitation _____ pleasure.

PART THREE

Using Prepositions

How to Use Part Three

This part explores the ways prepositions can be used in a sentence.

1. In each unit, observe the sentence patterns.

2. Read the example sentences aloud.

3. Think of another example sentence that follows the same pattern, and write it down.

4. Do the exercises and check your answers.

5. If you have any mistakes, go back and read the section again.

6. Repeat the entire exercise as many times as you need to, until you have no mistakes. This will help you memorize the patterns so that they "sound right," and you will soon be using them without having to think about them. Be sure to master each unit before proceeding to the next, as these patterns are tricky.

UNIT 1:
Prepositional Phrases

A prepositional phrase is a **preposition plus an object**.

There are three possible patterns:

preposition + noun
preposition + pronoun
preposition + verb + –ing

Preposition + Noun

Singular Nouns

NORMAL PATTERNS

preposition +	noun determiner	+/–	(descriptive adjectives)	+	singular common noun
with	a				pen
with	a		red		pen
with	a		new red		pen

SINGULAR NOUN DETERMINERS: a/an, the, one, this, that, any, each, every, another, either, neither, my, your, his, her, its, our, their, Mary's (or any other possessive noun)

EXCEPTION

preposition	+	ø	+	singular common noun
in				bed
to				school
at				school

Singular Proper Nouns

preposition	+	ø	+	proper noun
with				Mary
for				Mr. Jones

PRACTICE

1-1. Correct the mistakes in the following prepositional phrases. Write the correct phrases in the blank spaces.

1. with pen _____

2. for other girl _____

3. to Mary cousin _____

4. without book _____

5. from nice boy _____

6. between Mary and other girl   _____

7. in the Mary's house   _____

8. for the another apple   _____

9. next to tall boy   _____

10. near the Mr. Johnson's house   _____

Plural Nouns

NORMAL PATTERNS

preposition	+/–	(noun determiner)	+/–	(descriptive adjective)	+	plural common noun
for						apples
for		the				apples
for				red		apples
for		the		red		apples

PLURAL NOUN DETERMINERS: the, two (or any higher number), these, those, any, no, either, neither, other, some, both, few, enough, plenty of, a lot of, lots of, many, all, my, your, his, her, its, our, their, Mary's (or any possessive noun)

A <u>plural noun</u> not preceded by a noun determiner indicates <u>all of the group</u> or <u>in general</u>.

PLURAL PROPER NOUNS

preposition	+	the	+	proper noun
for		the		Joneses
for		the		United States

PRACTICE

1-2. Correct the mistakes in the following prepositional phrases. Write the correct phrases in the blank spaces.

1. for three apple   _____

2. without friend   _____

3. in United States   _____

4. from many country   _____

5. to a lots of places   _____

6. except this exercises   _____

7. with another friends   _____

8. at plenty of store   _____

9. by other teacher   _____

10. from the Smith   _____

Noncount Nouns

NORMAL PATTERNS

preposition	+/−	(noun determiner)	+/−	(descriptive adjective)	+	noncount noun
for						water
for		the				water
for				hot		water
for		this		hot		water

NONCOUNT NOUN DETERMINERS: the, this, that, any, no, either, neither, some, little, enough, a lot of, lots of, plenty of, much, all, my, your, his, her, its, our, their, Mary's (or any possessive noun)

A <u>noncount noun</u> not preceded by a noun determiner indicates <u>all of the group</u> or <u>in general</u>.

PRACTICE

1-3. Correct the mistakes in the following prepositional phrases. Write the correct phrases in the blank spaces.

1. for these furnitures _____

2. for a fresh air _____

3. with a new jewelry _____

4. without many hot water _____

5. with a few machinery _____

6. of a sugar _____

7. by mails _____

8. with too many junk _____

9. for a meat _____

10. for three equipment _____

Preposition + Pronoun

An **object pronoun** may replace a noun object.

TO REPLACE	USE	
the speaker	**me**	*The letter is for **me**.*
the person addressed	**you**	*The letter is for **you**.*
one male person (John)	**him**	*The letter is for **him**.*
one female person (Mary)	**her**	*The letter is for **her**.*
one thing (a book)	**it**	*The letter is about **it**.*
the speaker + one or more others	**us**	*The letter is for **us**.*

TO REPLACE	USE	
the people addressed	**you**	*The letter is for **you**.*
more than one person (John and Mary)	**them**	*The letter is for **them**.*
more than one thing (books)	**them**	*The letter is about **them**.*

If there is more than one object after a preposition, use the **object pronouns**:

*The letter is for **us**.*	*The letter is for **you** and **me**.*
*The letter is for **us**.*	*The letter is for **him** and **me**.*
*The letter is for **us**.*	*The letter is for **her** and **me**.*
*The letter is for **us**.*	*The letter is for **them** and **me**.*
*The letter is for **you**.*	*The letter is for **you** and **him**.*
*The letter is for **you**.*	*The letter is for **you** and **her**.*
*The letter is for **you**.*	*The letter is for **you** and **them**.*
*The letter is for **them**.*	*The letter is for **him** and **her**.*
*The letter is for **them**.*	*The letter is for **her** and **him**.*
*The letter is for **them**.*	*The letter is for **him** and **them**.*
*The letter is for **them**.*	*The letter is for **her** and **them**.*

PRACTICE

1-4. Change the underlined nouns to pronouns:

1. She paid for <u>the apples</u>. _____

2. He is excited about <u>the car</u>. _____

3. Do you study with <u>your classmates</u>? _____

4. The rug was made by <u>my grandmother</u>. _____

5. She made it for <u>my sister and me</u>. _____

6. We will give it to <u>our children</u>. _____

7. She is very fond of <u>that boy</u>. _____

8. They put the papers in <u>the trashcan</u> last night. _____

9. Please don't step on <u>the floor</u> until it is dry. _____

10. He hopes to get a call from <u>Sam</u> and <u>Mary</u> tomorrow. _____

11. It won't be the same without <u>David</u> and <u>Amy</u> and <u>you</u>. _____

12. There has been a lot of tension between <u>Susan</u> and <u>me</u>. _____

13. She lives near <u>John</u> and <u>me</u>. _____

14. They have been very kind toward <u>Sarah and the boys</u>. _____

15. She seems to be getting over <u>her problems</u>. _____

Preposition + Verb

A verb following a preposition should be in its **gerund** (basic verb + **ing**) form.

A pencil is used	for	**writing.**
We are excited	about	**going.**
They are happy	about	**coming.**
I am interested	in	**learning.**
She takes a nap	after	**eating.**
He is proud	of	**winning.**

Be careful with the word *to*. It may be a preposition or part of an infinitive.

To is a **preposition** after:

be accustomed to	She is accustomed to	**driving**	fast.
be used to	She is not used to	**driving**	in traffic.
look forward to	She is looking forward to	**driving**	home.
admit to	She admitted to	**driving**	my car.
opposed to	She is opposed to	**driving**	while drunk.
limited to	She is limited to	**driving**	during the day.

MORE EXAMPLES:

*I have to get accustomed **to getting** up early.*

*She isn't used **to working** all day.*

*The child admitted **to making** a mistake.*

*We are looking forward **to seeing** you soon.*

*They are opposed **to changing** the rules.*

*He is limited **to exercising** in the morning.*

To plus a basic verb forms an **infinitive**, and is not a preposition.

Use *to* + **basic verb** after the following verbs:

agree, appear, ask, be supposed, decide, expect, have, hope, intend, need, offer, plan, pretend, promise, refuse, seem, want, would like, used

EXAMPLES:

*He **agrees to help** with the arrangements.*

*She **appears to be** hurt.*

*They **asked to leave** early.*

*I **need to sleep**.*

*We **want to go** home.*

*Would you **like to play** tennis?*

Be careful with the expressions *be used to* and *used to*.

—be used to + gerund means "be accustomed to."

*I **am used to** working hard.*

*We **are** not **used to** working at night.*

—**used to** + basic verb means *did in the past*.

> I ***used to*** work hard when I was in college.
>
> We ***used to*** work at night, but now we work during the day.

PRACTICE

1-5. Fill in the blanks with the correct form of the verb:

1. She has to decide between _____ (study) and _____ (work).

2. That machine is great for _____ (exercise) the leg muscles.

3. He saved a lot of money by _____ (take) the bus to work.

4. Are you used to _____ (drive) on the freeway?

5. We decided against _____ (buy) that house.

6. They tried to stop her from _____ (move) so far away.

7. I am tired of _____ (cook) and _____ (clean).

8. He is really good at _____ (play) the guitar.

9. She is very close to _____ (win) the race.

10. You had better eat something before _____ (take) the medicine.

1-6. Choose <u>work</u> or <u>working</u> to complete the following:

1. She isn't used to _____ on Sundays.

2. He used to _____ every night.

3. I am opposed to _____ tomorrow.

4. She is supposed to _____ tomorrow.

5. He admits to _____ too little.

6. He agrees to _____ tomorrow.

7. We promise to _____ next week.

8. He would like to _____ every day.

9. They look forward to _____ here.

10. She expects to _____ here.

11. I am limited to _____ here.

12. Have you decided to _____ here?

13. They aren't used to _____ every day.

UNIT 2:
Prepositions in Questions

A. Basic Sentences with *Be*

STATEMENT PATTERN

subject	+	verb	+	preposition	+	object
The letter		is		to		John.
The letter		is		about		money.
The letter		is		from		Springfield.
The letter		is		from		Virginia.

YES/NO QUESTION PATTERN

verb	+	subject	+	preposition	+	object?
Is		the letter		to		John?
Is		the letter		about		money?
Is		the letter		from		Springfield?
Is		the letter		from		Virginia?

INFORMATION QUESTION PATTERN

question word	+	verb	+	subject	+	preposition?
Who(m)*		is		the letter		to?
What		is		the letter		about?
Where		is		the letter		from?
What state		is		the letter		from?
Which state		is		the letter		from?

Whom is used in writing and in formal speech. *Who* is used in conversation.

EXCEPTION:

The preposition *at* is not used with *where* or *what time*.

STATEMENTS:

The party is at my house.
The party is at ten o'clock.

QUESTIONS:

Where is the party?
What time is the party?

PRACTICE

2-1. Write a question that is answered by the <u>underlined</u> word in each statement.

1. <u>Yes</u>, the letter is from my mother.

   _____

2. <u>No</u>, I am not in Chicago.

   _____

3. We are from <u>California</u>.

   _____

4. They are from <u>San Francisco</u>.

   _____

5. The picture is of <u>my sister</u>.

   _____

6. The article is about <u>dieting</u>.

   _____

7. The class is at <u>seven-thirty</u>.

   _____

8. The concert is at <u>Memorial Stadium</u>.

   _____

B. Basic Sentences with Other Verbs

STATEMENT PATTERN

subject	+	verb	+	preposition	+	object
She		writes		to		John.
She		asks		about		money.
She		writes		from		Springfield.
She		writes		from		Virginia.

YES/NO QUESTION PATTERN

auxiliary verb	+	subject	+	verb	+	preposition	+	object?
Does		she		write		to		John?
Does		she		ask		about		money?
Does		she		write		from		Springfield?
Does		she		write		from		Virginia?

INFORMATION QUESTION PATTERN

question word	+	auxiliary verb	+	subject	+	verb	+	preposition?
Who(m)		does		she		write		to?
What		does		she		ask		about?
Where		does		she		write		from?
What state		does		she		write		from?
Which state		does		she		write		from?

EXCEPTION:

The prepositons *to* and *at* are not used with *where*.

STATEMENTS:

The letter is going to Chicago.
We are staying at the Forum Hotel.

QUESTIONS:

Where is the letter going?
Where are you staying?

PRACTICE

2-2. Write a question that is answered by the underlined word in each statement.

1. She works in the <u>furniture</u> department.

_____

2. He calls from <u>his office</u>.

_____

3. <u>No</u>, he doesn't text me.

_____

4. He sends email to <u>his boss</u>.

_____

5. <u>Yes</u>, he drives through Washington state.

_____

6. He drives through <u>Washington</u> state.

_____

7. They talk about <u>the garden</u>.

_____

8. They discuss it with <u>their neighbors</u>.

_____

9. He goes to <u>Europe</u> every summer.

_____

10. She makes cookies for <u>her children</u>.

_____

11. He works at <u>the airport</u>.

_____

12. He works at <u>four o'clock</u>.

_____

UNIT 3:
Prepositions in Noun Clauses

A question word often connects statements containing the verbs *know*, *understand*, *wonder*, *ask*, and *tell* with a noun clause (subject + verb combination).

introduction	+	question word	+	noun clause
I know				
I don't know				
Do you know		who		he is.(?)
I understand				
I wonder				
Ask him				
Tell us				

Basic Patterns for Prepositions in Noun Clauses:

A. CLAUSES WITH *BE*

introduction	+	question word	+	noun clause		
				subject	+ verb +	preposition
I know		who(m)		the letter	is	to.
I know		what		the letter	is	about.
I know		where		the letter	is	from.
I know		what state		the letter	is	from.
I know		which state		the letter	is	from.

B. CLAUSES WITH OTHER VERBS

introduction	+	question word	+	noun clause		
				subject	+ verb (object) +	preposition
I know		who(m)		she	writes letters	to.
I know		what		she	asks	for.
I know		where		she	writes	from.
I know		what state		she	writes	from.

PRACTICE

3-1. Complete each answer:

1. Where is she from?

   I don't know _____

2. Who(m) is he talking to?

   I don't know _____

3. What does she write with?

   I wonder _____

4. Who do they live with?

   I will ask them _____

5. Who(m) is this letter for?

   We know _____

6. What does he do that for?

   I don't understand _____

7. What company does she work for?

   She will tell me _____

8. Which bus is she coming on?

   I will ask her _____

9. Who(m) does she write letters to?

   I don't know _____

10. Which courses are you registered for?

    I don't understand _____

Prepositions in Adjective Clauses

An **adjective clause** can identify a noun. The clause comes right after the noun.

Basic Patterns for Prepositions in Adjective Clauses:

A. TO IDENTIFY A <u>PERSON</u>, AN ADJECTIVE CLAUSE CAN BEGIN WITH WHO(M), THAT, OR Ø:

person	+	introduction	+	*adjective clause*		
				subject	+ verb (object) +	preposition
The man		who(m)		she	writes	to
The man		that		she	writes	to
The man				she	writes	to
The people		who(m)		we	live	with
The people		that		we	live	with
The people				we	live	with
The doctor		who(m)		I	ask	for
The doctor		that		I	ask	for
The doctor				I	ask	for

Make sure the adjective clause is right after the noun:

> **The man who(m) she writes to**   *is my father.*
> **The people that we live with**   *are nice.*
> **The doctor I always ask for**   *isn't here.*

> *My father is*   **the man who(m) she writes to.**
> *I really like*   **the people that we live with.**
> *This is not*   **the doctor I always ask for.**

B. TO IDENTIFY A <u>THING</u>, AN ADJECTIVE CLAUSE CAN BEGIN WITH THAT OR Ø.

thing	+	introduction	+	*adjective clause*			
				subject	+ verb +	(object) +	preposition
the book		that		I	paid	ten dollars	for
the book				I	paid		for
the house		that		they	are looking		at
the house				they	are looking		at
the cities		that		we	work		in
the cities				we	work		in

Be sure to put the adjective clause directly after the noun.

> **The book that I paid ten dollars for**   *is great.*
> **The house they are looking at**   *is expensive.*
> **The cities that we work in**   *are far apart.*

I really like	*the book I paid ten dollars for.*
They might buy	*the house they are looking at.*
We love	*the cities we work in.*

PRACTICE

4-1. Combine each set of sentences into one sentence by forming an adjective clause.

1. The man is my father. She writes letters to him.

_____

2. The house is beautiful. My friends are looking at it.

_____

3. Those are the children. My daughter plays with them.

_____

4. The teacher isn't here. We talked to her yesterday.

_____

5. The piano is fabulous. He paid a lot of money for it.

_____

6. I am looking for the boy. I gave five dollars to him.

_____

7. She likes the neighbor. She goes to the movies with him.

_____

8. I lost the bag. I put my money in it.

_____

9. I found the jacket. I took my keys out of it.

_____

10. He can't remember the street. He parked on it.

_____

PART FOUR

Phrasal Verbs

A **phrasal verb** is a verb followed by a preposition that narrows or changes the meaning of the verb. Learn the verb and the preposition together as one unit.

There are three types of phrasal verbs:

nonseparable

separable

intransitive

Each has its own set of word-order patterns.

How to Use Part Four

1. Begin with Unit 1 and study the patterns described.

2. Read each example aloud.

3. Make up a new example sentence, write it down, and say it aloud.

4. Do the exercises, write your answers in your notebook, and check them with the key.

5. Keep doing the exercises until you have no mistakes.

6. Be sure to master each unit before proceeding to the next one.

EXAMPLE:

look for   search

Word Order

The object noun or pronoun immediately follows the preposition.

STATEMENT PATTERN

subject	+	verb-preposition	+	noun or pronoun
She		is looking for		John.
She		is looking for		him.

Incorrect:
~~She looks John for.~~
~~She looks him for.~~

Question Pattern 1 Use with *what*, *which*, *who(m)*, and *whose*.

question word	+	auxiliary verb	+	subject	+	verb	+	preposition?
What		are		you		looking		for?
Which book		were		you		looking		for?
Who(m)		are		you		looking		for?
Whose book		did		you		look		for?

Question Pattern 2 Use with *why*, *when*, and *how*.

question word	+	auxiliary verb	+	subject	+	verb-preposition		+	noun or pronoun
Why		are		you		looking	for		John?
When		did		you		look	for		him?
How long		have		you		been looking	for		him?
Where		have		you		looked	for		him?

Incorrect:
~~Why are you looking John for?~~
~~Why are you looking him for?~~

NOUN CLAUSES

Pattern 1 Use with *what*, *which*, *who(m)*, and *whose*.

introduction	+	question		+	*noun clause*			
		word	+	(object)	subject	+	verb	+	preposition
I don't know		what		book	you		are looking		for.
I don't know		which		book	you		are looking		for.
I don't know		who(m)			you		are looking		for.
I don't know		whose		book	you		are looking		for.

Pattern 2 Use with *why, where, when,* and *how.*

introduction	+	question word	+	subject	+	verb	+	preposition	+	object
I don't know		why		you		are looking		for		the book.
I don't know		where		you		have looked		for		it.
I don't know		when		you		looked		for		it.
I don't know		how		you		can look		for		it.

ADJECTIVE CLAUSES

Pattern 1

subject	+				*adjective clause*			
		who(m) that ø	+	subject	+	verb	+	preposition	+	verb
The man		who(m)		he		was looking		for		is my father.
The book		that		he		was looking		for		is on the table.

Pattern 2

subject	+	verb	+	object	+			*adjective clause*		
						who(m) that ø	+	subject	+	verb	+	preposition
I		see		the man		who(m)		you		are looking		for.
We		found		the book		that		you		were looking		for.

EXAMPLES OF NONSEPARABLE COMBINATIONS:

act like   behave in the same way as
*She **acts like** her sister. She **acts like** her.*

ask for   request
*They **asked for** information. They **asked for** it.*

beg off   make an excuse not to attend or participate
*He **begged off** going to the party. He **begged off** going.*

break into   enter forcefully
*Someone **broke into** the building. Someone **broke into** it.*

call on   ask one member of a group
*The teacher **called on** Tom. She **called on** him.*

care about   have affection for
*I **care about** my friends. I **care about** them.*

care for have affection for
*She **cares for** her roommates. She **cares for** them.*
like or desire something
*Do you **care for** more potatoes? (Do you want more?) No, I don't **care for** more. (No, I don't want any more.) No, I don't **care for** them. (No, I don't like them.)*

check into register
*They **checked into** the hotel. They **checked into** it.*
investigate
*The police **checked into** the situation. They **checked into** it.*

come across find by accident
*I **came across** these photos when I was cleaning out the closet.*
*I **came across** them.*

come after pursue in a negative way
*He **came after** my brother with a knife!*
*He **came after** him with a knife.*

count on expect someone to support you
*She **counts on** her mother for everything. She **counts on** her.*

fall for fall in love with
*She **fell for** the new employee. She **fell for** him.*
be tricked
*Don't **fall for** that old line! Don't **fall for** it.*

get in enter a vehicle that you cannot walk around in.
***Get in** the car. **Get in** it.*

get off remove one's self from a vehicle that you can walk around in; a personal vehicle; an animal that you can ride; a higher position
***Get off** the bus/bicycle/horse/ladder. **Get off** it.*

get on enter a vehicle that you can walk around in; a personal vehicle; an animal that you can ride
*Now you can **get on** the bus. **Get on** it!*

get over recover from
*It took him a long time to **get over** the tragedy.*
*It took him a long time to **get over** it.*

get with cooperate
***Get with** the program! You have to **get with** it!*

go for really like
*She really **goes for** tennis players. She really **goes for** them.*

go over review
*Can you **go over** the lesson with me? Can you **go over** it with me?*

go through   have a careful look at
Go through your papers and look for the document.
Please go through them and look for it.
experience a special period of time
He's going through a crisis. He's going through it.

go with   match; coordinate
This blouse doesn't go with my skirt.
This blouse doesn't go with it.
accompany; date
Are you going with John? Are you going with him?

hear from   have news of
We heard from Mary yesterday. We heard from her.

hear of   know about
I've never heard of that movie. I've never heard of it.

keep at   continue to pursue something
Keep at the job. Keep at it.

keep off   stay away from
Keep off the grass. You're supposed to keep off it.

look after   take care of
She'll look after their dog. She'll look after it.

look at   put one's eyes on
Look at this ad! Look at it!

look for   try to find
Will you help me look for my cat? Help me look for it!

look into   investigate
The police are looking into the case. They're looking into it.

look through   try to find among other things
She looked through her papers, but couldn't find the photo.
She looked through them, but couldn't find it.

pick at   agitate with one's fingernails
Don't pick at that scab! Stop picking at it!

pick on   abuse a member of a group
The teacher picks on Amy. She picks on her.

run across   find by accident
I ran across this chair at a flea market. I ran across it.

run for   be a candidate for office
Is he running for treasurer? Is he running for it?

run into   meet someone by accident
I ran into Jim at the mall. I ran into him.

run over	trample with a vehicle *That car **ran over** a squirrel. That car **ran over** it.*
see through	detect someone's true motives *It's easy to **see through** Jane. It's easy to **see through** her.*
see to	take responsibility for *The committee will **see to** the party preparations.* *The committee will **see to** them.*
show through	be transparent *His undershirt **shows through** his dress shirt.* *His undershirt **shows through** it.*
stand by	support *A loyal person **stands by** his friends. He **stands by** them.*
stand for	represent *That party **stands for** big changes. That party **stands for** them.* tolerate *The teacher won't **stand for** cheating. He won't **stand for** it.*
take after	be like *He sure **takes after** his father! He sure **takes after** him!*

PRACTICE

1-1. Rewrite each sentence, changing the noun object to a pronoun:

1. We asked for *the information*.

   _____

2. She is going to call on *Mary and Carolyn* next week.

   _____

3. They just got on *the bus to Chicago*.

   _____

4. I came across *some old family pictures*.

   _____

5. The policeman is coming after *you and Jessica*.

   _____

6. She ran into *some old friends* at the mall.

   _____

7. I am going to stand by *my friend*.

   _____

8. He just went through *all his papers.*

_____

9. We are looking for *Jason's wallet.*

_____

10. That boy takes after *his father.*

_____

1-2. **Write a question for each of the sentences in the previous exercise.**

Example:

1. What <u>did you ask for</u> _____ ?

2. Who(m) _____ ?

3. Which bus _____ ?

4. What _____ ?

5. Who(m) _____ ?

6. Who(m) _____ ?

7. Who(m) _____ ?

8. What _____ ?

9. Whose _____ ?

10. Who(m) _____ ?

1-3. **Use the phrasal verb and tense indicated to complete each sentence:**

1. I don't know what you _____ .

   (look for, present progressive)

2. He asked me what I _____ .

   (go through, past progressive)

3. She didn't tell us which hotel she _____ .

   (check into, past perfect)

4. I want to know who(m) he _____ .

   (care about, present)

5. I wonder what office she _____ .

   (run for, present progressive)

1-4. Complete each sentence using an adjective clause:

1. He was looking for a book.

    This is the book _____ .

2. Somebody broke into a house on this street.

    Is that the house _____ ?

3. She hopes to hear from that company soon.

    What is the name of the company _____ ?

4. The teacher picks on that group of students.

    That is the group of students _____ .

5. I have never heard of that place.

    That is a place _____ .

UNIT 2:
Must-Be-Separated Combinations

Certain verb-preposition combinations **must** be separated.

EXAMPLES:

call back   return a telephone call
get off   remove

Word Order

A **noun** or **pronoun** object comes between the verb and the preposition.

> *Please call **Sarah** back. Please call **her** back.*

> *Can you get **the wallpaper** off? Can you get **it** off?*

Incorrect:

> Please call back Sarah.
> Please call back her.
> Can you get off it?

EXAMPLES OF MUST-BE SEPARATED COMBINATIONS:

ask out   invite
*He **asked** Sally **out**. He **asked** her **out**.*

call back   return a call
*__Call__ Susan **back**. __Call__ her **back**.*

do over   repeat a task
*He **did** his project **over**. He **did** it **over**.*

drop by   deliver
*He **dropped** this note **by**. He **dropped** it **by**.*

drop in   place something in a receptacle
*Just **drop** the letter **in**. Just **drop** it **in**.*

get off   remove
*Can you **get** this wallpaper **off**? Can you **get** it **off**?*

have over   invite to one's home
*Let's **have** the Smiths **over**. Let's **have** them **over**.*

kick around   treat unfairly
*He **kicked** the little kids **around**. He **kicked** them **around**.*

kick out   force to leave
*They **kicked** Anne **out** of the group. They **kicked** her **out**.*

let down   disappoint
*She **let** the whole team **down**. She **let** us **down**.*

name after   give the same name as
*We **named** the baby **after** Paul. We **named** him **after** Paul.*

pass over	not promote on schedule *They **passed** Bill **over**. They **passed** him **over**.*
show around	give a tour *We'll **show** your guests **around**. We'll **show** them **around**.*
stand up	fail to appear for a date *She changed her mind, and **stood** the man **up**. She **stood** him **up**.*
start over	begin something again *It's not good: **start** the scene **over**. **Start** it **over**.*
turn around	change the direction of ***Turn** the rug **around** and it will fit. **Turn** it **around**.*
turn down	refuse a proposal *The editor **turned** her book **down**. He **turned** it **down**.*
turn off	become unattractive to *She **turned** Sam **off** when she acted so silly. She **turned** him **off**.*
wear out	exhaust someone *That exercise **wore** Tim **out**. It **wore** him **out**.*

PRACTICE

2-1. Express each of the following using a separated phrasal verb:

1. Pedro called me and I returned his call.

2. Patricia repeated the test in order to get a better grade on it.

3. We invited André to our house.

4. He disappointed his teacher.

5. My father's name is Connor. They named the baby Connor.

6. The teacher told Angela to leave the classroom immediately.

7. He said 'no' to Soo's invitation.

8. Jessica and I were really tired after the long swim.

9. The guide gave Jason and his family a tour of the campus.

10. They didn't promote Olivia.

2-2. Make a question for each "answer" in 2-1.

EXAMPLE: "She stood me up." Did she stand you up?

UNIT 3:
Separable Combinations

EXAMPLES:

cross out   something
                  delete something by marking it

look up   somebody
                  try to find information about somebody

Word Order

A **noun** object may follow the preposition.

> *He crossed out **the mistake**.*
>
> *She looked up **her old friend**.*

A **noun** object may precede the preposition.

> *He crossed **the mistake** out.*
>
> *She looked **her old friend** up.*

A **pronoun** object may precede, but not follow, the preposition.

> *He crossed **it** out.*
>
> *She looked **him** up.*

Incorrect: ~~He crossed out it.~~

Question Pattern 1

question word	+	auxiliary verb	+	subject	+	verb	+	preposition	+	noun object?
Why		did		he		cross		out		the mistake?
Why		did		she		look		up		her friend?

Question Pattern 2

question word	+	auxiliary verb	+	subject	+	verb	+	object	+	preposition?
Why		did		he		cross		the mistake		out?
Why		did		he		cross		it		out?
Why		did		she		look		her old friend		up?
Why		did		she		look		him		up?

NOUN CLAUSES

Pattern 1 Use with *why, when, how,* and *where*

introduction	+	question word	+		noun clause			
				subject	+	verb	+	preposition	+	noun object
I don't know		why		he		crossed		out		the mistake.
I don't know		when		he		crossed		out		the mistake.
I don't know		how		she		looked		up		her friend.
I don't know		where		she		looked		up		her friend.

Incorrect:

> ~~I don't know why he crossed out it.~~
> ~~I don't know how he looked up her.~~

Pattern 2 Use with *why*, *when*, *how*, and *where*

introduction	+	question word	+	subject	+	verb	+	object	+	preposition
I don't know		why		he		crossed		the mistake		out.
I don't know		when		he		crossed		it		out.
I don't know		how		she		looked		her friend		up.
I don't know		where		she		looked		him		up.

Pattern 3 Use with *what*, *which*, *who(m)*, and *whose*

introduction	+	question word	+	object	+	subject	+	verb	+	preposition
I don't know		what				he		crossed		out.
I don't know		what		mistake		he		crossed		out.
I don't know		which		mistake		he		crossed		out.
I don't know		whom				she		looked		up.
I don't know		whose		name		she		looked		up.

ADJECTIVE CLAUSES

Pattern

subject	+	verb	+	object	+	*adjective clause*							
						that who(m) ø	+	subject	+	verb	+	preposition	
This		is		the mistake		that		he		crossed		out.	
This		is		the mistake				he		crossed		out.	
He		is		the friend		whom		she		looked		up.	
He		is		the friend				she		looked		up.	

EXAMPLES OF SEPARABLE COMBINATIONS:

back up move a vehicle in reverse
*Back the car up. You need to **back** the car **up**. **Back** it **up**.*

blow down destroy by wind
*The wind **blew down** the barn. The wind **blew** the barn **down**. The wind **blew** it **down**.*

blow out extinguish with the force of one's breath
*The child **blew out** all the candles. The child **blew** all the candles **out**. She **blew** them all **out**.*

blow up cause to expand with the force of one's breath
*He **blew up** the balloons. He **blew** the balloons **up**. He **blew** them **up**.*

break down	destroy *They **broke** the door **down** to get in. They **broke down** the door. They **broke** it **down**.*
break in	use equipment for the first time *We **broke in** the new lawnmower. We **broke** the lawnmower **in**. We **broke** it **in**.*
break up	end a meeting or party *The police **broke up** the party. They **broke** the party **up**. They **broke** it **up**.*
bring back	return something ***Bring back** my book. **Bring** my book **back**. **Bring** it **back**.*
bring on	invite a challenge *The officer said to **bring on** the enemies. He said to **bring** the enemies **on**. He said to **bring** them **on**.*
bring up	introduce a topic for discussion *Don't **bring up** this idea at the meeting. Don't **bring** this idea **up**. Please don't **bring** it **up**.*
call off	cancel *She **called off** the wedding. She **called** the wedding **off**. She decided to **call** it **off**.*
call up	telephone ***Call up** your friends! **Call** your friends **up**! **Call** them **up**!*
carry out	remove something heavy ***Carry out** the sofa. Please **carry** the sofa **out**. Please **carry** it **out**.*
check off	remove from a list, indicating that it is no longer relevant *She **checked off** two tasks this morning. She **checked** two tasks **off**. She **checked** them **off**.*
check out	verify information *He **checked out** that information. He's **checking** that information **out**. He's **checking** it **out**.*
cheer up	put someone in better spirits *Let's go **cheer up** your mother. Let's go **cheer** your mother **up**. Let's go **cheer** her **up**.*
chew out	scold strongly *The coach **chewed out** the whole team. He **chewed** the whole team **out**. He really **chewed** them **out**.*
clean up	put back in order *We'll **clean up** the room after the party. We'll **clean** the room **up**. We'll **clean** it **up**.*
cross out	delete *She **crossed out** all my mistakes. She **crossed** all my mistakes **out**. She **crossed** (all of) them **out**.*

cut down	remove something tall with a saw or axe *They **cut down** the tree. They **cut** the tree **down**. They **cut** it **down**.*
cut out	remove with scissors or a knife *I **cut out** your article. I **cut** your article **out**. I **cut** it **out**.*
draw up	make a design on paper *The architect **drew up** the plans. She **drew** the plans **up**. She **drew** them **up**.*
drop off	deliver *She **dropped off** this package. She **dropped** this package **off**.* *She **dropped** it **off**.*
figure out	understand *I can't **figure out** this problem. I can't **figure** the problem **out**.* *I can't **figure** it **out**.*
fill in	write information on a blank space ***Fill in** the blanks. **Fill** the blanks **in**. **Fill** them **in**.*
fill out	fill in information on a form ***Fill out** the form. **Fill** the form **out**. **Fill** it **out**.*
fill up	add to capacity ***Fill up** the gas tank. **Fill** the gas tank **up**. **Fill** it **up**.*
get across	make someone understand *She **got across** the main idea. She **got** the main idea **across**.* *She **got** it **across**.*
get back	receive in return *You'll **get back** the money. You'll **get** the money **back**. You'll **get** it **back**.*
get out	remove *They **got out** the stain. They **got** the stain **out**. They **got** it **out**.*
give back	return something *We have to **give back** the tickets. We have to **give** the tickets **back**.* *We have to **give** them **back**.*
give out	distribute *She **gave out** pencils. She **gave** pencils **out**. She **gave** them **out**.*
hand in	give to a teacher or boss *We had to **hand in** our work. We had to **hand** our work **in**. We had to* ***hand** it **in**.*
hand out	distribute to a group *He's **handing out** the exams now. He's **handing** the exams **out** now.* *He's **handing** them **out**.*
hand over	give under force *She **handed over** the gun. She **handed** the gun **over**.* *She **handed** it **over**.*

hang up	suspend from a hook or hanger *Please **hang up** your clothes. Please **hang** your clothes **up**. Please **hang** them **up**.*
have on	be wearing *He **has on** a blue shirt. He **has** a blue shirt **on**. He **has** it **on**.*
hold up	keep high *Sue **held up** her hand. Sue **held** her hand **up**. She **held** it **up**.* rob *Two men **held up** the bus. Two men **held** the bus **up**. They **held** us **up**.*
knock out	hit until unconscious *The boxer **knocked out** two others. He **knocked** two others **out**. He **knocked** them **out**.*
leave out	omit *You **left out** David. You **left** David **out**. You **left** him **out**.*
look over	review carefully *He **looked over** her work. He **looked** her work **over**. He **looked** it **over**.*
look up	look in a book for information *I'll **look up** her address in the phone book. I'll **look** her address **up**. I'll **look** it **up**.*
make up	invent *She **made up** the story. She **made** the story **up**. She **made** it **up**.*
mark down	lower the price *She **marked down** the dresses. She **marked** the dresses **down**. She **marked** them **down**.*
pass in	submit homework, as a group *The students **passed in** their homework. The students **passed** their homework **in**. They **passed** it **in**.*
pass on	spread news to others *We **passed** the good news **on**. We **passed** it **on**.*
pass out	distribute to a group *The teacher **passed out** the test. The teacher **passed** the test **out**. He **passed** it **out**.*
pass up	not accept an opportunity *You **passed up** the chance to study in Europe. You **passed** the chance **up**. You **passed** it **up**.*
pay back	return a loan *You can **pay back** the money in ten years. You can **pay** the money **back** in ten years. You can **pay** it **back** in ten years.*
pick out	choose *She **picked out** a red dress. She **picked** a red dress **out**. She **picked** it **out**.*

pick up	collect *Pick up the box. Pick the box up. Pick it up.*
put back	return something to its place *She put back the candy. She put the candy back. She put it back.*
put down	stop holding *Put down the boxes. Put the boxes down over here. Put them down here.*
put off	postpone *She put off the party. She put the party off. She put it off.*
put on	begin wearing *He put on a sweater. He put a sweater on. He put it on.*
round off	estimate the closest whole number *He rounded off $39.95 to $40. He rounded $39.95 off to $40.* *He rounded it off to $40.*
set up	arrange *I set up the appointment. I set the appointment up. I set it up.*
show up	perform better than someone else *They were so good, they showed up the other teams. They showed the other teams up. They showed us up.*
take back	repossess *Did he take back the ring? Did he take the ring back? He took it back.* return to a store *She took back the shoes. She took the shoes back. She took them back.*
take down	disassemble *They took down the stage. They took the stage down.* *They took it down.* remove from a higher place *I took down the curtain. I took the curtain down. I took it down.*
take off	remove clothing *They took off their shoes. They took their shoes off.* *They took them off.*
take on	hire *They took on two new teachers. They took two teachers on. They took them on.*
take out	remove *He took out the rugs. He took the rugs out. He took them out.*
take up	shorten a garment *I took up the hem. I took the hem up. I took it up.*
tear down	demolish *They tore down our building. They tore our building down.* *They tore it down.*

tear off	remove paper or cloth quickly *He **tore off** the wrapper. He **tore** the wrapper **off**. He **tore** it **off**.*
tear out	remove from a book/notebook/magazine/etc. *Please don't **tear out** the pages. Please don't **tear** the pages **out**.* *Please don't **tear** them **out**.*
tear up	destroy by tearing *She **tore up** the letter. She **tore** the letter **up**. She **tore** it **up**.*
think over	consider an option *We'll **think over** your suggestion. We'll **think** your suggestion **over**. We'll **think** it **over**.*
throw out	put in the trash *I **threw out** your old sneakers. I **threw** your sneakers **out**.* *I **threw** them **out**.*
try on	test for fit *Try on these shoes. **Try** these shoes **on**. **Try** them **on**.*
try out	test a piece of equipment *Try out my laptop to see if you like it. **Try** my laptop **out**. **Try** it **out**.*
turn in	submit work *We have to **turn in** the essay by tomorrow. We have to **turn** the essay **in** by tomorrow. We have to **turn** it **in**.*
turn off	stop from operating *Turn off the lights. **Turn** the lights **off**. **Turn** them **off**.*
turn on	begin operating *He **turns on** the TV. He **turns** the TV **on**. He **turns** it **on**.*
turn over	put the other side up *She **turned over** the glasses. She **turned** the glasses **over**. She **turned** them **over**.*
turn up	increase the volume *Turn up the music! **Turn** the music **up**! **Turn** it **up**!*
wake up	stop from sleeping *Don't **wake up** the baby. Don't **wake** the baby **up**. Don't **wake** her **up**.*
wash out	remove with water *I can **wash out** the spot. I can **wash** the spot **out**. I can **wash** it **out**.*
wear out	use until it is no good *They **wore out** the carpet. They **wore** the carpet **out**. They **wore** it **out**.*
work out	solve a problem through effort *We can **work out** our problems. We can **work** the problems **out**.* *We'll **work** them **out**.*

wrap up	cover with paper *Shall I **wrap up** the package? Shall I **wrap** the package **up**? Shall I **wrap** it **up**?*
write down	note on paper ***Write down** my number. **Write** my number **down**. **Write** it **down**.*
write up	make a report on *She **wrote up** the wedding for the Star. She **wrote** the wedding **up**. She **wrote** it **up**.*

PRACTICE

3-1. Rewrite each sentence, changing the underlined nouns to pronouns:

Example: The wind blew down two trees. *The wind blew them down.*

1. The teacher came in and broke up <u>the party</u>.

_____

2. Don't bring up <u>that subject</u>.

_____

3. Are you going to call off <u>the wedding</u>?

_____

4. We will clean up <u>the mess</u>.

_____

5. I have to fill out <u>these forms</u>.

_____

6. She is trying to get <u>the mud</u> off her shoes.

_____

7. Did you give back <u>the money</u>?

_____

8. We looked up <u>your sister</u> in Pittsburgh.

_____

9. He always mixes up <u>the twins</u>.

_____

3-2. Rewrite each sentence two ways, changing the pronouns to the nouns indicated:

1. They looked it over. (the new house)
   <u>They looked the new house over.</u>
   <u>They looked over the new house.</u>

2. We are going to pass them in. (our papers)

   _____

   _____

3. He has to pay it back. (the money)

   _____

   _____

4. Did they kick her out? (Jennifer)

   _____

   _____

5. I hope she doesn't pass it up. (this opportunity)

   _____

   _____

UNIT 4:
Nonseparable Combinations with an Additional Preposition

With these combinations, the object noun or pronoun always goes after the verb.

EXAMPLES:

break up with	end a relationship *He **broke up with** her last week.*
check out of	teminate a hotel stay *We **checked out of** the hotel. We **checked out** of it.*
get out of	obtain release from an obligation; to leave a vehicle *She **got out of** jury duty. She **got out of** it.* *We **got out of** the car. We **got out of** it.*
be fed up with	be out of patience with a person or situation *The teacher kicked him out of class. She was **fed up with** his behavior.*
hang up on	end a phone call abruptly, usually in anger *I **hung up on** Sarah. She said something that made me furious, so I **hung up on** her.*
mix up with	confuse *Their careers are so similar that people often **mix** Alexa **up with** Michael. People **mix** her **up with** him.*
run out of	use up the entire supply of *She went to the store because she **ran out of** milk. She **ran out of** it.*
take out on	punish someone for someone else's misdeed *Eric had a tantrum in class, and the teacher **took** her frustration **out on** the whole class. She **took it out** on us.*

PRACTICE

4-1. Express each of the following with a nonseparable phrasal verb plus another preposition.

1. She wants to leave the car.

2. He ended the phone call with me abruptly.

3. We are using up all the milk.

4. The teacher calls John "Jim" and Jim "John."

5. He is mad at the boss, and is blaming me!

6. We need to leave the hotel officially.

7. I was released from lunch duty.

8. She is going to end her engagement to him.

When another preposition is added to a separable combination, the object, noun, or pronoun always goes between the verb and the two prepositions.

Pattern verb + non/pronoun + preposition + preposition + noun

EXAMPLE:

to take out of to remove something from within

Statement: *He took **the money** out of his back pocket.*
     *He took **it** out of his pocket.*

Question: *What did he take **the money** out of?*
     *Which pocket did he take **it** out of?*

Noun Clause: *I don't know which pocket he took **the money** out of.*
     *I don't know which pocket he took **it** out of.*

Adjective Clause: *This is the pocket (that) he **took the money** out of.*
     *This is the pocket he took **it** out of.*

EXAMPLE:

to give back to to return something to somebody

Statement: *We gave **the letter** back to her.*
     *We gave **it** back to her.*

Question: *Who(m) did you give **the letter** back to?*
     *Who(m) did you give **it** back to?*

Noun Clause: *I don't know who(m) we gave **the letter** back to.*
     *I don't know who(m) we gave **it** back to.*

Adjective Clause: *She is the girl who(m) we gave **it** back to.*
     *She is the girl we gave **the letter** back to.*

EXAMPLES OF SEPARABLE COMBINATIONS WITH AN ADDITIONAL PREPOSITION:

check out of   borrow from a library
     ***Check** that book **out** of the library. **Check** it **out**.*

get back from   have something returned
     *Did you **get** the book **back from** Kathy? Did you **get** it **back from** her?*

give back to   return to someone
     *He **gave** the papers **back to** Charles. He **gave** them **back to** him.*

hand in to   give to a teacher or boss
     ***Hand** your work **in to** the teacher. **Hand** it **in to** the teacher.*

hand out to	give to each member of a group She **handed** the exams **out to** the students. She **handed** them **out to** the students.
hand over to	give to an authority We had to **hand** the firecrackers **over to** the principal. We had to **hand** them **over to** the principal.
hang up on	place on a hook or hanger Can I **hang** my coat **up on** this rack? Can I **hang** it **up on** this rack?
mix up with	use for combining She **mixed** the ingredients **up with** a spoon. She **mixed** them **up with** a spoon.
run out of	force to leave a place Her dad **ran** everybody **out of** the house. He **ran** us **out of** the house.
take away from	remove forcibly from someone Her parents **took** the keys **away from** her. They **took** them **away from** her.
take out of	remove from a container She's **taking** the crayons **out of** the box. She's **taking** them **out of** the box.
tear out of	remove from a book or periodical You mustn't **tear** pages **out of** the book. You mustn't **tear** them **out**.
wash out of	remove a spot with water Try to **wash** the stain **out of** your skirt. Try to **wash** it **out of** your skirt.
write down on	note something on **Write** the address **down on** this card. **Write** it **down on** this card.

PRACTICE

5-1. Change each statement into a yes/no question. Change the underlined nouns to pronouns.

1. He brought <u>the books</u> up to the fourth floor.
   Did he bring them up to the fourth floor?

2. She is going to check <u>some books</u> out of the library.

   _____

3. He is trying to get <u>the spot</u> out of his shirt.

   _____

4. We got <u>our clothes</u> back from the dry cleaners.

   _____

5. He is going to hand <u>his letter of resignation</u> in to the manager tomorrow.

    _____

6. You should hang <u>your coat</u> up on the hanger.

    _____

7. She mixes <u>the dough</u> up with her fingers.

    _____

8. The police are going to run <u>the ruffians</u> out of town.

    _____

9. She takes <u>the groceries</u> out of the car herself.

    _____

10. I wrote <u>your number</u> down on a scrap of paper.

    _____

Intransitive Combinations

EXAMPLE:

act up   misbehave

There is no object; the word following the verb is now an **adverb**.

Statement Pattern

subject	+	verb	+	adverb
The child		acted		up

Question Pattern

(question word)	+	auxiliary verb	+	subject	+	verb	+	adverb?
Why		did		the child		act		up?

Noun Clause Pattern

introduction	+	question word	+	subject	+	verb	+	adverb
I don't know		why		the child		acted		up.

Adjective Clause Pattern

subject	+	who that	+	verb	+	adverb	+	verb
The child		who		acted		up		is in the kitchen.

EXAMPLES OF INTRANSITIVE VERB + ADVERB COMBINATIONS:

act out   misbehave
*The kids **act out** more at the end of the year.*

act up   misbehave
*The kids always **act up** when their parents go out.*

add up   make sense
*She's a good student, but she hates school. It doesn't **add up**.*

back down   weaken one's stance
*He fought hard, but **backed down** when he saw that it was impossible to convince us.*

back off   stop aggressive behavior
*She was yelling at the policeman, but **backed off** when he started to handcuff her.*

blow away   disappear in the wind
*The newspaper came, but it **blew away** in the storm.*

blow out	explode (a tire) *When we were driving to Texas, the tire **blew out**.*
blow over	lose importance *They had a big argument, but it **blew over**, and they're friends again.*
blow up	explode *He didn't know it was a bomb, and it **blew up** in his hand.* become angry *When he heard what we did, the principal **blew up**.*
break down	show sorrow *The girl **broke down** at her grandmother's funeral.*
break out	suddenly have spots or sores on one's body *I heard you had the measles. When did you first **break out**?*
break up	end a relationship *They seemed so happy together; it's too bad they **broke up**.*
burn down	be destroyed by fire (a building) *We found out too late, and the barn **burned down**.*
burn up	be destroyed by fire (an object) *All of our photos and books **burned up**.*
butt in	interrupt *We were having a nice conversation until she **butted in**.*
calm down	tranquilize one's self *She was upset, but she **calmed down** quickly.*
carry on	keep working *Their leader got sick, but they **carried on** bravely.*
catch on	understand *After doing the homework exercises, he finally **caught on**.*
catch up	attain the expected level *She should go on the trip, but she'll have to **catch up** when she returns.*
cheer up	improve one's mood *I sure wish you would **cheer up**.*
chicken out	become too afraid to participate *She was supposed to do a parachute jump, but she **chickened out** at the last minute.*
chip in	add to a collection of money for a benefit *We're collecting for the Red Cross. Can you **chip in**?*
clam up	refuse to talk *When they started asking him questions, he **clammed up**.*
close down	stop business *I loved that shop; too bad it **closed down**.*

close up	stop business for the day *Please come back tomorrow; we're **closing up** now.*
come about	happen *He got into big trouble; now, how did that **come about**?*
come out	declare one's homosexuality publicly *She **came out** three years ago.*
come through	behave as everyone hopes *He didn't want to help, but in the end he **came through**.*
come to	regain consciousness *She fainted, but **came to** a few seconds later.*
crack down	become stricter *The students acted out so often that the principal decided to **crack down**.*
crop up	appear unexpectedly (an obstacle) *Some problems have **cropped up** recently.*
cut back	reduce spending *Because of the slow economy, most people have to **cut back**.*
drag on	continue for too long *The dull show **dragged on** until eleven o'clock.*
drop by	visit unexpectedly *My friends **dropped by**, and I was still in pajamas.*
drop in	visit unexpectedly *Come see us. Just **drop in** any time.*
drop off	fall asleep *He always **drops off** while watching TV.*
drop out	stop going to school *It's too bad he **dropped out**; now he'll have trouble getting a good job.*
eat out	eat at a restaurant *More people **eat out** than ever before.*
fall down	collapse *My mother **fell down** and broke her hip.*
fall over	hit the ground *The tall trees **fell over** during the storm.*
fall through	fail to occur *Our vacation plans **fell through** at the last minute.*
get along	not fight *Do you **get along** with your roommate?*
get around	be active *My dad just got back from Europe; he really **gets around**.*

get by	barely manage to survive	
	*She has little money, but she **gets by**.*	
get through	finish	
	*When are you going to **get through**?*	
get up	leave bed	
	*What time do you **get up**?*	
give in	surrender	
	*When she saw the gun, she **gave in** and turned over the money.*	
give up	stopped trying	
	*After years of trying to save her marriage, she **gave up**.*	
go by	pass	
	*Time seems to **go by** faster when you're having fun.*	
go on	happen	
	*What's **going on** in the basement? I hear a lot of noise.*	
go out	stop functioning	
	*The lights **went out** last night during the storm.*	
goof off	waste time	
	*You're supposed to be working. Stop **goofing off**!*	
grow up	become an adult	
	*You are so silly. Sometimes I think you'll never **grow up**.*	
hang around	not leave	
	*We told them to go home, but they keep **hanging around**.*	
hang out	spend leisure time	
	*Where does he **hang out** in the evening?*	
keep out	not enter	
	*The building is condemned. You must **keep out**.*	
live on	not die	
	*She was a great influence, and her spirit will **live on**.*	
look out	take notice	
	***Look out**! There's a car coming!*	
luck out	be fortunate	
	*There were no more tickets, but I **lucked out** and got one from a stranger.*	
make out	manage	
	*How did you **make out**? Did the interview go well?*	
make up	return to a relationship	
	*They broke up last week, but now have **made up**.*	
nod off	fall asleep	
	*She always **nods off** in class.*	

pan out (not)	end unsuccessfully *Their new business didn't **pan out**, and they need jobs.*
pass away	die *His father **passed away** last year.*
pass out	lose consciousness *She was dancing, and all of a sudden **passed out**.*
pull over	move a car off the road *The policeman told him to **pull over**.*
run around	party a lot *He used to be responsible, but now he just **runs around**.*
show up	surprisingly appear *Even the teachers **showed up** at the rally.*
slip up	make a mistake *The error is my fault. I **slipped up**.*
stand by	not leave *The flight has been canceled. **Stand by** for more information.*
stand out	be emphasized *The bold printing makes the message **stand out**.*
stand up	get to one's feet *If you want to volunteer, please **stand up**.*
take off	begin to fly *What time does the plane **take off**?*
take over	assume control *What will we do if that political party **takes over**?*
throw up	vomit *The woman was so upset that she **threw up**.*
turn in	go to bed *He came home exhausted, and **turned in** early.*
turn out	finish *The party **turned out** well, thanks to your help.*
turn up	appear, uninvited *A lot of people we didn't know **turned up** at the party.*
wake up	stop sleeping ***Wake up**! You're late for school!*
watch out	take notice; be careful *He'll get into trouble if he doesn't **watch out**.*
work out	end successfully *I sure hope your new job **works out**.* exercise *She's in great shape. You can tell that she **works out**.*

PRACTICE

6-1. **Rewrite each sentence, using an intransitve verb-adverb combination in place of the underlined verb.**

1. The children <u>misbehaved</u>.
   The children acted up.

2. I hope the boss doesn't <u>lose his temper</u> because we are late.

   _____

3. I'm so glad you <u>came to visit</u>.

   _____

4. Please try to <u>be still and quiet</u>.

   _____

5. Do you think they will <u>understand the rules quickly</u>?

   _____

6. What time did you <u>fall asleep</u>?

   _____

7. It is important to <u>become mature</u>.

   _____

8. Those kids <u>act silly and do nothing</u> all day.

   _____

9. He <u>fainted in class</u>.

   _____

10. We passed the exam; we <u>were very fortunate</u>.

    _____

UNIT 7:
Intransitive Verb-Adverb Combinations Followed by a Preposition

EXAMPLE 1:

to get along with to live in harmony with

Statement:	*She **gets along with** her roommates.*
	*She **gets along with** them.*
Question:	*Who(m) does she **get along with**?*
Noun Clause:	*It doesn't matter who(m) she **gets along with**.*
Adjective Clause:	*Those are the roommates [who(m)] she **gets along with**.*

EXAMPLE 2:

to get through with to finish something that requires effort

Statement:	*They have **to get through** with their exams.*
	*They have **to get through** with them.*
Question:	*What do they have **to get through** with?*
Noun Clause:	*I don't care what they have **to get through** with.*
Adjective Clause:	*These are the exams (that) they have **to get through** with.*

EXAMPLES OF VERB-ADVERB-PREPOSITION COMBINATIONS:

add up to	total
	*The bill **adds up to** $366.*
be up for	be in the mood to
	***Are** you **up for** a movie tonight?*
bone up on	research or study
	*You should **bone up on** politics before the meeting.*
brush up on	review
	*She's **brushing up on** European history before her trip.*
catch up with	attain the same level as
	*I'm sure he'll **catch up with** the others soon.*
close in on	entrap
	*The police **closed in on** the gang and handcuffed them all.*
come down with	become sick with
	*The kids **came down with** colds.*
crack down on	become stricter with
	*They're **cracking down on** illegal immigration.*
cut back on	use less of
	*She had to **cut back on** sugar.*

drop in on	visit unexpectedly *My old high school friend **dropped in on** me last night.*
drop out of	stop attending school *Her boyfriend **dropped out of** college.*
face up to	confront *You're going to have to **face up to** reality and accept that your children have moved to their own places.*
fall in with	become involved with *He **fell in with** a rough crowd.*
feel up to	be well enough to *Do you **feel up to** a walk in the park?*
fill in for	substitute for *I have another commitment. Can you **fill in for** me?*
find out about	learn information *How did you **find out about** her new boyfriend?*
get ahead of	overtake *If you don't study, the others will **get ahead of** you.*
get around to	finally do *When are you going to **get around to** fixing the faucet?*
get away from	separate one's self from *You have to **get away from** here.*
get away with	misbehave and not be found out *They cheated on the exam and **got away with** it.*
get out of	be released from an obligation *How did you **get out of** washing the dishes?*
get through with	finish a difficult experience *When does he **get through with** chemotherapy?*
give up on	no longer have hope for *He let her down so many times that she finally **gave up on** him.*
go in for	be interested in *Do you **go in for** motorcycles?*
go out for	audition for a team *He's **going out for** the football team; I hope he makes it.*
go out with	date *She's **going out with** Paul on Saturday night.*
go through with	endure an event, even with second thoughts *Divorce is a big step. Are you really going to **go through with** it?*

hang out with	spend leisure time with *Who are you **hanging out with** these days?*
keep away from	not associate with *Her mother told her to **keep away from** that crowd.*
keep up with	maintain the same level as *You run too fast; I can't **keep up with** you.*
look back on	remember *It's fun to **look back on** all the fun we had together.*
look down on	feel superior to *You must never, ever, **look down on** other people.*
look in on	make sure that all is in order *Thank you for **looking in on** my mother every evening.*
look up to	admire and respect *We will always **look up to** our mother and father.*
make up with	reestablish a relationship *They're not fighting anymore; he **made up with** her.*
put up with	tolerate *She refused to **put up with** his laziness, and kicked him out.*
run around with	spend leisure time with questionable people *I heard he was **running around with** a gang.*
run out of	exhaust the supply of *We **ran out of** gas in the middle of nowhere.*
stand in for	substitute for *She couldn't come, so her sister is **standing in for** her.*
stand up for	support or witness *All of his friends **stood up for** him at the trial.*
try out for	audition for *He is **trying out for** the part of the king in the school play.*
watch out for	be wary of ***Watch out for** potholes in the road!*

PRACTICE

7-1. Rewrite each sentence, using a verb-adverb-preposition expression in place of the underlined words.

1. My sister is going to <u>stop dating</u> her boyfriend tonight.
   My sister is going to break up with her boyfriend tonight.

2. I don't understand how she <u>tolerates</u> her new roommate.

   _____

3. He is looking for another teacher to <u>substitute for</u> him tomorrow.

   _____

4. The doctor told her to <u>drink less</u> coffee.

   _____

5. If you have a cold, you should <u>avoid</u> other people as much as possible.

   _____

6. It is hard for the smaller children to <u>maintain the pace of</u> the big ones.

   _____

7. We have to go to the store; we have <u>exhausted our supply of</u> milk for the baby.

   _____

8. The children are <u>exhausted from</u> playing all day.

   _____

9. They will have to <u>confront</u> the facts.

   _____

10. We all <u>respect and admire</u> our boss.

    _____

Phrasal Verbs Used as Nouns

Many phrasal verbs are commonly used as nouns. There are three ways to write these nouns:

as two separate words

EXAMPLE:

rip off   a rip off a robbery
*I had to pay fifteen dollars to park my car. What a **rip off**!*

with a hyphen between the two words

EXAMPLE:

stand-in   a stand-in a substitute
*She worked as a **stand-in** when the manager was on vacation.*

as one word

EXAMPLE:

turnout   a turnout the size of an audience
*We had a great **turnout** for our baseball game.*

Unfortunately, there is no good rule or guideline to help us know which of the three forms to use. Many organizations have their own style manual to specify the usage they prefer.

Use these combinations as singular or plural nouns; use noun-determiners and descriptive adjectives as usual.

EXAMPLES OF PHRASAL VERBS USED AS NOUNS:

blowout   a tire that has burst
*We had a **blowout** on the highway.*

breakdown   a collapse
*Rioters crowded the streets, and there was a general **breakdown** of order.*

break-in   an illegal or forced entry into a room or building
*We had a **break-in** at the office last night; several computers were stolen.*

break-up   a separation caused by disagreement
*The young girl was unhappy about the **break-up** with her boyfriend.*

close-up   a photograph of someone's face
*That photographer is very good at **close-ups**.*

come-on   an incentive
*The free T-shirts at the game were a **come-on** to get more people to buy tickets.*

cover up   an attempt to hide the truth
*The **cover-up** of the crime made it difficult to investigate.*

getaway   a vacation
*That travel agency advertises exotic **getaways**.*

giveaway   something that can be obtained for free
*There were a lot of prizes and **giveaways** at the fair.*

hand-me-down   clothing used first by an older child and later by a younger one
*As the youngest child in a big family, almost all her clothes were **hand-me-downs**.*

handout   free food or supplies
*Many homeless people survive on **handouts**.*

hangout   a place where friends often go for relaxation or entertainment
*The bar on the corner is their favorite **hangout**.*

hang-up   a psychological problem
*Her insecurity is one of her **hang-ups**.*

kickback   money received by a controlling agent in a business transaction
*We believe somebody got a **kickback** in that business deal.*

leftovers   food saved for another meal
*We have **leftovers** for a week after a big holiday meal.*

letdown   a return to normal life after a time of excitement
*It was a big **letdown** for her to go back to work after her long vacation.*

lookout   a place for observing the activities of others
*The detective had a great **lookout** from the tenth floor of that building.*

makeup   paint for the face
*Most women look better with a little **makeup**.*

markdown   merchandise that has been reduced in price
*The **markdowns** are in the basement of the store.*

mix-up   confusion caused by an error
*There were a lot of **mix-ups** during our tour; most of the information we received about prices, hours of operation, and transportation was incorrect.*

pullover   a sweater that you put on by pulling it over your head
***Pullovers** are comfortable and attractive.*

pushover   a gullible person
*Her husband is a **pushover**; he will buy anything from a slick salesman.*

rip-off   a high price for something of lesser value
*He paid too much for that antique chair; it was a **rip-off**.*

show-off   a person who constantly demonstrates his talents
*I don't like to dance with him because he is a big **show-off**.*

stand-in   a substitute
*The **stand-in** for the main actor did a great job.*

step up   an improvement in status
*The new house is a **step up** for him.*

takeoff   departure of an airplane
*The **takeoff** was smooth, but the landing was difficult.*

takeover	the assumption of control, management, or responsibility of another group *There have been a lot of **takeovers** of big companies this year.*
tryouts	auditions *If you want to be on the team, come to the **tryouts** tomorrow afternoon.*
turnaround	a change in attitude *When he met her he went from depressed to cheerful; it was a complete **turnaround**.*
turnout	the number of people attending an event *The **turnout** for the office picnic was great; almost everybody came.*
workout	a session of exercise *A daily **workout** can improve your disposition.*
write-up	an article in a newspaper or a magazine *There was a big **write-up** about our friend in last week's paper.*

PRACTICE

8-1. Write the appropriate nouns in the blanks.

1. Our tire burst on the highway. We had a _____.

2. My friend is going to a psychologist to try to get rid of her _____.

3. The beach is private and quiet; it is a perfect _____ for a busy couple.

4. The woman carefully applied lipstick, powder, and mascara; she was an expert at putting on _____.

5. She paid two thousand dollars for that old, broken-down car. What a _____!

6. That soccer player always gets the ball and dances around with it. He is a big _____.

7. If you want to audition for the school chorus, come to the auditorium for _____ on Thursday at four o'clock.

8. The kids always go there to relax after school. It's their favorite _____.

9. Walking fast for an hour every day is a good _____.

10. Be sure to read the review of the show in the newspaper. It was an excellent _____.

UNIT 9:
Phrasal Verbs Used
as Adjectives

Verb-preposition combinations are used as adjectives in some common expressions.
When used as adjectives before nouns, these combinations are hyphenated.

carry-out/take-out food
food prepared and sold to be eaten somewhere else
*She lives alone and thrives on **carry-out food**.*

check-out counter
the place where the cashier is located
*Please take all your purchases to the **check-out counter**.*

drive-by shooting
a crime involving the indiscriminate use of a gun from a vehicle
*The wounded people were victims of a **drive-by shooting**.*

drive-in restaurant/ movie; drive-through bank/carwash
a business where people enjoy the services without leaving their cars
***Drive-in movies** were popular in the fifties, but not anymore.*

hand-me-down clothes
used clothes
*In order to save money, the student wore **hand-me-down clothes**.*

left-over food
prepared food saved from a previous meal
***Left-over food** is never as good as it was when it was fresh.*

run-down neighborhood
a neglected area
*There are too many **run-down neighborhoods** in the city.*

stand-up comic
an entertainer who stands at a microphone and tells jokes
*He made quite a bit of money as a **stand-up comic**.*

sit-down dinner/ lunch/meal
a meal where the food is served at the table, rather than buffet style.
*They had a wonderful **sit-down dinner** at their wedding reception.*

wake-up call
a telephone call ordered by a hotel guest to help him wake up
*Our plane is leaving early in the morning, so we will need a **wake-up call**.*

wind-up toy
a mechanical toy that works by turning a key
*The children love to play with **wind-up toys**.*

PRACTICE

9-1. Fill in each blank with a verb-preposition combination used as an adjective:

1. You can pay for your groceries at the _____ counter.

2. I'm cooking dinner at home tonight; I'm really tired of _____ food.

3. Whenever I check into a hotel, I ask for a _____ call for the next morning.

4. The politicians promised to help clean up the _____ neighborhoods around the city.

5. It is very convenient to deposit your checks at a _____ bank.

PART FIVE

Prepositions as Nouns, Adjectives, and Verbs

In the following examples, a preposition has been added to the beginning of the original word, making it more specific.

UNIT 1:
Nouns

In the following examples, a preposition has been added to the beginning of the original word, making it more specific.

byline   a line at the beginning of an article with the author's name
*His article was published, and he was pleased to see his name on the **byline**.*

bypass   a route that goes around a city, rather than through it
*Taking the **bypass** saves a lot of time.*

a surgical operation that avoids the main organ
*Her father had a heart **bypass** last month.*

downgrade   a change to a lower quality
*His new position is a **downgrade** in salary, but he is happier.*

downpour   a heavy rain
*The streets are flooded after that **downpour** yesterday.*

downswing   a reduction in business activity
*There was a **downswing** in the first quarter of the year.*

downtown   the heart of a city
*Let's go **downtown** tonight and have fun.*

input   the contribution of ideas
*We really need your **input** for this proposal.*

off chance   an unlikely possibility
*He called me on the **off chance** that I would be available.*

offshoot   a branch
*That group is an **offshoot** of a national organization.*

outbreak   an eruption
*There has been an **outbreak** of the flu in this city.*

outlaw   a criminal
*The cowboy films always have heroes and **outlaws**.*

outpost   a place of business far away from city life
*His store is a little **outpost** in the middle of nowhere.*

outpouring   an abundance
*There was an **outpouring** of sympathy for the widow.*

output   production
*Our **output** for the month was huge; we made a lot of money.*

overkill   failure caused by too much effort
*The salesman talked so much that the client lost interest; it was complete **overkill**.*

overpass   a bridge that extends over a road
*An **overpass** is being built at that intersection; it will ease the traffic situation.*

throughway	highway *You should go on the **throughway**; it's much faster.*
underdog	the team or person not expected to succeed *It's exciting when the **underdog** wins in a tournament.*
underpass	a road built underneath another road *To get on the main highway, you need to get on the **underpass** first.*
underpinnings	foundation *If the **underpinnings** are strong, the building will be safe.*
update	the latest information *The television stations are giving us an **update** on the tragedy every five minutes.*
upheaval	a disruption *There is a big **upheaval** going on in our office; a lot of people are being transferred.*
upstart	ambitious newcomer *The new assistant tried to change our office procedures during her first week. What an **upstart**!*
upsurge	increase in activity *There was an **upsurge** during the second quarter, thank goodness!*
upswing	increase in activity *There has been a steady **upswing** this year.*

Certain expressions use prepositions in noun form.

backup	someone who can substitute if necessary *I think I am well enough to do the job; if not, my colleague is here as a **backup**.*
the ins and outs	all of the details *After owning a restaurant for twenty years, he knows all **the ins and outs** of the business.*
the ups and downs	the good things and the bad things *We learn to cope with **the ups and downs** of life.*

PRACTICE

1-1. Fill in each blank with a preposition-noun combination:

1. That business lost money during the _____ in August.

2. The arrival of tourists in the spring means a big _____ in business activity.

3. At the meeting they asked for _____ from everybody in the department.

4. Our boss gives us an _____ on the company's activities at the end of every month.

5. You'd better get a flu shot in case there is an _____ of the flu next winter.

UNIT 2:
Adjectives

In the following examples, a preposition has been added to the beginning of the original word, making it more specific.

backup   reserve
*There is a **backup** crew in case you need help.*

bygone   past
*In **bygone** days, the pace of life was slower.*

downbeat   unhappy
*He has been **downbeat** ever since his girlfriend left town.*

for-profit   money-making
*That group looks like a charity, but it is really a **for-profit** operation.*

in-class   activity done in the classroom, rather than as homework
*We have to write an **in-class** composition.*

incoming   being received
*The **incoming** mail should go in that pile.*

off-color   obscene
*I really hate his **off-color** remarks.*

offshore   in the ocean or sea
*They are trying to regulate the **offshore** drilling of oil.*

off-the-cuff   spontaneous
*Her **off-the-cuff** remarks prove her to be very well informed.*

ongoing   currently in progress
*Everyone is sick of the long **ongoing** investigation.*

online   pertaining to the Internet
***Online** services get better every day.*

outgoing   extroverted
*He is one of the most **outgoing** young people I have ever met.*

out-of-the-way   far away, and not on the main road
*He proposed to her at a romantic, **out-of-the-way** restaurant.*

overbearing   domineering
*Life is stressful when you have an **overbearing** boss.*

overdone   ruined from cooking too long
*The dinner wasn't good; the meat was raw and the vegetables were **overdone**.*

overextended   too busy
*Her life is very stressful because of her **overextended** schedule.*

overjoyed   very happy
*He was **overjoyed** when he heard the news.*

overpaid   receiving more money than one is worth
*The organization has a few **overpaid** employees.*

underdone   not cooked long enough
*The meat was **underdone**, so we put it back in the oven.*

underpaid   paid less than one is worth
*The workers at that factory are **underpaid**.*

upbeat   in a good mood
*Everybody is **upbeat** because of the holidays.*

upmarket   stylish and expensive
*The new mall has only **upmarket** shops; there are no discount stores there.*

In the following expressions, prepositions are used in the form of adjectives:

the downside   the negative aspect
*The **downside** of my new job is that I have to work on Saturdays.*

the in crowd/   what is currently popular
thing/place   *In high school, she was always part of **the in crowd**.*
*Body piercing was **the in thing** in the early nineties.*
*That nightclub is **the in place** for the over-thirty crowd.*

the inside story   information known only by the people concerned
*The tabloid newspapers always claim to have **the inside story**, but it is usually only speculation.*

the upside   the positive aspect
***The upside** of the new job is that there will be a lot of international travel.*

PRACTICE

2-1. Fill in each blank with a preposition-adjective combination with the indicated meaning:

1. We were _____ (thrilled) at the news.

2. She got the information through her _____ (Internet) contacts.

3. Many people are _____ (given too much work) and _____ (given very low wages).

4. Her new boyfriend is friendly and _____ (extroverted).

5. During the interview they explained the _____ (positive) and the _____ (negative) of working there.

UNIT 3:
Verbs

In the following examples, a preposition has been added to the beginning of a verb, giving it more specific meaning.

bypass	to go around a city to avoid the downtown traffic *If you are in a hurry, you can **bypass** Philadelphia by taking the alternate route.*
downgrade	to lower in quality or status *They **downgraded** her job, so she is looking for another one.*
download	to add software to a computer *She **downloaded** a new program this morning.*
outdo	to surpass *She is very ambitious; she wants to **outdo** everybody.*
outlaw	to make illegal *They have **outlawed** smoking in many public places.*
outpace	to go faster *The men **outpaced** the boys right from the beginning of the race.*
overcome	to conquer *She **overcame** her shyness and made a lot of friends.*
overdo	to work too hard *After the operation, the doctor told him not to **overdo** it.*
overtake	to reach and then surpass *We knew him when he was just learning to dance, but he **overtook** us and is now a professional.*
overturn	to change from a negative situation to a positive one *There has been a big **overturn** in the school system.*
overwhelm	to surprise in the extreme *The teacher was **overwhelmed** by the party the students gave in her honor.*
undercut	to succeed by offering a lower price than one's competitors *Discount stores usually **undercut** the department stores.*
update	announce the latest news *Have they **updated** the hurricane warning?*
upgrade	to raise in quality or status *She is earning more money because they **upgraded** her job.*
withdraw	to stop participating *It is a shame you have to **withdraw** from the class.*
withhold	keep money that will be owed to you at a later date *The government **withholds** part of your salary for income tax.*

In the following expressions, prepositions are used in the form of verbs.

to "**down**" something	to drink something very fast *After the race, he **downed** four glasses of water.*
to "**up**" something	to increase something *I wish I had bought that coat last year; they have **upped** the price.* *The gym workout is getting easier; it's time to **up** the weights on the machines.*

PRACTICE

3-1. Fill in each blank with an appropriate preposition-verb combination:

1. In an effort to save money, they are going to _____ (decrease the status of) a lot of jobs.

2. I hope they can _____ (conquer) all of their difficulties.

3. That team didn't have enough players and they had to _____ (cancel participation) from the tournament.

4. He bought her a huge diamond ring, hoping to _____ (surprise and impress) her.

5. Do you think they will ever _____ (prohibit) guns in this country?

Appendices

Appendices

Appendix 1: Answer Key

Part One

1-1   1. story   2. complaint   3. jokes   4. learn
5. told   6. unkind   7. excited   8. twenty
dollars   9. finished   10. scattered

1-2   1. We are not about to go there.   2. She did
an about-face.

1-3   1. The president's announcement brought
about riots.
2. Is your great-grandmother able to get
about by herself?

2-1   1. sofa   2. hang   3. principal   4. cruelty
5. article

2-2   1. The policeman went above and beyond
the call of duty.
2. Even the president is not above the law.

3-1   1. swim   2. street   3. library   4. state

3-2   1. I came across this recipe in my mother's
cookbook.
2. Her brother tried to get it across that she
should be quiet.
3. I hope to get my message across to the
audience.

4-1   1. read the instructions   2. your name
3. the school bus   4. studying   5. day

4-2   1. After all is said and done, we will be
happy.
2. David didn't study for the test, but he
got a good grade after all.

4-3   1. She takes after her dad.
2. The baby was named after her
grandmother.
3. The babysitter looks after the children on
Thursday afternoons.

5-1   1. suitcase   2. current   3. age   4. windows
5. dark hair   6. loan   7. the flu   8. gun control

5-2   1. It goes against the grain that teacher
salaries are so low.
2. They became prosperous against all odds.
3. We're up against the state champions
tomorrow night.

6-1   1. late   2. five classes

6-2   1. We asked if we could look around, and
they said to go ahead.
2. They were just trying to get ahead.
3. His brother is trying to get ahead of him
at tennis.

7-1   1. path   2. work

7-2   1. You thought we were angry, but we were
just pretending all along.

7-3   1. It's important to get along with your
classmates.

8-1   1. ourselves   2. winners   3. flowers

9-1   1. house   2. world   3. corner   4. scarf
5. moping   6. snooped   7. twenty-five
dollars   8. five o'clock

9-2   1. Drive around back.
2. You have to turn around.
3. She's giving him the run around.

9-3   1. She really gets around.
2. Can you show me around the campus?
3. We are just hanging around.
4. His older brother kicks him around.

10-1   1. works   2. captain

11-1   1. school 2. 123 Oak Street 3. smiled
       4. computer 5. war 6. latest 7. 75 miles
       per hour 8. 40 cents per pound
       9. 3,000 feet 10. the news

11-2   1. They are at work.
       2. Don't try to do everything at once.
       3. We arrived at last.
       4. We were happy at first.
       5. He's at an advantage.
       6. I keep her at arm's length.
       7. I don't know what he's getting at.
       8. He made a pass at me.

11-3   1. The child picked at the scab.

12-1   1. the store 2. came 3. call

12-2   1. The officer told her to step back/to move
       back.
       2. I wanted to get back at her.
       3. I'll get back to you when I have the
       information.
       4. We need to cut back on movies.

13-1   1. a lot of people 2. four P.M. 3. the judge

14-1   1. Maria 2. Mrs. Martínez's and Miss Evans's
       classes 3. idea 4. problems

14-2   1. The bus is behind (schedule).
       2. You are behind the times.

15-1   1. normal 2. mine

15-2   1. It was below the belt.

16-1   1. other people 2. pillow 3. cheating

17-1   1. sit 2. walk

17-2   1. Her comment was beside the point.
       2. The teacher is beside herself.

18-1   1. All the girls 2. my brothers

19-1   1. fence 2. five 3. Monday and Friday
       4. 33 and 40 5. New York and California
       6. decide

19-2   1. Between you and me, I am not voting for
       that politician.

20-1   1. Chicago 2. homework

20-2   1. His behavior was beyond the pale/belief.

21-1   1. Monday

22-1   1. carpenter 2. 5 P.M. 3. gallon 4. 1,800
       5. babysitting 6. rocks 7. 10 points

22-2   1. By all means, ask for help if you need it.
       2. She is kind by nature.
       3. By the way, don't forget the meeting
       next week.
       4. Some people work by night and sleep by
       day.
       5. She was (all) by herself.
       6. I found this old photo by chance.
       7. Do you by any chance know my father?

22-3   1. He stood by me when I needed help.
       2. Could you run that story by me again?
       3. She gets by.
       4. Can we stop by/drop by this afternoon?
       5. I go by your house on my way home
       from work.

23-1   1. work 2. each other 3. three hours

24-1   1. lack of experience 2. traffic

25-1   1. slide 2. tree 3. street

25-2   1. He hung the picture upside down.

25-3   1. The government is cracking down on homelessness.
2. I hope you don't come down with a cold.
3. Julia's mother will calm her down.
4. Please tell your dog to back down.
5. Please don't let your teacher down.
6. Are you going to turn the offer down?
7. Let's buy the computer when the price comes down.
8. She looks down her nose at the newcomers.
9. It's a good idea to write your passwords down.
10. Stop putting me down in front of your friends.

26-1   1. sleep 2. football game

27-1   1. Abe 2. Saturdays and Sundays

28-1   1. our house 2. honest

29-1   1. surprise 2. relaxation 3. tickets
4. winning 5. a warm coat 6. difficult
7. cat 8. grabs 9. leaving 10. bill 11. free
12. happy 13. drove 14. good 15. music
16. good 17. actress 18. higher wages

29-2   1. Please help me for once.
2. We didn't trust the travel guidebook, so we went there and saw for ourselves.
3. You're on time—for a change!
4. He decided to stop calling her once and for all.
5. It was very hot, so I decided to go for a swim.
6. We cannot change the situation now; we will stay quiet for the time being.

29-3   1. They stood up for the mayor.
2. He (really) cares for his mom.
3. She is trying out for the play next week.
4. The university will not stand for cheating.
5. No thank you. I don't care for dessert.

30-1   1. hears 2. deleted 3. graduate
4. took off 5. 9 A.M. to 5 P.M. 6. $60,000 to $70,000 7. see 8. tired 9. crying 10. tell

31-1   1. car 2. notebook 3. chorus 4. 80s
5. 30 minutes 6. used paper 7. hand
8. portions 9. this 10. the rain. 11. black and white 12. rhythm 13. style 14. treat
15. grades

31-2   1. He will have to pass a driving test in addition to a written test.
2. A ban on smoking on campus is in the air.

31-3   1. Someone broke in last night.
2. We were having a private conversation, and he kept butting in.
3. You should check in at the hotel as soon as you arrive.
4. Before the plane lands, you have to fill in this form.
5. Count me in!

32-1   1. him 2. tennis court

33-1   1. experiences 2. class

34-1   1. house 2. surprise

35-1   1. to the mall 2. Australia

36-1   1. stomped 2. debt 3. trouble

36-2   1. I don't want to get into trouble!

36-3   1. They talked me into going with them.
2. I wonder if I'll run into anybody I know at the game.

37-1   1. mangoes 2. crazy 3. argue

38-1   1. near 2. her job

39-1   1. me and Taylor 2. favorite

40-1   1. the alphabet 2. private 3. mathematics
4. fourth 5. loaves 6. noise 7. a couple
8. the sky 9. rid 10. disgust

40-2   1. I didn't have the right of way.
2. We needed a change of scenery.

41-1   1. jumped 2. close to 3. school 4. lights

41-2   1. This is off the record, but I heard that the
teacher is going to a different school.
2. His behavior is off the wall.
3. That bar is off limits to the kids.
4. My sister hit it off with my friends.
5. She is better off.

41-3   1. They called the wedding off.
2. I was nodding off during the meeting.
3. Hey—knock it off!
4. He was laid off.
5. His bad manners put everyone off.
6. What time does your plane take off?

42-1   1. standing 2. boardwalk 3. house
4. street 5. hands and knees 6. gloves
7. weekends 8. health care 9. basketball
team 10. order

42-2   1. I'm trying to log on.
2. My computer is on the blink.
3. Elena is always on time.
4. She has a crush on the camp counselor.
5. On your mark, get set, go!

42-3   1. We have to get on the bus now.
2. It's hard for her to put her clothes on.
3. It's too bad you missed out on the party.
4. Don't let those bullies pick on your little
sister.
5. You can log on here.

43-1   1. floor 2. cheated

44-1   1. ice cream 2. bed

45-1   1. sat

46-1   1. threw 2. style 3. ran 4. office
5. breath 6. Three 7. kindness

46-2   1. He asked me out. 2. They have checked
out (of the hotel) 3. He dropped out
(of school) when he was sixteen. 4. She
passed out in class. 5. Please pick out four
apples. 6. The firemen put out the fire.
7. I spilled coffee on the sofa and tried
to get the spot out. 8. They work out
together.

47-1   1. car

48-1   1. building 2. head 3. fence 4. dogs
5. state line 6. the speed limit
7. hotel room 8. money

48-2   1. She is head over heels in love with him.
2. That course is over my head.

48-3   1. Nobody was there when he fell over.
2. The police officer pulled me over.
3. He was passed over.
4. We are thinking your offer over.
5. Could you please look over these
contracts?

49-1   1. your office 2. sixty-five

50-1   1. red light 2. window 3. course
4. illness 5. embassy

50-2   1. Do you think he will come through?
2. Our contract fell through.
3. She showed us through the museum.

51-1   1. day 2. city

52-1   1. home 2. school 3. flight 4. handed
5. best pianist 6. neighborhood 7. adapt
8. dust 9. obedient 10. a quarter
11. book club 12. gallon

52-2   1. He texts me from time to time.
2. Are you used to the climate here?

52-3   1. She came to a few minutes ago.
2. I am looking forward to your visit.

53-1   1. steps 2. contributes 3. hospitable
4. directed

54-1   1. midnight 2. April

55-1   1. gifts 2. seven 3. laws 4. impression
5. Canada

56-1   1. sad 2. thermal underwear

57-1   1. 12 P.M. 2. learn

58-1   1. hopped 2. hill 3. street 4. scrape
5. game 6. pieces

58-2   1. She kept walking up and down the room.
2. I hope you make up your mind soon.
3. It's up to you.
4. The workers are up in arms.
5. I can't go because I'm up to my ears in work.

58-3   1. My mom blew up when she found out.
2. Please don't bring that topic up at the meeting.
3. He will need to do extra work in order to catch up to the other children.
4. I hope this news will cheer you up.
5. Please hurry up!
6. Keep up the good work!
7. She can't keep up with you.
8. I hope she doesn't pass up this opportunity.
9. She wrote up her ideas.

59-1   1. dance 2. furnished 3. pride 4. toys
5. problems 6. a new company 7. harmony
8. broke up 9. shouting 10. these shoes

59-2   1. They were charged with starting the fire.
2. Down with the dictator/tyrant!
3. She gets along with her roommate.

59-3   1. I can't put up with his attitude.
2. I don't know how he gets away with his crimes.
3. Let's get on with it!

60-1   1. neighborhood 2. ten minutes 3. sight

61-1   1. her coat 2. training wheels 3. paying

61-2   1. She was without a doubt my best teacher.
2. We will finish tomorrow without fail.
3. That is without question.
4. The new boss began to work without ceremony.

Part Two

1-1.

1.   in, in, on, at, in

2.   since

3.   for

4.   at, on, by

5.   on, of, for/in

6.   on, at, around/at, until

7.   at, in

8.   after

9.   through/during

10.   during

11.   At

12.   up

2-1A.

1. on
2. in
3. near
4. far from
5. over
6. in back of/behind
7. at the top of
8. at the bottom of
9. next to
10. against
11. between
12. among

2-1B.

in, in, at, on, at, on, in, at, at, at, in, in, at, on, at, in, on, in

3-1.

1. across
2. up
3. over
4. away from
5. out of
6. down
7. back to
8. into
9. toward
10. through
11. along
12. past
13. around
14. onto
15. off

4-1.

1. about
2. over
3. under
4. between
5. plus
6. from
7. into
8. of

5-1.

1. in
2. in
3. during
4. on
5. in
6. on
7. During
8. On
9. In
10. on

6-1.

1. in
2. on
3. on
4. in
5. in
6. in
7. on
8. in
9. on
10. on

7-1.

1. of
2. on
3. in
4. on
5. of
6. in
7. of
8. on
9. in
10. on

8-1.

1. like
2. above
3. about
4. of
5. about
6. about
7. with
8. of
9. like
10. with

9-1.

1. in
2. on
3. with, on
4. have, on
5. in
6. on
7. in
8. with, on
9. on
10. in

10-1.

1. about
2. about/over
3. about
4. in
5. about
6. on
7. in
8. at
9. in
10. on
11. over
12. in
13. at
14. of/about
15. over
16. in
17. at
18. of
19. on
20. about

11-1.

1. to
2. for
3. on
4. for
5. to
6. to/for
7. for
8. to
9. to
10. for
11. for
12. to/for

12-1.

1. out of
2. under
3. in
4. at
5. on
6. in
7. in
8. on
9. on
10. in
11. in
12. on
13. out of
14. in
15. under

13-1.

1. of
2. out of/from
3. with
4. from
5. of
6. off
7. out of
8. from
9. off
10. of

14-1.

1. of
2. for
3. to
4. for
5. at/with

6. about
7. at
8. in
9. of
10. of
11. with
12. about
13. about
14. for
15. about

15-1.

1. with
2. about
3. to
4. on
5. to
6. to/with
7. with
8. with
9. to
10. about

15-2.

1. to
2. with
3. toward
4. on
5. to
6. to
7. on
8. at
9. about
10. with

15-3.

1. in
2. with
3. in
4. in
5. in
6. in
7. with
8. in
9. with
10. with

Part Three

1-1.

1. with a pen
2. for a girl/for this girl/for that girl/for another girl
3. to Mary's cousin
4. without a book
5. from a nice boy
6. between Mary and another girl
7. in Mary's house
8. for another apple
9. next to a/the tall boy
10. near Mr. Johnson's house

1-2.

1. for three apples
2. without friends
3. in the United States
4. from many countries
5. to lots of places/to a lot of places
6. except these exercises
7. with other friends
8. at plenty of stores
9. by other teachers
10. from the Smiths

1-3.

1. for this furniture
2. for fresh air
3. with new jewelry
4. without much hot water
5. with a little machinery
6. of sugar
7. by mail
8. with too much junk
9. for meat
10. for equipment

1-4.

1. them
2. it
3. them
4. her
5. us
6. them
7. him
8. it
9. it
10. him and her/them
11. you
12. her and me/us
13. us
14. them
15. them

1-5.

1. studying, working
2. exercising
3. taking
4. driving
5. buying
6. moving
7. cooking, cleaning
8. playing

9. winning

10. taking

1.6.

1. working
2. work
3. working
4. work
5. working
6. work
7. work
8. work
9. working
10. work
11. working
12. work
13. working

2-1.

1. Is the letter from your mother?
2. Are you in Chicago?
3. Where are you from?/What state are you from?
4. What city are they from?
5. Who is the picture of?
6. What is the article about?
7. What time is the class?
8. Where is the concert?

2-2.

1. What/Which department does she work in?
2. Where does he call from?
3. Does he send email to text you?
4. Who(m) does he send email to?
5. Does he drive through Washington state?
6. What state does he drive through?
7. What do they talk about?
8. Who(m) do they discuss it with?

9. Where does he go every summer?

10. Who(m) does she make cookies for?

11. Where does he work?

12. What time does he work?

3-1.

1. where she is from.
2. who(m) he is talking to.
3. what she writes with.
4. who(m) they live with.
5. who(m) this letter is for.
6. what he does that for.
7. what company she works for.
8. which bus she is coming on.
9. who(m) she writes letters to.
10. which courses I am registered for.

4-1.

1. The man [who(m)] she writes letters to is my father.
2. The house (that) my friends are looking at is beautiful.
3. Those are the children [who(m)] my daughter plays with.
4. The teacher [who(m)] we talked to yesterday isn't here.
5. The piano (that) he paid a lot of money for is fabulous.
6. I am looking for the boy [who(m)] I gave five dollars to.
7. She likes the neighbor [who(m)] she goes to the movies with.
8. I lost the bag (that) I put my money in.
9. I found the jacket (that) I took my keys out of.
10. He can't remember the street (that) he parked on.

Part Four

1-1.

1. We asked for it.
2. She is going to call on them next week.
3. They just got on it.
4. I came across them.
5. The policeman is coming after you.
6. She ran into them at the mall.
7. I am going to stand by him/her.
8. He just went through them.
9. We are looking for it.
10. That boy takes after him.

1-2.

1. did you ask for?
2. is she going to call on?
3. did they just get on?
4. did you come across?
5. is the policeman coming after?
6. did she run into at the mall?
7. are you going to stand by?
8. did he just go through?
9. wallet are you looking for?
10. does that boy take after?

1-3.

1. are looking for.
2. was going through.
3. had checked into.
4. cares about.
5. is running for.

1-4.

1. he was looking for.
2. somebody broke into.
3. she hopes to hear from?
4. the teacher picks on.
5. I have never heard of.

2-1.

1. I called him/Pedro back.
2. Patricia did the test/it over.
3. We invited André/him over.
4. He let his teacher/her/him down.
5. They named the baby/him after my father.
6. The teacher kicked Angela/her out (of the classroom).
7. He turned Soo/her down.
8. The long swim wore Jessica and me/us out.
9. The guide showed Jason and his family/ them around.
10. They passed Miriam/her over.

2-2.

1. Did you call Pedro/him back?
2. Did she do the test/it over?
3. Did you invite André/him over?
4. Did he let his teacher/her/him down?
5. Did they name the baby/him after your father?
6. Did the teacher kick Angela/her out?
7. Did he turn Soo/her down?
8. Did the long swim wear Jessica and you/ you (all) out?
9. Did the guide show Jason and his family/ them around?
10. Did they pass Miriam/her over?

3-1.

1. The teacher came in and broke it up.
2. Don't bring it up.
3. Are you going to call it off?
4. We will clean it up.
5. I have to fill them out.
6. She is trying to get it off her shoes.
7. Did you give it back?
8. We looked her up in Pittsburgh.
9. He always mixes them up.

3-2.

1. They looked the new house over./They looked over the new house.
2. We are going to pass our papers in./We are going to pass in our papers.
3. He has to pay the money back./He has to pay back the money.
4. Did they kick Jennifer out?/Did they kick out Jennifer?
5. I hope she doesn't pass this opportunity up./I hope she doesn't pass up this opportunity.

4-1.

1. She wants to get out of the car.
2. He hung up on me.
3. We are running out of milk.
4. The teacher mixes John up with Jim.
5. He is taking it out on me!
6. We need to check out of the hotel.
7. I got out of lunch duty.
8. She is going to break up with him.

5-1.

1. Did he bring them up to the fourth floor?
2. Is she going to check them out of the library?
3. Is he trying to get it out of his shirt?
4. Did we get them back from the dry cleaners?
5. Is he going to hand it in to the manager tomorrow?
6. Should you hang it up?
7. Does she mix it up with her fingers?
8. Are the police going to run them out of town?
9. Does she take them out of the car herself?
10. Did I write it down on a scrap of paper?

6-1.

1. The children acted up.
2. I hope the boss doesn't blow up because we are late.
3. I'm so glad you dropped in.
4. Please try to calm down.
5. Do you think they will catch on?
6. What time did you drop off?
7. It is important to grow up.
8. Those kids hang around all day.
9. He passed out in class.
10. We passed the exam; we lucked out.

7-1.

1. My sister is going to break up with her boyfriend tonight.
2. I don't understand how she puts up with her new roommate.
3. He is looking for another teacher to fill in for him tomorrow.
4. The doctor told her to cut back on coffee.
5. If you have a cold, you should keep away from/stay away from other people as much as possible.
6. It is hard for the smaller children to keep up with the big ones.
7. We have to go to the store; we have run out of milk for the baby.
8. The children are worn out from playing all day.
9. They will have to face up to the facts.
10. We all look up to our boss.

8-1.

1. blowout
2. hang-ups
3. getaway
4. makeup
5. rip-off

6. show-off
7. tryouts
8. hangout
9. workout
10. write-up

9-1.

1. check-out
2. carry-out/take-out
3. wake-up
4. run-down
5. drive-through

Part Five

1-1.

1. downswing
2. upsurge

3. input
4. update
5. outbreak

2-1.

1. overjoyed
2. online
3. overworked, underpaid
4. outgoing
5. up, down

3-1.

1. downgrade
2. overcome
3. withdraw
4. overwhelm
5. outlaw

Appendix 2: Index of Phrases

PRECEDING PREPOSITION OR OTHER PARTICLE/S	NOUN OR VERB	FOLLOWING PREPOSITION	PAGE NUMBER
be	abhorrent	to	165–166
in one's	absence		89
an	absence	of	116
to	abuse someone	(all) through	160
from one's	accent		82
be	acceptable	to	165–166
in	acceptance		94
be	accessible	for	71
in	accord	with	194–195
on	account	of	117
on	account	of	131
in	accounting		90
be	accustomed	to	166–167
an	ache	in one's …	92
be	aching	with	196–197
to	act	against	23
to	act	as	34
to	act	for someone	72
to	act	like	107
to	act	up	184
against an	action		23
in	action		94
go into	action		105
in one's	actions		85
to	adapt	to	166–167
to	add	on	136
to	add	to	167
to	add	up (to)	184
to	add something	on (to)	136
in	addition		94–95
in	addition	to	96
to	adhere	to	167
be	adjacent	to	169–170
in	administration		90
under an	administration		178
to	admit	to	166–167
something/nothing	adorable	about	13
be beneath	adultery		48
in	adulthood		85
in	advance		85
to	advance	in	95
at an	advantage		39
	advice	for	69
on the	advice	of	131

PRECEDING PREPOSITION OR OTHER PARTICLE/S	NOUN OR VERB	FOLLOWING PREPOSITION	PAGE NUMBER
to	advise	about	12
to	advise someone	of	115
be	affectionate	to	167
be	affectionate	toward	174
in the	affirmative		92–93
to	affix	to	167
in the	afternoon		85
(all) through the	afternoon		160
on nice	afternoons		129
at one's	age		38
under	age		177
with	age		195
one's	age is	against	24
through an	agency		161
be	aghast	at	37
to	agree	about	11
to	agree	on	136
to	agree	to	166–167
to	agree	with	194–195
in	agreement	with	91
an	agreement	with	194–195
in	agreement	with	194–195
toward an	agreement		175
be	ahead	of	26
in	aid	of	91
to one's	aid		165
to	aim	at	36
have an	air	about	13
in the	air		96–97
on the	air		134
with an	air		191–192
in the	air force		90
on an	airplane		128
an	airplane	to	164
in an	airplane (small)		84
off	alcohol		121
in an	alcove		84
in	alignment		90
in	alignment	with	91
after	all		21
	all	along	27
in	all		94–95
	all	of	113
be	allergic	to	166–167
an	allergy	to	166–167
of	aluminum		115
be	amazed	at	37

PRECEDING PREPOSITION OR OTHER PARTICLE/S	NOUN OR VERB	FOLLOWING PREPOSITION	PAGE NUMBER
in	analysis		94–95
of	anger		114–115
with	anger		196–197
with	anger		191–192
from an	angle		81
be at an	angle	to	170–171
be	angry	about	11
in	anguish		88–89
in	anguish	of	117
of	anguish		114–115
an	animal	of	111–112
out of	animosity		145
for one's	anniversary		72
on one's	anniversary		133
an	annoyance	to	165–166
to the	annoyance	of	117
be	annoying	to	165–166
	another	of	113
an	answer	for	69
an	answer	to	164
an	answer	to	166–167
in	answer	to	94–95
the	answer	to	168
the	antidote	to	168
out of	anxiety		145
be	anxious	about	12
be	anxious	for	70
	any	of	113
like	anything		107
at an	apartment		35
an	appeal	to	166–167
to	apply	for	70
to	apply	to	167
in	appreciation	of	91
be	appreciative	to	167
in	apprehension		92–93
in	approbation		92–93
in	approval		92–93
on	approval		134
on	approval		135–136
an	aptitude	for	74
in	architecture		90
within an	area		199
to	argue	about	11
to	argue	against	23
to	argue	among	29
to	argue	over	153
to	argue	with	184–188
an	argument	about	11
have an	argument	with	184–188
in an	argument	with	91
toward an	argument		175
arm–in–	arm	with	89
at	arm's length		38
be up in	arms	about	184
in the	army		90
to	arrange	above	16
to	arrange	into	104–105
on one's	arrival		133
with the	arrival	of	196–197
an	article	about	11
an	article	on	132
in an	article		84
be	ashamed	of	117
to	ask	about	11
to	ask	for	70
to	ask someone	out	146–148
an	assault	on	133–134
in	assent		92–93
to	assist	in	95
the	assistant	to	169
in an	association		85
on the	assumption	of	131
	assurance	about	11
be	astonished	at	37
to one's	astonishment		165–166
be	astounded	at	37
to	attach	to	167
to	attach something	with	193
be	attached	to	169
an	attack	on	133–134
at	attention		37
pay	attention	to	166–167
be	attentive	to	167
in an	attic		84
after one's	attitude		20
one's	attitude	toward	174
something/nothing	attractive	about	13
be	attributable	to	169
to	audition	for	70
on the	authority	of	131
be	available	for	71
be	available	to	167
above	average		16

APPENDICES

PRECEDING PREPOSITION OR OTHER PARTICLE/S	NOUN OR VERB	FOLLOWING PREPOSITION	PAGE NUMBER
on	average		129
under	average		177
an	aversion	to	166–167
an	award	to	165
to	award	to	165
be	aware	of	117
in	awe	of	88–89
be	awkward	with	191–192
around	back		30
be back to	back		170–171
on the	back	of	112
to	back	down (from)	64
to	back	off	122–123
to	back	up	184
one's	background is	against	24
something/nothing	bad	about	13
be	bad	at	38
be	bad	for	71
	bad	of someone	118
in	bad weather		86–87
in	badminton		93
a	bag	of	112
by the	bag		56
in a	bag		84
to	bake	for	69
against one's	balance		24
in a	balcony		84
on the	balcony		126
a	ban	on	132
to	bang	against	23
to	bank	on	129
in	banking		90
in	bankruptcy		92
go into	bankruptcy		105
by the	barrel		56
through a	barricade		158
through a	barrier		158
a	barrier	to	168
in	baseball		93
be	based	on	129
in a	basement		84
be	bashful	about	12
be	basking	in	95
to	bat something	over	152
in a	bathing suit		89–90
to	battle	over	153
to	be	about	13
to	be	across from	18
to	be	after	20
to	be	ahead of	26
to	be	back from	42
to	be	in back of	43
to	be	beside	49
to	be	for	75
to	be	from	79
to	be	like	107
to	be	off	120
to	be	on	128–129
to	be	out of	144
to	be	out of	144
to	be	over	151
to	be	over	152
to	be	through with	159
to	be	under	177
to	be	up	182
to	be	up to	184–188
to	be	with	190
to	be	with	194–195
to	be	with	195
to	be	with	190
to	be	with	197
to	be	with	192–193
off the	beach		120
on the	beach		126
on the	beach		127
be	beaming	with	196–197
to	beat	against	23
to the	beat	of	169
to	beat	to a pulp	169–170
with all one's	beauty		196–197
	because	of	117
in	bed		84
to	bed		164
to	beg	for	70
to	beg	off	122–123
to	begin	with	195
at the	beginning		36
from the	beginning		79
from the	beginning	of	81
from	beginning	to end	81
on	behalf	of	131
to	behave	like	107
after one's	behavior		20
on one's best	behavior		134–135

PRECEDING PREPOSITION OR OTHER PARTICLE/S	NOUN OR VERB	FOLLOWING PREPOSITION	PAGE NUMBER
one's	behavior	toward	174
beyond	belief		53
be	belligerent	with	191–192
to	belong	to	169
below the	belt		47
on the	bench		134–135
go around the	bend		30
to	bend	over	151
be	beneficial	to	165–166
to one's	benefit		165
at	best		39
be for the	best		75
to	bet	on	129
be	better	for someone	71
be	better	from	81–82
be	better	off	122
for	better or	for worse	75
in	between		51
the great	beyond		53
on a	bicycle		128
a	bill	for	73
against a	bill		23
against one's	bill		24
in	bills		90
with the	bills		196–197
to	bind	to	171
through	binoculars		161
a	bird	of	111–112
on one's	birth		133
with the	birth	of	196–197
for one's	birthday		72
on one's	birthday		133
quite a	bit	about	11
into	bits		104–105
in	black		89–90
in the	black		88–89
in	black and white		88
to the	blare	of	169
be	blessed	with	191
	blind	in	95
on the	blink		134–135
around the	block		30
to	blow	down	63
to	blow	into	104
to	blow	off	120
to	blow	over	154
to	blow	toward	174

PRECEDING PREPOSITION OR OTHER PARTICLE/S	NOUN OR VERB	FOLLOWING PREPOSITION	PAGE NUMBER
to	blow	up	184
to	blow something	down	63
to	blow something	into	104
to	blow something	off	120
to	blow something	out	146–148
to	blow something	up	184
above	board		17
across the	board		18
go by the	board		57
on the	board		132
on	board		134
on the	boardwalk		126
in a	boat (small)		84
in	bold		88
to	bone	up on	184
a	book	about	11
in a	book		84
a	book	on	132
to	book someone	for	71
a	boost	to	168
to	boot	up	184–188
on the	border	of	127
to	bore	to death	169–170
be	bored	from	81–82
be	bored	with	192
be	boring	to	165–166
to	borrow	from	79
to	borrow something	from	79
under a	boss		178
	both	of	113
to	bother	about	12
a	bother	to	165–166
on the	bottom	of	127
to	bounce	on	127
out of	bounds		145
within	bounds		199
have a	bout	with	193–194
a	bowl	of	112
a	box	of	112
by the	box		56
in a	box		84
through the	boxes		159–160
in	braces		89–90
to	brag	about	11
in	braids		89–90
a	brand	of	112
of	brass		115

PRECEDING PREPOSITION OR OTHER PARTICLE/S	NOUN OR VERB	FOLLOWING PREPOSITION	PAGE NUMBER
to	break	down	63
to	break	in (on)	97
to	break	into	104
to	break	into	104–105
to	break	into	106
to	break	off	120
to	break	out	146–148
to	break	up	184–188
to	break	up (with)	195
to	break something	down	63
to	break something	in	97
to	break something	off	122–123
to	break something	up	184–188
at	breakfast		35
for	breakfast		72
over	breakfast		153
(all) through	breakfast		160
to	breakfast		164
above	breaking the law		16
beneath	breaking the law		48
a	breath	of	114
out of	breath		144
a	bridge	to	164
in the game of	bridge		93
in	brief		88
to	bring	about	14
to	bring	back	42
to	bring	back to	42
to	bring	down	63
to	bring	down	63
to	bring	from	79
to	bring	on	136
to	bring	to	165
to	bring something	down	63
to	bring something	in	87
to	bring something	through	158
to	bring something	up	182
to	bring something	up	184–188
on the	brink		134–135
to	broadcast something	all over the…	153
at a	brunch		35
to	brush	up (on)	184–188
to	brush something	off	120
by the	bucket		56
on a	budget		134–135
be over one's	budget		151

PRECEDING PREPOSITION OR OTHER PARTICLE/S	NOUN OR VERB	FOLLOWING PREPOSITION	PAGE NUMBER
to	build	for	69
to	build	on	136
to	build something	on (to)	136
to	build something	out of	144–145
in a	building		84
through a	building		158
through the	building		159–160
within a	building		199
by the	bunch		56
in	bunches		90
in	bundles		90
to	burn	down	63
to	burn	up	184–188
to	burn something	up	184–188
to	burst	in	87
to	burst	into flames	106
to	bury something	under	177
on a	bus		128
a	bus	to	164
at a	bus stop		35
by the	bushel		56
in	business	with	90
on	business		131
do	business	with	194–195
in	busloads		93
to	butt	against	23
to	butt	in	97
to	butt	in	87
to	buy	for	69
to	buy	from	79
a good	buy	on	132
to	buy something	for	73
to	buy something	from	79
the	buzz	of	114
to the	buzz	of	169
by and	by		57
in	cahoots	with	91
in	cahoots	with	194–195
on the	calculations	of	131
on	call		134
to	call	back	43
to	call	for	70
to	call	from	79
to	call	on	138
above the	call of duty		17
to	call someone	up	184–188
to	call something	off	122–123

PRECEDING PREPOSITION OR OTHER PARTICLE/S	NOUN OR VERB	FOLLOWING PREPOSITION	PAGE NUMBER
to	calm someone	down	64
on	calories		130
to	campaign	against	23
to	campaign	for	70
a	can	of	112
in the game of	canasta		93
in a	canoe		84
be	capable	of	115–116
in	capital letters		88
the	captain	of	111
in	captivity		92
in a	car		84
a	card	to	164
of	cardboard		115
in a game of	cards		93
to	care	about	11
to	care	for	76
under the	care	of	178
with	care		191–192
to	care for someone	(all) through	160
be	careless	of	118
through	carelessness		161
in	carloads		93
to	carry	above	16
to	carry	back to	42
to	carry	down	63
to	carry	on (with)	138
to	carry	through with	161
to	carry	to extremes	169–170
to	carry	to the limits	169–170
to	carry	to	165
to	carry something	out	143
to	carry something	over	152
to	carry something	through	161
to	carry something	through	158
to	carry something	up	182
to	carve something	out of	144–145
in	case	of	94–95
in any	case		94–95
in that	case		94–95
in one's	case		94–95
the	case	to	169
in	cash		90
at the	cash register		37
on	cassette		130
to	catch	on (to)	138
to	catch	up on	184–188

PRECEDING PREPOSITION OR OTHER PARTICLE/S	NOUN OR VERB	FOLLOWING PREPOSITION	PAGE NUMBER
to	catch	up (with)	184–188
in a	category		85
the	category	of	112
be	caught	with	191
be	caused	by	56
on the	ceiling		126
to	celebrate	among	29
to	celebrate	with	195
at a	celebration		35
in	celebration	of	91
of	celebration		116
to	center	on	137
in	centimeters		91
in a	century		85
without	ceremony		201
be	certain	of	117
to one's	chagrin		165–166
in a	chair		84
a	challenge	for	72
the	challenge	of	117
a	challenge	to	165–166
be	challenging	for	71
by	chance		57
by (any)	chance		57
off	chance		122–123
for a	change		75
in	change		90
a	change	in	95
a	change	of pace	116–117
a	change	of scenery	116–117
with the	change		196–197
in	chaos		88–89
in	charge		92
on the	charge	of	131
be	charged	with	197
against one's	charges		24
be	charitable	toward	174
with all one's	charm		196–197
be	charming	about	11
be	charming	to	167
off the	charts		122–123
to	chase something	from	79
to	chat	with	190
to	cheat	on	137
to	cheat	(all) through	160
above	cheating		16
be beneath	cheating		48

PRECEDING PREPOSITION OR OTHER PARTICLE/S	NOUN OR VERB	FOLLOWING PREPOSITION	PAGE NUMBER
a	check	for	73
in	check		92
to	check	in	97
to	check	into	106
to	check	out	146–148
to	check	out (of)	146–148
to	check something	in	97
to	check something	off	122–123
to	check something	out	146–148
in	checks		90
tongue in	cheek		88
to	cheer	at	37
to	cheer	for	75
to	cheer	up	184–188
to	cheer someone	up	184–188
in the game of	chess		93
to	chew someone	out	146–148
to	chicken	out (on)	146–148
to	chide someone	for	71
in	childhood		85
to	chill	to the bone	169–170
to	chip	in	97
in a	choir		85
to	choke	on	130–131
to	choose	as	34
to	choose	between	51
to	chop	off	120
to	chop	up	184
in	chorus		88
in a	chorus		85
at	church		35
in	church		84
to	church		164
off	cigarettes		121
in a	circle		90
in	circulation		92
under the	circumstances		178
to	cite someone	for	71
a	citizen	of	111–112
in a	city		84
of a	city		111
the	city	of	112
all over the	city		153
through the	city		158
all through the	city		159–160
within a	city		199
to	clash	with	193–194

PRECEDING PREPOSITION OR OTHER PARTICLE/S	NOUN OR VERB	FOLLOWING PREPOSITION	PAGE NUMBER
to	clash	with	196
at a	class		35
in	class		84
a	class	of	112
of	clay		115
to	clean	up	184–188
to	clean	with	193
to	clean something	off	120
to	clean something	up	184–188
to	clean something	with	193
to	clear something	off	120
to	clear something	with	193
to	climb	on	127
to	climb	over	152
a	climb	to	164
to	climb	up	182
to	cling	on	128
to	close	down	64
to	close	in (on)	97
to	close	out (of)	146–148
be	close	to	170–171
to	close	up	184–188
be	close	up	184–188
to	close	with	195
to	close something	down	64
to	close something	up	184–188
through the	closets		159–160
through the	clouds		158
in a	club		85
of a	club		111
a	clue	to	168
under a	coach		178
off the	coast		120
in the	coast guard		90
in a	coat		89–90
in a	cocoon		84
in	code		88
over	coffee		153
in	coins		90
in the	cold		86–87
be	cold	to	167
in	cold blood		89
in	cold weather		86–87
to	collaborate	with	194–195
in	collaboration	with	91
in	collaboration	with	194–195
to	collect	from	79

PRECEDING PREPOSITION OR OTHER PARTICLE/S	NOUN OR VERB	FOLLOWING PREPOSITION	PAGE NUMBER
to	collect something	from	79
in	collusion	with	91
in	color		88
in a	color		89–90
the	color	of	112
the	color	of	114
off	color		122–123
to	color	with	193
in	combination	with	91
to	come	about	14
to	come	across	19
to	come	after	20
to	come	back from	42
to	come	down	63
to	come	down	63
to	come	down with	64
to	come	from	79
to	come	in	87
to	come	into	104
to	come	off	120
to	come	out of	143
to	come	through	161
to	come	to	164
to	come	to	172
to	come	up to	184–188
to	come	up with	184–188
in	comfort		88–89
be	comfortable	with	192
on	command		131
in	commemoration	of	91
to	comment	about	11
out of	commission		144
be	committed	to	169
on a	committee		132
be beneath	committing a crime		48
in	common	with	91
on	compact disc		130
of a	company	of	111
be	comparable	to	168
be	comparable	with	196
to	compare	to	168
to	compare	with	196
to	compare something	with	196
	compared	to	168
in	comparison	with	91
in	comparison		94
out of	compassion		145

PRECEDING PREPOSITION OR OTHER PARTICLE/S	NOUN OR VERB	FOLLOWING PREPOSITION	PAGE NUMBER
with	compassion		191–192
to	compensate someone	for	71
in	compensation	for	91
to	compete	for	70
to	compete	with	193–194
in	competition	with	91
be in	competition	with	193–194
to	complain	about	11
to	complain	of	115
a	complaint	about	11
about	complete		13
in	compliance		92–93
in	compliance	with	194–195
to	comply	with	194–195
be	composed	of	115
beyond	comprehension		53
be	comprised	of	115
at the	computer		37
on the	computer		130
on the	computer		130
in	computers		90
to	concentrate	on	137
against a	concept		23
be	concerned	about	12
be	concerned	with	192–193
at a	concert		35
in	concert		88
in	concert	with	194–195
in	conclusion		94
in	conclusion		94–95
toward a	conclusion		175
to	concur	with	194–195
in	concurrence	with	194–195
in	condition		88–89
get into	condition		105
on	condition		134–135
to	conduct	for someone	72
one's	conduct	toward	174
at a	conference		35
in	confidence		89
to	confine	to	171
in	confinement		92
in	conflict	with	91
in	conflict		92
to	conflict	with	193–194
be in	conflict	with	193–194

APPENDICES

PRECEDING PREPOSITION OR OTHER PARTICLE/S	NOUN OR VERB	FOLLOWING PREPOSITION	PAGE NUMBER
be	confused	about	12
be	confusing	to	165–166
in	confusion		88–89
in	confusion		92–93
to	congratulate someone	for	71
	congratulations	on	133
in	conjunction	with	91
be	connected	to	169
in	connection	with	91
be	conscientious	of	118
be	conscious	of	117
in	consent		92–93
to	consent	to	166–167
be	considerate	to	167
be	considerate	toward	174
under	consideration		178
under	construction		178
to	contact	about	12
in	contact	with	91
through a	contact		161
a	container	of	112
in	contempt		92–93
be	content	with	192
have a	contest	with	193–194
out of	context		144
in a	continent		84
under a	contract		178
a	contract	with	194–195
on the	contrary		137
in	contrast		94
to	contrast	with	196
to	contribute something	toward	175
in	control		92
out of	control		144
have	control	over	152
under the	control	of	178
under	control		178
a	conversation	about	11
in	conversation		94
to	converse	with	190
to	cook	for	69
to	cook	to perfection	169–170
be	cool	toward	174
to	cooperate	in	95
to	cooperate	with	194–195

PRECEDING PREPOSITION OR OTHER PARTICLE/S	NOUN OR VERB	FOLLOWING PREPOSITION	PAGE NUMBER
in	cooperation	with	91
in	cooperation	with	194–195
the	coordinator	of	111
of	copper		115
to	copy	from	79
be	cordial	to	167
in a	corner		84
in a	corner		92
on the	corner		126
through the	correspondence		159–160
the	cost	of	112–113
in	costume		89–90
of	cotton		115
on the	council		132
to	count	on	129
to	count	out	146–148
to	count	up to	184–188
to	count someone	in	97
at a	counter		35
across the	country		18
in a	country		84
of a	country		111
all over the	country		153
through the	country		158
all through the	country		159–160
within a	country		199
within a	county		199
a	couple	of	113
with	courage		191–192
off	course		121
on	course		134
through (with) a	course		159
on the	court		126
the	cover	to	169
to	cover	up	184–188
to	cover something	with	193
be	covered	in	95
to	crack	down (on)	64
to	craft something	out of	144–145
be	crafted	from	81
to	cram	into	104
to	cram something	with	193
to	crash	against	23
to	crash	into	104
the	crash	of	114
to	crawl	about	13
to	crawl	across	18

PRECEDING PREPOSITION OR OTHER PARTICLE/S	NOUN OR VERB	FOLLOWING PREPOSITION	PAGE NUMBER	PRECEDING PREPOSITION OR OTHER PARTICLE/S	NOUN OR VERB	FOLLOWING PREPOSITION	PAGE NUMBER
to	crawl	back to	42	in	curls		89–90
to	crawl	out of	143	against the	current		24
to	crawl	all over the …	153	with the	current		195
be	crazy	about	12	be	curt	with	191–192
like	crazy		107	through the	curtains		158
be	crazy	of someone	118	be	customary	for someone	71
to	create	for	69	through	customs		158
to	create something	out of	144–145	to	cut	back (on)	43
be	created	from	81	to	cut	down	63
on	credit		130	to	cut	in/into	87
a	credit	to	165–166	to	cut	into	104–105
be up a	creek		184	to	cut	off	120
to	creep	up	182	to	cut	with	193
on the	crew		132	to	cut something	down	63
with the	crime		196–197	to	cut something	out	143
to	criticize someone	for	71	to	cut something	with	193
to	cross	over	152	to	cut ties	with	195
to	cross something	out	143	something/nothing	cute	about	13
be	crucial	for	71	at a	dance		35
be	crucial	to	165–166	to	dance	for	69
be	crude	of someone	118	to	dance	with	190
be	cruel	of someone	118	to	dance something	with	190
be	cruel	to	167	be	dancing	with	196–197
above	cruelty		16	in	danger		88–89
out of	cruelty		145	get into	danger		105
on a	cruise		130	out of	danger		145
a	cruise	to	164	in the	dark		92
to	cruise	up	183	out of	date		144
to	cruise	with	195	be up to	date		184
to	crush	against	23	towards	dawn		176
have a	crush	on	136	day after	day		21
to	cry	about	11	by	day		57
to	cry	for	70	by the	day		56
to	cry	in	92–93	a	day	of	116
the	cry	of	114	(all) through the	day		160
a	cry	of	114–115	over the next few	days		153
to	cry	over	153	a	dearth	of	116
to	cry	(all) through	160	in	death		85
with a	cry		191–192	on one's	death		133
be	crying	with	196–197	with the	death	of	196–197
of	crystal		115	a	debate	against	23
of a	culture		111	a	debate	among	29
by the	cup		56	at a	debate		35
a	cure	for	69	in	debate	with	91
a	cure	for	70	in a	debate	with	91
be	cured	of	116–117	a	debate	on	132
out of	curiosity		145	against one's	debt		24

PRECEDING PREPOSITION OR OTHER PARTICLE/S	NOUN OR VERB	FOLLOWING PREPOSITION	PAGE NUMBER
in	debt		92
go into	debt		105
in a	decade		85
of the	decade		111
to	decide	between	51
a	decline	in	95
a	decrease	in	95
with the	decrease	in	196–197
to	dedicate something	to	165
to	dedicate something	with	195
be	dedicated	to	169
in	dedication	of	91
a	dedication	to	165
in one's	deeds		85
in	defeat		92–93
in	defeat		85
in	deference	to	89
in	defiance		92–93
to	delete something	from	79
in	delight		92–93
of	delight		114–115
to the	delight	of	165–166
to one's	delight		165–166
with	delight		191–192
be	delighted	for someone	72
be	delighted	with	192
be	delightful	of someone	118
to	deliver	to	165
in	demand		92
on	demand		135–136
one's	demeanor	toward	174
on one's	departure		133
with the	departure	of	196–197
to	depend	on	129
to	depend	on	137–138
be	dependent	on	129
go into a	depression		105
a	depth	of	112–113
to	derive	from	79
of a	descent		111
to	describe	to	165
to	design	for	69
a	desire	of	117
at a	desk		35
in	desolation		92–93
in	despair		88–89
in	detail		88

PRECEDING PREPOSITION OR OTHER PARTICLE/S	NOUN OR VERB	FOLLOWING PREPOSITION	PAGE NUMBER
through	determination		161
a	detriment	to	165–166
be	detrimental	to	165–166
be	developed	from	81
to	devote	to	165
be	devoted	to	167
on the	diamond (baseball)		126
the	dictator	of	111
under a	dictator		178
under the	dictatorship	of	178
in a	dictionary		84
to	die	of	116–117
to	die	on someone	137
off one's	diet		121
on a	diet		134–135
to	differ	from	80
to	differ	with	193–194
be	different	from	79
to	dig	with	193
to	dig something	with	193
of	dignity		118
in	dimes		90
at	dinner		35
for	dinner		72
over	dinner		153
(all) through	dinner		160
to	dinner		164
towards	dinnertime		176
in	dire straits		88–89
to	direct	for someone	72
to	direct someone	toward	174
in this/that	direction		87
under the	direction	of	178
the	directions	for	70
the	directions	to	168
at a	disadvantage		39
to	disagree	with	193–194
a	disagreement	about	11
have a	disagreement	with	193–194
be	disappointed	with	192
in	disappointment		92–93
to one's	disappointment		165–166
in	disarray		88–89
in	disaster		88–89
to one's	discomfort		165–166
at a	discount		38
a	discount	on	132

PRECEDING PREPOSITION OR OTHER PARTICLE/S	NOUN OR VERB	FOLLOWING PREPOSITION	PAGE NUMBER
a	discredit	to	165–166
at one's	discretion		40
with	discretion		191–192
to	discuss something	among	29
a	discussion	about	11
a	discussion	on	132
under	discussion		178
in a	discussion	with	190
in	disdain		92–93
with	disdain		191–192
in	disgrace		88–89
in	disgrace		92–93
to one's	disgrace		165–166
in	disguise		89–90
in	disgust		92–93
to the	disgust	of	117
to one's	disgust		165–166
above	dishonesty		16
on	disk		130
in	dismay		92–93
in	disobedience		92–93
in	disorder		88–89
on	display		134
by	disposition		57
in	dispute	with	91
be	disrespectful	of	117
in	dissent		92–93
to	dissociate something	from	79
at a	distance		38
be	distasteful	to	165–166
to	distinguish something	from	80
with	distress		191–192
to	distribute	among	29
to	distribute	to	165
a	distrust	of	117
a	disturbance	to	165–166
be	disturbing	to	165–166
to	dive	off	120
to	divide	in/into	87
to	divide	into	104–105
to	divide	up	184–188
to	do	about	11
to	do	for	69
to	do someone	in	97
to	do something	for	73

PRECEDING PREPOSITION OR OTHER PARTICLE/S	NOUN OR VERB	FOLLOWING PREPOSITION	PAGE NUMBER
to	do something	over	154
to	do well	by someone	58
under a	doctor		178
in	dollars		90
to	donate	to	165
to	donate something	toward	175
a	donation	to	164
about	done		13
be	done	by	56
through a	door		158
door to	door		168
the	door	to	169
out of	doors		145–146
to	dote	on	137
in	doubt		88–89
without a	doubt		201
	down	with	197
by the	dozen		56
by the	dozens		57
to	drag	around	31
in	drag		89–90
to	drag	on	133
to	drag something	up	182
to	drape something	on	128–129
to	drape something	over	152
to	draw	around	30
to	draw	up	183
to	draw	with	193
to	draw something	in	87
to	draw something	with	193
in a	drawer		84
through the	drawers		159–160
in	dread		88–89
be	dreadful	to	167
to	dream	about	11
to	dream	of	115
to	dream	up	183
in one's	dreams		85
in a	dress		89–90
to	dress	up	184–188
to	drift	with	195
to	drink	out of	143
to	drink	with	190
to	drink something	with	190
over	drinks		153
to	drip	onto	140
to	drip something	on	127

PRECEDING PREPOSITION OR OTHER PARTICLE/S	NOUN OR VERB	FOLLOWING PREPOSITION	PAGE NUMBER
to	drip something	onto	140
to	drive	across	18
to	drive	against	24
to	drive	around	30
to	drive	around	31
to	drive	back to	42
to	drive	back from	42
to	drive	down	63
go for a	drive		75
to	drive	for someone	72
to	drive	from	79
to	drive	away from	79
in	drive		92
to	drive	into	104
to	drive	off	120
to	drive	on	133
to	drive	out of	143
to	drive	over	152
to	drive	all over the . . .	153
to	drive	to	164
to	drive	to distraction	169–170
to	drive	to insanity	169–170
to	drive	up	183
to	drive	with	195
to	drive something	into	104
to	drive something	off	120
to	drive something	out of	143
to	drive something	over	152
to	drop	by	58
by the	drop		56
to	drop	in	97
to	drop	in (on)	97
to	drop	off	122–123
to	drop	out of	146–148
to	drop something	by	58
to	drop something	in	84
to	drop something	in	87
to	drop something	on	127
to	drop something	onto	140
be	drowning	in	95
off	drugs		121
to	drum	up	183
be	drunk	from	81–82
to	dry something	with	193
in	duplicate		88
towards	dusk		176
off	duty		121

PRECEDING PREPOSITION OR OTHER PARTICLE/S	NOUN OR VERB	FOLLOWING PREPOSITION	PAGE NUMBER
on	duty		134
to	dwell	on	137
to	dwell	over	152
	each	of	113
be	eager	for	70
an	ear	for	74
at the	earliest		39
in	earnest		89
be up to one's	ears	in	184
on	earth		126
at	ease		37
be	easy	on	137
to	eat	out	146–148
to	eat	out of	143
to	eat	with	190
to	eat	with	193
to	eat something	with	190
to	eat something	with	193
on	edge		134
on the	edge		134–135
on the	edge	of	127
for all one's	education		74
with all one's	education		196–197
in the	eighties		85
	either	of	113
of	elation		114–115
to	elect	as	34
on	electricity		130
to	eliminate something	from	79
an	embargo	on	132
to one's	embarrassment		165–166
to	empathize	with	194–195
an	encumbrance	on	132
in an	encyclopedia		84
at the	end		36
in the	end		94
on the	end	of	127
to	end	with	195
toward an	ending		175
against an	enemy		23
get up (enough)	energy		183
be	engaged	to	169
in	English		88
the	enjoyment	of	117
	enough	of	113
in	entertainment		90

PRECEDING PREPOSITION OR OTHER PARTICLE/S	NOUN OR VERB	FOLLOWING PREPOSITION	PAGE NUMBER
with	enthusiasm		191–192
through an	entrance		158
be	envious	of	117
to	erase something	from	79
to	erase something	with	193
to	err	on	137
through an	error		161
the	essays	of	111
be	even	with	196
in the	evening		85
towards	evening		176
on nice	evenings		129
	evidence	on	132
the	evil	of	118
through (with)	exams		159
be	excellent	at	38
to	exchange something	for	73
in an	exchange	with	91
be	excited	about	12
the	excitement	of	117
of	excitement		114–115
to	exclaim	in	92–93
be	exclusive	to	169
on an	excursion		130
for	exercise		71
of	exercise		116
be	exhausted	from	81–82
something/nothing	exotic	about	13
to	expel someone	for	71
to	expel someone	from	79
for all one's	experience		74
with	experience		195
for all one's	expertise		74
to	explain	to	165
an	explanation	to	164
to	expound	on	132
with an	expression		191–192
to	extend	to	164
on the	exterior	of	127
an	eye	for	74–75
in the	eye		92
under the	eye	of	178
of	fabric		115
through the	fabric		158
to	fabricate something	out of	145
about	face	about	14
be face to	face	(with)	170–171
to	face	up to	184–188
in	fact		94–95
at a	factory		35
on the	faculty		132
without	fail		201
after one's	failure		20
to	faint	on someone	137
in	fairness		89
of a	faith		111
of	faith		118
be	faithful	to	167
to	fall	down	63
to	fall	for	76
to	fall	into	104
to	fall	off	120
to	fall	on	130–131
to	fall	on	127
to	fall	onto	140
to	fall	out (of)	143
to	fall	over	154
to	fall	through	161
to	fall	to	164
to	fall	out (with)	195
to	fall asleep	on	137
something/nothing	familiar	about	13
in a	family		85
of a	family		111
keep within the	family		199
be	famous	for	71
by	far		57
something/nothing	fascinating	about	13
be	fascinating	to	165–166
in	fashion		88
out of	fashion		144
to	fashion something	out of	144–145
be	fashioned	from	81
to	fasten	around	30
to	fasten	with	193
be	fat	from	81–82
through the	fault	of	161
with all one's	faults		197
a	favor	to	165
at the	fax machine		37
for	fear	of	75
in	fear		88–89

PRECEDING PREPOSITION OR OTHER PARTICLE/S	NOUN OR VERB	FOLLOWING PREPOSITION	PAGE NUMBER
a	fear	of	117
of	fear		114–115
out of	fear		145
with	fear		196–197
with	fear		191–192
be	feared	for	71
the	feel	of	112–113
the	feel	of	114
to	feel	up to	184–188
with	feeling		191–192
one's	feelings	toward	174
in	feet		91
on the	fence		126
on the	fence		134–135
of	festivity		116
	few	of	113
a	few	of	113
in a	few words		88
on the	field		126
on the	field		126
all over the	field		153
on a	field trip		130
in	fifties		90
in the	fifties		85
to	fight	against	23
to	fight	against	24
to	fight	among	29
to	fight	for	70
in a	fight	with	91
to	fight	over	153
to	fight	with	193–194
to	figure something	out	146–148
in a	file		84
through the	files		159–160
to	fill	in (for)	97
to	fill in	for someone	72
to	fill something	in	97
to	fill something	out	146–148
to	fill something	up	184–188
to	fill something	with	193
on	film		130
in the	final analysis		94–95
to	find	out (about)	11
to	find something	out	146–148
to	find something	under	177
to	find something	under	178
to	fine someone	for	71

PRECEDING PREPOSITION OR OTHER PARTICLE/S	NOUN OR VERB	FOLLOWING PREPOSITION	PAGE NUMBER
about	finished		13
be	finished	with	195
on	fire		134
at	first		36
something/nothing	fishy	about	13
in	fives		90
be	flexible	with	191–192
on a	flight		130
a	flight	to	164
to	flirt	around	31
to	float	over	151
to	float	with	195
to	float something	over	151
on the	floor		126
all over the	floor		153
against the	flow		24
with the	flow		195
to	fly	around	30
to	fly	back to	42
to	fly	back from	42
to	fly	from	79
to	fly	into	104
to	fly	over	151
to	fly	to	164
to	fly	toward	174
to	fly something	in	87
to	fly something	over	151
out of	focus		144
in the	fog		86–87
through the	fog		158
in	foggy weather		86–87
in a	folder		84
in	folds		90
to	follow something	through	161
be	fond	of	117
on	food		130
to	fool	around (with)	31
on	foot		128
in the game of	football		93
		for	money	71
against a	force		23
against the	force		24
to	force something	on	136
to	force something	through	158
be beneath	forgery		48
to	forget	about	11
a	form	of	112

PRECEDING PREPOSITION OR OTHER PARTICLE/S	NOUN OR VERB	FOLLOWING PREPOSITION	PAGE NUMBER
be	formed	of	115
be	forthcoming	with	191–192
at a	forum		35
be	found	with	191
on all	fours		128
be	frank	with	191–192
in a	fraternity		85
for	free		73
down a	freeway		63
to	freeze	to death	169–170
through a	friend		161
be	friendly	to	167
be	friendly	toward	174
be	friendly	with	191–192
in	friendship		89
a	friendship	with	194–195
from	front	to back	80
to	frost something	with	193
to	frown	at	36
with a	frown		191–192
be	frustrated	with	192
the	frustration	of	117
of	frustration		114–115
through	frustration		161
on	fuel		130
in	full		88
be	fuming	with	196–197
for	fun		71
in	fun		89
like	fun		107
of	fun		116
at a	function		35
at a	funeral		35
through a	funnel		158
something/nothing	funny	about	13
be	furnished	with	191
in the	future		85
to	gain weight	on	130
by the	gallon		56
at a	game		35
off one's	game		121
(all) through the	game		160
all through the	garden		159–160
on	gas		130
out of	gas		144
through a	gate		158
to	gaze	into	104

PRECEDING PREPOSITION OR OTHER PARTICLE/S	NOUN OR VERB	FOLLOWING PREPOSITION	PAGE NUMBER
in	gear		92
of a	gender		111
in	general		94–95
under a	general		178
through the	generosity	of	161
be	generous	with	191–192
of a	genus		111
to	get	about	14
to	get	ahead (of)	26
to	get	along with	27
to	get	around	31
to	get	around to	31
to	get	back from	42
to	get	back	43
to	get	back at	43
to	get	back to	43
to	get	by	58
to	get	in	97–98
to	get	in	87
to	get	into	104
to	get	off	120
to	get	off	122–123
to	get	on	138
to	get	on	127
to	get	on	128
to	get	out (of)	146–148
to	get	out of	143
to	get	over	152
to	get	through (with)	159
to	get	to	164
to	get	up	184–188
to	get	along with	194–195
to	get	on with	197
to	get away	from	79
to	get away	with	197
to	get sick	on	137
to	get someone	back	43
to	get someone	for	71
to	get something back	to/from	42
to	get something	across to	19
to	get something	across (to)	24
to	get something	for	69
to	get something	from	79
to	get something	in	84
to	get something	in	97–98
to	get something	into	104

PRECEDING PREPOSITION OR OTHER PARTICLE/S	NOUN OR VERB	FOLLOWING PREPOSITION	PAGE NUMBER
to	get something	off	120
to	get something	off	121
to	get something	off	122–123
to	get something	on	128
to	get something	on	138
to	get something	out	143
to	get something	out (of)	143
to	get something	up	184–188
be	getting	at	40
a	gift	for	69
a	gift	to	164
a	gift	to	165
to	give	in	98
to	give	up (on)	184–188
to	give something	back (to/from)	42
to	give something	out	143
to	give something	to	165
to	give something	to	165
to	give something	toward	175
to	give something	up	184–188
be	glad	about	12
to	glare	at	36
of	glass		115
through the	glass		158
through	glasses		161
with	glee		196–197
with	glee		191–192
to	glue something	on	127
to	glue something	to	167
be	glued	to	167
to	go	about	13
to	go	across	18
to	go	after	20
to	go	against	23
to	go	against	24
to	go	ahead	26
to	go	ahead	26
to	go	around (with)	31
to	go	back to	42
to	go	by	59
to	go	down	63
to	go	down	63
to	go	for	76
to	go	in for	76
to	go	for	70
to	go	out for	71
to	go	in	87

PRECEDING PREPOSITION OR OTHER PARTICLE/S	NOUN OR VERB	FOLLOWING PREPOSITION	PAGE NUMBER
to	go	into	104
to	go	off	120
to	go	on	133
to	go	on	128
to	go	out with	146–148
to	go	out (of)	143
to	go	over	152
to	go	through (with)	159
to	go	through	159–160
to	go	to	164
to	go	toward	174
to	go	toward	175
to	go	up	182
to	go	up	183
to	go	with	190
to	go	with	195
to	go	with	196
to	go away	in	92–93
to	go out	for	70
to	go quiet	on	137
toward a	goal		175
of	gold		115
in the game of	golf		93
something/nothing	good	about	13
be	good	at	38
for	good		74
be	good	for someone	71
in	good	with	91
be	good	of	118
be	good enough	for someone	71
in	good hands	with	92
in	good weather		86–87
to	goof	around	31
to	goof	off	122–123
to	gossip	about	11
through	gossip		161
above	gossiping		16
be beneath	gossiping		48
in	government		90
to	grab	at	36
to	grab something	out of	143
up for	grabs		72–73
with	grace		191–192
be	gracious	to	167
be	gracious	toward	174
to	graduate	from	79
a	graduate	of	111–112

PRECEDING PREPOSITION OR OTHER PARTICLE/S	NOUN OR VERB	FOLLOWING PREPOSITION	PAGE NUMBER
for one's	graduation		72
against the	grain		25
through the	grapevine		161
be	grateful	for	71
be	grateful	to	166–167
be	gratifying	to	165–166
with	gratitude		191–192
be	great	at	38
through	greed		161
be	greedy	for	70
with a	greeting		191–192
in	grief		92–93
to	grieve	over	153
to	grin	at	36
to	grind	to a pulp	169–170
to	grind	to dust	169–170
to	groan	about	11
a	groan	of	114–115
on the	ground		126
on solid	ground		126
in a	group		90
in a	group		85
of a	group		111
a	group	of	115
in	groups		90
in	groups	of a number	93
to	grow	up	184–188
to	growl	at	36
the	growl	of	114
to	grumble	at	37
with a	grumble		191–192
with a	grunt		191–192
to	guard	against	24
on	guard		134
to	guess	at	37
with the	guests		196–197
a	guide	to	168
to	guide someone	toward	174
the	gush	of	114
to	gush	over	153
in a	hall		84
in/into	halves		87
hand–in–	hand		89
off	hand		122–123
on	hand		134–135
on the other	hand		137

PRECEDING PREPOSITION OR OTHER PARTICLE/S	NOUN OR VERB	FOLLOWING PREPOSITION	PAGE NUMBER
to	hand over something	for	154
to	hand something	out among	29
to	hand something	in (to)	87
to	hand something	out (to)	143
to	hand something	over (to)	154
to	hand something	to	165
lay	hands	on	137
on one's	hands and knees		128
with a	handshake		191–192
to	hang	above	16
to	hang	against	23
to	hang	around with	32
to	hang	around	31
to	hang	on	128–129
to	hang	out with	146–148
to	hang	over	151
to	hang	up (on)	184–188
to	hang one's head	in	92–93
to	hang something	on	128–129
to	hang something	over	151
to	hang something	over	152
to	hang something	up	184–188
for	happiness		71
in	happiness		92–93
the	happiness	of	117
of	happiness		114–115
of	happiness		116
with	happiness		196–197
with	happiness		191–192
be	happy	about	12
be	happy	for someone	72
be	happy	with	192
to	harass	about	12
be	hard	on	137
from	hard work		81
to	hark	back to	42
be	harmful	to	165–166
to	harmonize	with	194–195
in	harmony		88
in	harmony	with	91
in	harmony	with	194–195
to	harp	on	137
in a	hat		89–90
be	hateful	of	118
the	hatred	of	117
with	hatred		191–192

PRECEDING PREPOSITION OR OTHER PARTICLE/S	NOUN OR VERB	FOLLOWING PREPOSITION	PAGE NUMBER
to	have it	out with	193–194
to	have something	on	128
to	have something	over	154–155
to	have something	over	152
to	head	for	73
the	head	of	111
be	head	over heels	154
be over one's	head		151
to	head	toward	174
to	head	toward	175
in bad/good	health		88–89
in (the field of)	health		85
be	healthy	for	71
be	healthy	from	81–82
to	heap something	on	136
to	heap something	with	193
to	hear	about	11
to	hear	from	79
to	hear	of	115
out of one's	hearing		145
within	hearing		199
sick at	heart		37
in one's	heart		94–95
in the	heat		86–87
to	heave	against	23
to	heave something	up	182
down at the	heels		39
the	height	of	112–113
under	height		177
one's	height is	against	24
in a	helicopter		84
beyond	help		53
	help	for	69
to	help	in	95
through	help		161
a	help	to	165–166
to	help	toward	175
to	help	with	194–195
to	help someone	(all) through	160
be	helpful	for someone	71
be	helpful	to someone	165–166
be	helpful	with	191–192
from	here		81
the	hero	of	111
the	heroine	of	111
to	hide	from	82
to	hide	under	177

PRECEDING PREPOSITION OR OTHER PARTICLE/S	NOUN OR VERB	FOLLOWING PREPOSITION	PAGE NUMBER
to	hide something	from	79
to	hide something	under	177
in the game of	hide–and–seek		93
in	high heels		89–90
down a	highway		63
off the	highway		120
on the	highway		126
on the	highway		127
a	highway	to	164
up the	highway		182
to	hike	to	164
to	hike	toward	174
on the	hill		126
to	hint	at	37
for	hire		72
the	hiss	of	114
to	hit	against	23
to	hit	at	36
to	hit	in	92
to	hit it	off	121
to	hit something	over	152
to	hit something	with	193
in the game of	hockey		93
to	hold	above	16
to	hold	against	23
on	hold		134
to	hold	to	171
to	hold	to	167
to	hold	up	184–188
to	hold something	over one's head	151
to	hold something	on	127
to	hold something	over	151
to	hold something	up	184–188
through a	hole		158
for the	holidays		72
over the	holidays		153
at	home		35
be	honest	with	191–192
on a	honeymoon		130
to the	honk	of	169
in	honor	of	91
of	honor		118
on the	honor roll		132
to	honor someone	for	71
to	hoot	at	37
to	hop	off	120

PRECEDING PREPOSITION OR OTHER PARTICLE/S	NOUN OR VERB	FOLLOWING PREPOSITION	PAGE NUMBER
to	hop	on	127
to	hop	onto	140
to	hop	out of	143
to	hop	over	152
to	hope	for	70
in	hordes		93
on the	horizon		126
to one's	horror		165–166
be	hospitable	to	167
be	hospitable	toward	174
at a	hospital		35
be	hostile	to	167
in	hot weather		86–87
at a	hotel		35
hour after	hour		21
by the	hour		56
within the	hour		199
over the next few	hours		153
at a	house		35
on the	house		135
all over the	house		153
all through the	house		159–160
house to	house		168
to	hover	over	151
to	howl	at	36
the	howl	of	114
with a	hug		191–192
to	hum	along with	27
the	hum	of	114
to the	hum	of	169
in the	humidity		86–87
with	humility		191–192
by the	hundreds		57
in	hundreds		90
in	hundreds		93
be	hungry	for	70
in a	hurry		88–89
to	hurry	up	184–188
be	hurt	in	92
be	hurtful	to	165–166
the	hush	of	114
go into	hysterics		105
to	ice something	with	193
against an	idea		23
behind an	idea		45
an	idea	for	69
an	idea	for	70

PRECEDING PREPOSITION OR OTHER PARTICLE/S	NOUN OR VERB	FOLLOWING PREPOSITION	PAGE NUMBER
be far from	ideal		68
the	ideas	of	111
be	ignorant	of	118
be	ignorant	of	115–116
to	ignore someone	(all) through	160
of that	ilk	of	111
(all) through one's	illness		160
be	impatient	for	70
be	impatient	with	191–192
be	important	for	71
be	important	to	169
be	important	to	165–166
be	impossible	for someone	71
be	impressed	with	192
under the	impression		178
the	improvement	in	95
in	inches		91
on one's	income		130
be	inconsiderate	of	117
be	inconsiderate	to	167
an	increase	in	95
with the	increase	in	196–197
be	indebted	to	166–167
with	indifference		191–192
be	indignant	at	37
one's	inexperience is	against	24
be	inferior	to	168
under the	influence	of	178
with all one's	influence		196–197
to	inform someone	of	115
	information	for	69
an	inhabitant	of	111–112
be	inhospitable	toward	174
in	ink		88
to	insert something	in	84
on the	inside	of	127
to	install something	over	151
on	instinct		131
the	instructions	for	70
the	instructions	to	168
in (the field of)	insurance		90
of	integrity		118
with all one's	intelligence		196–197
of good/bad	intentions		118
be	interested	in	95
something/nothing	interesting	about	13
on the	interior	of	127

PRECEDING PREPOSITION OR OTHER PARTICLE/S	NOUN OR VERB	FOLLOWING PREPOSITION	PAGE NUMBER
on the	Internet		130
on the	Internet		135
through an	intersection		158
to	introduce	to	165
to	invest	in	95
under	investigation		178
an	invoice	for	73
be	involved	in	90
be	involved	with	192–193
of	iron		115
at the	ironing board		37
be	irresponsible	of someone	118
off the	island		120
at	it		37
out of	it		145–146
in	italics		88
the	jacket	to	169
in	jail		84
in	jail		92
to	jail		164
in	jeans		89–90
by the	job		56
a	job	for	69
to	jog	along	27
a	joke	about	11
to	joke	about	11
in	journalism		90
on a	journey		130
the	joy	of	117
of	joy		114–115
with	joy		196–197
with	joy		191–192
to	judge	between	51
to	jump	about	13
to	jump	around	31
to	jump	back to	42
to	jump	in	87
to	jump	off	120
to	jump	on	127
to	jump	onto	140
to	jump	out of	143
to	jump	over	152
to	jump	up	182
within a	jurisdiction		199
on the	jury		132
of	jute		115
to	keep	above	16

PRECEDING PREPOSITION OR OTHER PARTICLE/S	NOUN OR VERB	FOLLOWING PREPOSITION	PAGE NUMBER
to	keep	against	23
to	keep	at it	37
to	keep	from	81–82
to	keep	in	98
to	keep	off	121
to	keep	on	133
to	keep	on _____ing	133
to	keep	out (of)	146–148
to	keep	up (with)	184–188
to	keep alive	on	130
to	keep away	from	79
to	keep someone	from	82
to	keep something	from	79
to	keep something	on	128
to	keep something	up	184–188
to	keep something	with	190
to	key	in	98
the	key	to	168
the	key	to	169
to	kick	in	92
to	kick	in	98
to	kick	off	122–123
to	kick somebody	out	143
to	kick someone	around	32
for	kicks		71
to	kill something	off	122–123
in	kilos		91
be	kind	about	12
be	kind	of someone	118
a	kind	of	112
be	kind	to	167
after one's	kindness		20
out of	kindness		145
through	kindness		161
with	kindness		191–192
under a	king		178
with a	kiss		191–192
in a	kitchen		84
a	knack	for	74
to	kneel	beside	49
the	knob	to	169
to	knock	against	23
to	knock	in	92
to	knock	on	127
to	knock someone	out	146–148
to	knock something	off	122–123
to	know	about	11

PRECEDING PREPOSITION OR OTHER PARTICLE/S	NOUN OR VERB	FOLLOWING PREPOSITION	PAGE NUMBER
to	know something	about	11
to	know something	from	80
for all one's	knowledge		74
be	known	for	71
a	lack	of	116
be	lacking	in	95
on	land		126
in (the field of)	landscaping		90
by and	large		57
at	last		36
for	later		74
at the	latest		39
to	laugh	about	11
to	laugh	at	36
to	laugh	at	37
to	laugh	(all) through	160
the	laughter	of	114
above the	law		17
against the	law		23
in (the field of)	law		90
within the	law		199
on the	lawn		126
to	lay	off	121
to	lay someone	off	122–123
to	lay something	against	23
to	lay something	in	84
to	lay something	in	87
to	lay something	on	128–129
to	lead someone	toward	174
a	leader	of	111
to	lean	against	23
to	lean	on	128
to	lean	over	151
to	lean	toward	175
to	learn	of	115
at	least		39
of	leather		115
to	leave	for	73
to	leave	from	79
on	leave		134
to	leave	with	190
to	leave something	out	143
to	leave something	with	190
to	leave something	with	190
a	lecture	about	11
at a	lecture		35
in a	lecture		84

PRECEDING PREPOSITION OR OTHER PARTICLE/S	NOUN OR VERB	FOLLOWING PREPOSITION	PAGE NUMBER
to	leer	at	36
on the	left	of	127
in the	leg		92
to	lend	to	165
at	length		36
a	length	of	112–113
through	lenses		161
a	lesson	for	70
to	let someone	down	64
a	letter	for	69
a	letter	to	164
through the	letters		159–160
be	level	with	196
the	lid	to	169
to	lie	about	11
to	lie	against	23
to	lie	around	31
to	lie	on	128
to	lie	over	152
to	lie	under	177
to	lie (down)	beside	49
in	lieu	of	91
for	life		74
in	life		85
(all) through one's	life		160
in	light	of	94–95
through a	light		158
a	limit	to	171
under the	limit		177
within the	limit(s)		199
off	limits		122–123
to	limp	across	18
to	limp	off	120
in a	line		90
in	line		90
on	line		134–135
on the	line		134–135
out of	line		145
to	line	up	184–188
in	lines		90
on the	list		132
to	listen	to	166–167
to	listen	up	184–188
from	listening		81
very	little	about	11
little by	little		57
	little	of	113

PRECEDING PREPOSITION OR OTHER PARTICLE/S	NOUN OR VERB	FOLLOWING PREPOSITION	PAGE NUMBER
a	little	of	113
to	live	across from	18
to	live	off	122
to	live	on	130
to	live	on	133
to	live	over	152
to	live	through	159
to	live	with	190
a	load	of	112
	load something	on	136
to	load something	on	127
a	loaf	of	112
against one's	loan		24
on	loan		134
be	located	over	152
to	lock up	against	24
to	log	on	138
to	long	for	70
to	look	about	13
to	look	after	22
to	look	around	31
to	look	at	36
to	look	back on	42
to	look	back to	42
to	look	down on	64
to	look	for	70
to	look	in (on)	98
to	look	into	104
to	look	into	106
to	look	like	107
to	look	out (for)	146–148
to	look	over	151
to	look	over	152
to	look	all over the …	153
to	look	through	159–160
to	look	toward	174
to	look	up to	184–188
with a	look		191–192
to	look forward	to	172
to	look good	with	196
to	look something	over	154–155
to	look something	up	184–188
to	look up something	under	178
to	lose weight	on	130
the	loser	of	111
a	lot	of	113
	lots	of	113

PRECEDING PREPOSITION OR OTHER PARTICLE/S	NOUN OR VERB	FOLLOWING PREPOSITION	PAGE NUMBER
be	lousy	at	38
in	love		88–89
a	love	of	117
out of	love		145
with	love		191–192
be in	love	with	192
be	loved	by	56
be	loved	for	71
in	lower case		88
be	loyal	to	167
out of	loyalty		145
to	luck	out	146–148
out of	luck		144
through	luck		161
at	lunch		35
for	lunch		72
over	lunch		153
(all) through	lunch		160
to	lunch		164
at a	luncheon		35
towards	lunchtime		176
to	lurk	around	31
be above	lying		16
be beneath	lying		48
on the	machine		130
be	mad	about	12
like	mad		107
be	made	by	56
be	made	from	81
be	made	of	115
be	made up	of	115
in a	magazine		84
to	mail	from	79
to	mail something	out	143
to	make	for	69
to	make	of	112
to	make	out	146–148
to	make	up (with)	184–188
to	make	up	184
to	make a pass	at	36
to	make a toast	to	165
to	make do	on	130
to	make something	for	73
to	make something	out of	144–145
to	make something	up	184–188
to	make something	up to	184–188
in	make–up		89–90

PRECEDING PREPOSITION OR OTHER PARTICLE/S	NOUN OR VERB	FOLLOWING PREPOSITION	PAGE NUMBER
out of	malice		145
at a	mall		35
to	manage	for someone	72
under the	management	of	178
the	manager	of	111
in a	manner		89
after one's	manners		20
	many	of	113
to	march	around	31
to	march	on	133–134
to	march	toward	174
in the	marines		90
on the	mark		134–135
on your	mark		137
to	mark something	down	64
to	mark something	off	122–123
to	mark something	up	184–188
be	married	to	169
have a	match	with	193–194
under the	maximum		177
from	May	to September	80–81
the	mayor	of	111
under a	mayor		178
as for	me		34
(all) through the	meal		160
be	mean	about	12
be	mean	of someone	118
be	mean	to	167
be	meaningful	to	165–166
above	meanness		16
out of	meanness		145
by all	means		57
the	measurement	of	112–113
in	medicine		90
off one's	medicine		121
of	meditation		116
at a	meeting		35
a	member	of	111
a	memo	to	164
a	memorial	to	165
from	memory		81
in	memory	of	91
be	menacing	toward	174
to	mention	to	165
at one's	mercy		39
in a	mess		88–89
a	message	for	69

PRECEDING PREPOSITION OR OTHER PARTICLE/S	NOUN OR VERB	FOLLOWING PREPOSITION	PAGE NUMBER
of	metal		115
in	meters		91
a	method	of	111
a	method	of	115
on	microfilm		130
through a	microscope		161
towards	mid–afternoon		176
in the	middle	of	112
towards	midnight		176
by a	mile		57
in	miles		91
within	miles	of	199
in the	military		90
in a	million		87
make up one's	mind		184
be	mindful	of	117
under the	minimum		177
within	minutes		199
with	mirth		196–197
through	misinformation		161
to	miss	out on	138
on a	mission		130
through a	mistake		161
to	mix something	up (with)	184–188
to	moan	about	11
a	moan	of	114–115
at the	moment		37
a	moment	of	116
on	Monday (or any day)		55
out of	money		144
with all one's	money		196–197
in	monopoly		93
month after	month		21
by the	month		56
of the	month		111
the	month	of	116
(all) through the	month		160
over the next few	months		153
a	monument	to	165
in a bad/good	mood		88–89
to	mope	around	31
of high/low	morals		118
in the	morning		85
(all) through the	morning		160
on nice	mornings		129
at	most		39

PRECEDING PREPOSITION OR OTHER PARTICLE/S	NOUN OR VERB	FOLLOWING PREPOSITION	PAGE NUMBER
	most	of	113
on a	motorcycle		128
in	mourning		88–89
of	mourning		116
to	move	about	13
to	move	across	18
to	move	against	23
to	move	against	24
to	move	around	31
to	move	back to	42
to	move	back from	42
to	move	down	63
to	move	down	63
to	move	in	87
to	move	into	104
to	move	off	120
to	move	on	133
to	move	onto	140
to	move	to	164
to	move	to tears	169–170
to	move	toward	174
to	move	up	182
with the	move	to	196–197
to	move away	from	79
to	move something	into	104
to	move something	off	120
to	move something	onto	140
to	move something	out	143
to	move something	out of	143
to	move something	up	182
to	move something	with	193
a	movie	about	11
at the	movies		35
	much	of	113
be above	murder		16
be beneath	murder		48
in	music		88
	music	of	111
the	music	of	114
to the	music	of	169
to	nail	to	167
to	nail something	over	151
to	nail something	with	193
the	name	of	112
to	name someone	after	22
be	nasty	about	12
one's	nationality is	against	24

PRECEDING PREPOSITION OR OTHER PARTICLE/S	NOUN OR VERB	FOLLOWING PREPOSITION	PAGE NUMBER
a	native	of	111–112
by	nature		58
for	naught		75
in the	navy		90
be	necessary	for	71
a	necessity	of	116
a	need	for	70
in	need		88–89
a	need	of	116
a	need	of	117
to	need someone	for	70
through	negligence		161
to	negotiate	with	194–195
all through the	neighborhood		159–160
be	nervous	about	12
in a	nest		84
in	neutral		92
the	news	about	11
	news	for	69
on the	news		133
in a	newspaper		84
through a	newspaper		161
be	next	to	170–171
be	nice	about	12
something/nothing	nice	about	13
be	nice	of someone	118
be	nice	to	167
in	nickels		90
night after	night		21
at	night		36
(all) through the	night		160
on rainy	nights		129
in the	nineties		85
in	no time		86
to	nod	off	122–123
to	nod one's head	in	92–93
the	noise	of	114
to the	noise	of	169
to	nominate	as	34
to	nominate someone	for	70
against a	nomination		23
	none	of	113
towards	noon		176
under the	norm		177
above	normal		16
by a	nose		57
a	nose	for	74–75

PRECEDING PREPOSITION OR OTHER PARTICLE/S	NOUN OR VERB	FOLLOWING PREPOSITION	PAGE NUMBER
in a	notebook		84
through the	notes		159–160
	nothing	for	69
for	nothing		73
be	notorious	for	71
the	novels	of	111
by	now		56
in the	nude		89–90
a	nuisance	to	165–166
under a	number		177
of	nylon		115
be	obedient	to	167
to	object	to	166–167
an	objection	to	166–167
be	objective	about	12
be	obligated	to	169
be	obnoxious	to	165–166
an	obstacle	to	168
to	obtain	from	79
on	occasion		129
on the	occasion	of	133
against all	odds		24
neither	of		113
	off	with	197
an	offer	to	164
at an	office		35
run for	office	for	70
in an	office		84
in an	office		85
to the	office		164
in	oil		88
be an	old hand	at	38
at	once		36
for	once		75
	once and	for all	75
one by	one		58
after	one's own heart		21
beyond	one's wildest dreams		53
in	ones		90
beside	oneself		49
(all) by	oneself		57
be	open	to	167
be	open	with	191–192
to	open something	with	193
to	operate	for someone	72
in one's	opinion		94–95
the	opinion	of	111
with	optimism		191–192
be	optimistic	about	12
(all) through the	ordeal		160
in	order		90
in	order	to	91
on	order		134
out of	order		145
against	orders		23
on the	orders	of	131
under	orders		178
out of the	ordinary		144
of an	organization	of	111
by the	ounce		56
in	ounces		91
after one's	outburst		20
on an	outing		130
on the	outside	of	127
on the	outskirts	of	127
on one's	own		134–135
to	pack something	with	193
by the	package		56
a	package	of	112
on the	page	of	127
on	page one, two, etc.		126
in	pain		88–89
a	pain	in one's	92
a	pain	in the neck	92
in	pain		92–93
to	paint	with	193
to	paint something	over	152
to	paint something	with	193
to	paint something	with	193
the	paintings	of	111
beyond the	pale		53
of	paper		115
on	paper		130
a	paper	on	132
through the	papers		159–160
be on a	par	with	196
at a	parade		35
be	parallel	to	170–171
be	parallel	with	196
at a	park		35
in	park		92
through the	park		158
to the	park		164

PRECEDING PREPOSITION OR OTHER PARTICLE/S	NOUN OR VERB	FOLLOWING PREPOSITION	PAGE NUMBER
at a	parking lot		35
on	parole		134
the	part	to	169
to	part	with	195
to	part company	with	195
to	participate	in	95
in	particular		94–95
a	partnership	with	194–195
in	partnership	with	194–195
in	parts		87
into	parts		104–105
at a	party		35
to	pass	on something	11
to	pass	out	146–148
to	pass	to	165
to	pass out	among	29
to	pass someone	over	154–155
to	pass someone	over	154–155
to	pass something	in	87
to	pass something	on	138
to	pass something	out	143
to	pass something	up	184–188
through a	passage		158
out of	passion		145
in the	past		85
out of the	past		145–146
to	paste	to	167
to	paste something	on	127
down a	path		63
on the	path		126
a	path	to	164
up the	path		182
be	patient	with	191–192
on the	patio		126
a	pattern	for	70
a	pattern	of	112
the	paucity	of	116
to	pay someone	for	71
to	pay something/someone	back	42
behind in	payments		45
on the	payroll		132
at	peace		37
for	peace		71
something/nothing	peculiar	about	13
in	pencil		88
in	pennies		90

PRECEDING PREPOSITION OR OTHER PARTICLE/S	NOUN OR VERB	FOLLOWING PREPOSITION	PAGE NUMBER
the	people	of	111–112
about	perfect		13
be far from	perfect		68
to	perform	for	69
(all) through the	performance		160
a	period	of	116
through a	periscope		161
be above	perjury		16
be beneath	perjury		48
be	perpendicular	to	170–171
to	persist	in	95
in	person		89
to	pertain	to	169
be	pertinent	to	169
be	pessimistic	about	12
to	petition	for	70
a	petition	to	164
to	pick	as	34
to	pick	at	40
to	pick	between	51
to	pick	off	120
to	pick	on	137
to	pick	on	138
to	pick	up	184–188
to	pick something	out	146–148
to	pick something	over	154–155
to	pick something	up	184–188
a	picture	of	114
by the	piece		56
a	piece	of	112
in	pieces		87
into	pieces		104–105
in a	pile		90
	pile something	on	136
in	piles		90
to	pin	to	167
by the	pint		56
through a	pipe		158
have	pity	on	136
out of	pity		145
to	place	above	16
to	place	against	23
from one	place	to another	80–81
in	place		84
out of	place		144
all over the	place		153
place to	place		168

PRECEDING PREPOSITION OR OTHER PARTICLE/S	NOUN OR VERB	FOLLOWING PREPOSITION	PAGE NUMBER	PRECEDING PREPOSITION OR OTHER PARTICLE/S	NOUN OR VERB	FOLLOWING PREPOSITION	PAGE NUMBER
to	place something	in	84	to	point something	out to	146–148
to	place something	in	87	to	poke	about	13
to	place something	into	104	to	poke	in	92
to	place something	over	151	under a	policy		178
to	place something	over	152	be	polite	to	167
to	place something	under	177	in	politics		90
against a	plan		23	in the game of	polo		93
behind a	plan		45	of	polyester		115
a	plan	for	69	in	ponytails		89–90
to	plan	for	73	be	poor	in	95
a	plan	for	70	to	pop	up	182
to	plant something	with	193	be	popular	for	71
a	plaque	to	165	for all one's	popularity		74
of	plastic		115	on the	porch		126
a	plate	of	112	in	portions		87
of	platinum		115	from a	position		81
to	play	about	11	be	possible	for someone	71
to	play	against	23	to	pounce	on	127
to	play	along with	27	by the	pound		56
to	play	among	29	to	pound	on	127
to	play	around	31	in	pounds		91
at a	play		35	to	pour something	in	87
to	play	for	69	to	pour something	into	104
to	play	like	107	to	pour something	on	127
to	play	(all) through	160	to	pour something	out of	143
(all) through the	play		160	to	pour something	over	152
to	play	with	190	in	power		92
to	play a game	with	190	have	power	over	152
all over the	playground		153	with all one's	power		196–197
the	plays	of	111	at a	practice		35
to	plead	for	70	for	practice		72
be	pleasant	to	167	for	practice		71
be	pleased	for someone	72	in	practice		94
be	pleased	with	192	out of	practice		144
be	pleasing	to	165–166	a	practitioner	of	111
for	pleasure		71	in	praise	of	91
the	pleasure	of	117	to	praise someone	for	71
with	pleasure		191–192	to	pray	about	11
	plenty	of	113	to	pray	for	70
behind a	plot		45	of	prayer		116
to	plow something	with	193	in one's	prayers		85
the	poems	of	111	against the	precepts		23
in	poetry		88	be	precious	to	165–166
the	poetry	of	111	be	predicated	on	129
beside the	point		49	to	prefer	to	166–167
to	point	toward	174	be	preferable	to	168
from one's	point of view		81	be	preferable	to	165–166

PRECEDING PREPOSITION OR OTHER PARTICLE/S	NOUN OR VERB	FOLLOWING PREPOSITION	PAGE NUMBER	PRECEDING PREPOSITION OR OTHER PARTICLE/S	NOUN OR VERB	FOLLOWING PREPOSITION	PAGE NUMBER
a	preference	for	75	in	publishing		90
on the	premise	of	131	to	pull	against	23
be	prepared	for	70	to	pull	back to	42
in one's	presence		89	to	pull	down	63
at	present		36	to	pull	into	104
a	present	for	69	to	pull	off	120
a	present	to	164	to	pull	over	154–155
to	present	to	165	to	pull a gun/knife	on	133
a	present	to	165	to	pull something	in	87
to	preside	over	152	to	pull something	off	120
under the	presidency	of	178	to	pull something	off	122–123
the	president	of	111	to	pull something	out of	143
under a	president		178	to	pull something	over	154–155
to	press	on	133	to	pull something	over	152
to	press	to	167	to	pull something	through	158
put	pressure	on	137	to	pull something	toward	174
to	prevent someone	from	82	to	punch	in	92
to	prey	on	137	to	punish someone	for	71
at a	price		38	for	purchase		72
the	price	of	112–113	on	purpose		131
with	pride		191–192	to	push	against	23
under a	principal		178	to	push	back to	42
against the	principles		23	to	push	down	63
in	print		88	to	push	for	75
in	private		89	to	push	into	104
with the	problems		196–197	to	push	to the limits	169–170
with all one's	problems		197	to	push	toward	175
by	profession		58	to	push something	in	84
a	professor	of	111	to	push something	in	87
under a	professor		178	to	push something	off	120
a	program	about	11	to	push something	on	136
at a	program		35	to	push something	out of	143
a	program	for	70	to	push something	through	158
behind a	project		45	to	push something	toward	174
a	project	for	69	to	push something	under	177
a	project	for	70	to	put	above	16
with a	promise		191–192	to	put	against	23
be	promised	to	169	to	put	around	30
against a	proposal		23	be	put	out	145–146
a	proposal	to	164	to	put	up with	197
at the	prospect	of	36	to	put something	back	43
to	protect	against	24	to	put something	by	59
to	protect something	from	79	to	put something	down	64
be	proud	of	117	to	put something	in	84
be	proud	of	115–116	to	put something	in	87
be	provided	with	191	to	put something	into	104
in	public		89	to	put something	off	122–123

PRECEDING PREPOSITION OR OTHER PARTICLE/S	NOUN OR VERB	FOLLOWING PREPOSITION	PAGE NUMBER
to	put something	on	128
to	put something	on	136
to	put something	on	127
to	put something	out	143
to	put something	over	152
to	put something	under	177
to	put something	with	190
to	put together	from	81
to	puzzle	over	153
for all one's	qualifications		74
to	quarrel	with	193–194
have a	quarrel	with	193–194
by the	quart		56
in	quarters		90
to	question	about	11
a	question	for	69
in	question		94–95
a	question	to	164
with a	question		191–192
of	quiet		116
to	race	around	30
to	race	back to	42
of a	race	of	111
a	race	to	164
to	race	up	182
in the game of	racquetball		93
on the	radio		135
in a	rage		88–89
with	rage		196–197
a	raid	on	133–134
in the	rain		86–87
to	rain	on	127
with the	rain		196–197
in	rainy weather		86–87
to	ram something	in	87
within	range		199
to	rat	on	137
of	rayon		115
out of	reach		144
within	reach		199
to	react	in	92–93
to	react	to	166–167
after one's	reaction		20
in	reaction		92–93
a	reaction	to	166–167
to	read	about	11
to	read	on	133

PRECEDING PREPOSITION OR OTHER PARTICLE/S	NOUN OR VERB	FOLLOWING PREPOSITION	PAGE NUMBER
to	read	to	165
to	read something	over	154
at a	reading		35
of	reading		116
about	ready		13
be	ready	for	70
by the	ream		56
to	rebel	at	37
a	receipt	for	73
on	receipt		135–136
to	receive	from	79
to	receive something	through	158
a	recipe	for	70
to	recommend	to	165
on the	recommendation	of	131
on	reconnaissance		131
off the	record		122–123
on	record		130
on	record		134
through the	records		159–160
through	red tape		159
of	reflection		116
on	reflection		135–136
with	regard		191–192
to	register	for	70
against the	regulations		23
to	reimburse someone	for	71
to	rejoice	at	37
to	relate	to	166–167
be	related	to	169
a	relation	to	166–167
a	relationship	with	194–195
for	relaxation		71
to	release something	from	79
be	relevant	to	169
in	relief		92–93
of	relief		114–115
to	relieve someone	of	116–117
against a	religion		23
of a	religion	of	111
to	rely	on	129
a	remark	to	165
to	remind someone	about	12
to	remind someone	of	115
be	reminiscent	of	115
to	remove something	from	79
for	rent		72

PRECEDING PREPOSITION OR OTHER PARTICLE/S	NOUN OR VERB	FOLLOWING PREPOSITION	PAGE NUMBER
to	rent something	for	73
be	repentant	of	117
be	repentant	of	115–116
to	reply	to	166–167
a	reply	to	166–167
to	report	about	11
a	report	on	132
to	report	on	132
to	reprimand someone	for	71
be	repulsive	to	165–166
by	reputation		58
a	request	for	73
on	request		131
a	request	to	164
to one's	rescue		165
in	research		90
the	research	on	132
in the	reserves		90
to	reside	over	152
a	resident	of	111–112
show	respect	for	75
out of	respect		145
be	respectful	of	117
be	respectful	to	167
to	respond	to	166–167
a	response	to	166–167
be	responsible	of someone	118
to	rest	against	23
at	rest		37
to	rest	beside	49
of	rest		116
to	rest	on	128
to	rest	under	177
at a	restaurant		35
to	restrict	to	171
a	restriction	on	132
in	return		94
in	return		94–95
to	return	to	164
at a	reunion		35
to	reveal	to	165
in	reverse		92
in	reverse		94–95
to	revert	to	166–167
to	reward someone	for	71
a	rhythm	for	74

PRECEDING PREPOSITION OR OTHER PARTICLE/S	NOUN OR VERB	FOLLOWING PREPOSITION	PAGE NUMBER
in	rhythm		88
in	rhythm	with	91
to the	rhythm	of	169
be	rich	in	95
be	rich	in	95
be/get	rid	of	116–117
to	ride	across	18
to	ride	around	30
to	ride	down	63
to	ride	on	128
to	ride	to	164
to	ride	with	195
be	ridiculous	for someone	71
be	right	about	12
about	right		13
on the	right	of	127
on the	rink		126
to	rip something	out of	143
to	rise	to the occasion	164
at	risk		37
on the	river		127
down a	road		63
off the	road		120
on the	road		134–135
on the	road		126
on the	road		127
a	road	to	164
up the	road		182
up the	road		182
to the	roar	of	169
be above	robbing		16
to	rock	to sleep	169–170
off one's	rocker		121
on the	rocks		126
to	roll	down	63
to	roll	off	120
on a	roll		134–135
to	roll	all over the …	153
to	roll something	off	120
on	roller blades		128
on the	roof		126
	room	for	75
in a	room		84
up and down the	room		184
be	rough	on	137
to	round	up	183